BETWEEN THE ICON AND THE IDOL

# THEOPOLITICAL VISIONS

SERIES EDITORS:

Thomas Heilke
D. Stephen Long
and C. C. Pecknold

Theopolitical Visions seeks to open up new vistas on public life, hosting fresh conversations between theology and political theory. This series assembles writers who wish to revive theopolitical imagination for the sake of our common good.

Theopolitical Visions hopes to re-source modern imaginations with those ancient traditions in which political theorists were often also theologians. Whether it was Jeremiah's prophetic vision of exiles "seeking the peace of the city," Plato's illuminations on piety and the civic virtues in the Republic, St. Paul's call to "a common life worthy of the Gospel," St. Augustine's beatific vision of the City of God, or the gothic heights of medieval political theology, much of Western thought has found it necessary to think theologically about politics, and to think politically about theology. This series is founded in the hope that the renewal of such mutual illumination might make a genuine contribution to the peace of our cities.

FORTHCOMING VOLUMES:

James Reimer
*Toward an Anabaptist Political Theology: Law, Order, and Civil Society*

David Deane
*The Matter of the Spirit: How Soteriology Shapes the Moral Life*

# Between the ICON and the IDOL

The Human Person and the Modern State in Russian Literature and
Thought—Chaadayev, Soloviev, Grossman

ARTUR MRÓWCZYŃSKI-VAN ALLEN

*Translated by* Matthew Philipp Whelan
*Foreword by* William T. Cavanaugh

CASCADE *Books* · Eugene, Oregon

BETWEEN THE ICON AND THE IDOL
The Human Person and the Modern State in Russian Literature and Thought—
Chaadayev, Soloviev, Grossman

Theopolitical Visions 16

Cascade Books
An Imprint of Wipf and Stock Publishers
199 W. 8th Ave., Suite 3
Eugene, OR 97401

www.wipfandstock.com

ISBN 13: 978-1-4982-1471-1

*Cataloging-in-Publication data:*

Mrówczyński-Van Allen, Artur.

    Between the icon and the idol : the human person and the modern state in Russian literature and thought—Chaadayev, Soloviev, Grossman / by Artur Mrówczyński-Van Allen ; translated by Matthew Philipp Whelan ; foreword by William T. Cavanaugh.

    p.; 23 cm—Includes bibliographical references.

    ISBN 13: 978-1-61097-816-3

    Theopolitical Visions 16

    1. Philosophy, Russian—19th century. 2. Philosophy, Russian—20th century. 3. Religious thought—Russia—Sources. 4. Christianity and politics—Catholic Church. 5. Political theology. 6. Church and state. I. Whelan, Matthew Philipp. II. Cavanaugh, William T. III. Title. IV. Series.

BL2747.8 .M67 2013

Manufactured in the USA.

Dedicated to my wife, Mercedes

# Contents

# Foreword

The present book is two things. It is a sketch of the intellectual and political history of the Russian Idea, a fascinating constellation of concepts that took shape among Christian and Jewish thinkers in the nineteenth and twentieth centuries. It is also a contribution to political theology as it is currently practiced in the West. The author is convinced that the Russians have something extremely important to add to the current ferment of political theology in the West. He is not alone; one thinks of Dorothy Day and Rowan Williams who, in different ways, have plumbed the riches of Dostoevsky, Berdyaev, Bulgakov, and others for ways to heal what ails modernity.

Artur Mrówczyński-Van Allen is in many ways uniquely situated to appreciate the contributions the East can make to the West. He is a Polish Roman Catholic scholar of Russian thought, and director of the Slavic Studies Department of the International Center for the Study of the Christian Orient in Granada, Spain. He has seen his native Poland make the transition from a communist state to one dominated by neoliberal capitalism, and he has seen his adopted country shake off an authoritarian right-wing regime allied with the Catholic Church and plunge headlong into an intense process of secularization. In both cases Mrówczyński-Van Allen is reluctant to celebrate the transition in any straightforward way. In both cases he sees continuities between authoritarian states and liberal ones, where others see only positive change. And in both cases, Mrówczyński-Van Allen thinks that the East has something valuable to offer the West in learning how to resist some of the negative pathologies of modernity.

As Christian political theology has increasingly questioned the religious/secular and religion/politics dualisms, Mrówczyński-Van Allen shows how Russian thinkers since the nineteenth century have refused such dichotomies in favor of a comprehensive theocentric vision that unites all reality in a God-ruled world. The dualisms break down in both directions:

the true Kingship of Christ is proclaimed, while the religion of the state is critiqued. The truncation of modern reason and its severing from metaphysics is only superficially a separation of reason from its opposite; in truth, modern reason is a species of irrationality, and its institutionalization in either the Marxist or the utilitarian state is in fact the establishment of a new, albeit false, religion. In a Promethean act, humanity deifies its own will. The result is the terrible loneliness of modernity, the abstract, individual, self-legislating subject, who, thus isolated, is defenseless in the face of the divinized collective, be it the nation, the state, the market, or the inexorable progress of history.

At the heart of the Russian Idea is the conviction that we are not alone. We are brought into being by community with God and with one another. The Athanasian idea that God became human so that humans might become divine is not the Promethean seizing of divinity, but its reception as gift. As Chaadayev makes plain, it is God, not humans, who writes on the *tabula rasa* of the human soul. Freedom is not the self-creation of individual destiny but an embrace of the eternal destiny of humankind, in which we participate with one another, all made equally in the image of God. Philosophy for the Russians is not detached abstraction but an act of participation in the vital intellectual and moral experience of theosis. The Eucharist, then, is the font of both philosophy and politics, for in it we discover our true identity as one with God and with one another.

The present study deftly weaves together the stories of great Russian thinkers to present a holistic vision in which the theological and the political are not seen as separate enterprises. The result is a kind of manifesto for a sane politics centered in the basic and inescapable questions of human nature. We cannot fashion a politics without asking and giving at least preliminary answers to the questions, "Who are we?" and "What are we here for?"

Totalitarian systems function because they have answers, albeit false ones, to these questions. Mrówczyński-Van Allen gets to the heart of the matter by writing of the idol of totalitarianism. Totalitarianism is a type of idolatry, which is to say that it is a fundamentally theological phenomenon. This idolatry takes different forms, more overtly religious in the East, more apparently secular in the West. Even in its more secular, Kantian form, however, politics is still in search of a god without God, a deified self that self-legislates. The question of politics remains fundamentally theological.

The theological roots of politics are most evident in the totalitarian impulse to sanctify the state, which becomes the deified "we" to whom the individual person is sacrificed. The state is not simply the apparatus created by a society or by an ideology to put its will into action. The state is much more than an instrument or tool. In totalitarian societies, the state has enormous creative power. The state itself comes to have a life of its own, a will and initiative and mind of its own. One of the greatest predictive errors Marx made was in believing that the state would eventually wither away and an elevated humanity take its place. Humans cannot replace God. Once God has been banished, God will necessarily reappear in idolatrous form, a colossal active and personal agent of providence in history. The state is simply the immanentized version of a properly theological concept, as Carl Schmitt saw so clearly.

Mrówczyński-Van Allen draws on his experiences in communist Poland, where clearly, to borrow his words, the memory of totalitarianism has not yet been converted to the mere past. And yet the reader knows that this exercise in confronting the idolatry of totalitarianism has much more than communism and Nazism in view. Mrówczyński-Van Allen's comments about the state do not apply only to such contexts, but find resonance in liberal democratic states as well. The link is the tendency in modernity to reduce the political to an oscillation between the individual and the state. The totalitarian state clearly intends to eliminate all those forms of organic community that rival the absolute loyalty of the individual to the state. This god is a jealous god. But the dynamic of individualization is no less endemic to liberal states, where secularization demands that talk of substantive common goals and *teloi* be privatized. We cannot hold a religion in common; what we can agree upon in a liberal society are merely the procedures and techniques necessary to maximize the freedom of individuals to pursue their visions of human meaning with a minimum of interference from others. The liberal state is no less a savior, in other words, but it saves us from each other. As in totalitarian societies, it is civil society, and not the state, that withers.

Mrówczyński-Van Allen's diagnosis is therefore no less relevant after the fall of the Berlin Wall. And his proposed cure is no less salutary. He appeals to the work of Grossman and other voices from the East to oppose the idolatry of the deified self with the icon, which opens up a distance in which giving and forgiving can occur. Eastern voices are so helpful because they refuse to quarantine theological questions; the borders between theology, politics, and literature are fluid and porous, because they are all a part of an integrated life. The holism of totalitarianism must be opposed by another kind of holism that replaces the idol with the icon. At the same time, the aspiration of secularism to separate politics from theology, and power from love, must be opposed by a politics based on an opening of human persons to God and to each other, the kind of self-donation found in Grossman, and for Christians, on the Cross.

Mrówczyński-Van Allen's work is a valuable contribution to the opening of the West to voices from the East. It is a contribution as well to a politics of generosity and beauty.

William T. Cavanaugh
DePaul University

# Acknowledgments

I wish to express my sincere gratitude to two teachers and friends: the Archbishop of Granada, Francisco Javier Martinez, and Professor Sebastian Montiel. This work is in large measure the result of the friendship with which they have honored me. I also want to thank Professor William T. Cavanaugh, for his support and for having contributed significantly to my own thought. I want to thank Aaron Riches for help with the preparation of this edition. In addition, I owe a great debt of gratitude to Matthew Philipp Whelan for his extraordinary effort translating this book; in fact, his work was much more than that of a mere translator.

I must also thank my academic colleagues in the Archdiocese of Granada in the International Centre for the Study of the Christian Orient, especially to Olga Tabatadze, and the Institute of Philosophy Edith Stein for their friendship and dialogue, which has contributed in various ways to the outcome of this book.

Christian thought never occurs in abstraction. The thought that is finally expressed in these pages would not have been possible without the lived experience of faith with which I have been graced in my little community of the Santo Domingo parish of Granada of the Neo-Catechumenal Way.

Finally, and especially, I thank my family: my wife, Mercedes, to whom I dedicate this book, and our children—Ines, Blanca, Alvaro, Martin, Elena, Victoria, Hugo, Jacobo, and Mateo—for their love, kindness, and patience.

# Prologue

*I saw the human face of God, and my soul has been saved.*
—Saint John of Damascus

In the corner facing the entrance to the main room, an icon presides over the house. In this way the *oikos* renders visible its membership and participation in the *ecclesia*. Like an icon set in the iconostasis of a church, the household icon likewise displays the ordinary interpenetration of what is sacred and what is human. It refuses the lie that the secular is the opposite of the divine.

Whenever we have occasion to enter one of these houses—these houses that, throughout Eastern Europe, are increasing in number—and bow before the icon, we worship the Creator who became a creature, taking flesh in the womb of the Virgin Mary. At the same time, we recognize our own vocation and nature as icon. Perhaps we could describe the whole history of the world, just as we could describe the local histories of our communities and our lives, as the discovery before what and before whom we have bowed. Perhaps we could describe these histories in terms of moments in which the awareness of our own nature as icon, created in the image and likeness of God, permits us to glimpse the plentitude of what is truly human, which was revealed to us in the Incarnate Word, and to see not only ourselves but others as icons.

The decision before what and before whom to bow therefore expresses both who we are and who others are for us. Perhaps this whole matter can be summarized in the question, do I bow before the icon or the idol? Or, to put it in more contemporary terms, are we citizens—that is, clients, consumers, or slaves—or are we children—that is, sons and daughters, and therefore free persons? Someone might argue that the choice may not be so stark, that intermediate solutions are possible, and so on. I confess, however, that I am not able to locate myself under the description "brother citizen." So I simply choose "brother," bowing before the True Icon, worshiping the Father.

⌐⌐

The increasingly evident totalitarian character of the modern state raises the question of the state's nature and origin. Many of history's most eminent thinkers have addressed this issue, which is anything but abstract: from classic studies on the nature of the *polis* or *civitas* and the threat of tyranny, to modern and contemporary texts dedicated to the totalitarianisms of our recent past. The present work outlines a proposal for the interpretation of totalitarianism from within a tradition of Russian thought. It is a tradition that, having largely shielded itself from the influence of the philosophical principles that led to the emergence of modern totalitarianism, also suffered that totalitarianism directly. By rejecting the separation between supernatural and natural, or between religion and politics, this tradition of Russian philosophy facilitated a characteristic way of interpreting the modern world, as well as itself, known as the Russian Idea. The Russian Idea, especially as it found expression in Russian literature, was uniquely able to describe the drama of the modern human person under totalitarian rule. This mode of philosophical reflection was nurtured from the same sources as the Orthodox iconographic tradition. In this tradition, the icon is not some abstract aesthetic expression; rather, it reveals a specific way of being. It reveals, in other words, an ontology and an anthropology.

The present work arises from the desire to show not only the basic features of this mode of philosophical reflection and its roots within Russian culture, literature, and philosophy, but also the extraordinary ability of such reflection to generate a culture and a literature. Chapter 1 presents the genesis of Russian philosophy, focusing on Vladimir Odoevsky and on Peter Chaadayev, particularly the latter. Chapter 2 treats the Russian Idea, especially with reference to its most distinguished representative, Vladimir Soloviev. Chapter 3 journeys through the life and work of the twentieth-century Russian writer Vasily Grossman, who with absolute mastery and extraordinary wisdom interpreted the totalitarian nature of contemporary society and identified the idolatrous nature of the modern state. Over the course of these three chapters, we will look at this tradition of Russian thought in its philosophical, theological, and literary expressions in order to signal the possibility of rediscovering the human person's identity as icon and the modern state as one of the many metamorphoses of the idol. Moreover, I hope to show that this tradition of Russian thought—the Russian Idea—uniquely identifies the idol of the state because it has been able to preserve a sense of the human person as icon, even in the work of authors who were not Christians, such as that of Vasily Grossman.

The contents of chapters 1 and 2 draw upon work developed within the research program of the Slavic Studies Department of the International Center for the Study of the Christian Orient in Granada, Spain. They are also fruit of the kind invitations of my colleagues and friends of the Department of Philosophy at the Saint Tikhon Orthodox University in Moscow to deliver lectures during the Annual Theological Lectures series, held under the aegis of the Synodal Theological Commission of the Patriarchate of the Russian Orthodox Church.[1] Chapter 3 resulted from the Second International Vasily Grossman Convention, at which I had the opportunity to present a paper titled "Literature and the Totalitarian State—the Icon and the Idol—from Soloviev to Grossman." This conference was organized by the Life and Fate Study Center in Turin, Italy, on whose steering committee I serve as a member.[2]

I want to take this opportunity, as I did then, at the beginning of the conference in Turin, to thank those who made it possible, many years ago, for a young student from a communist country to enjoy the few spaces of freedom that were then available. That freedom especially came to us through what is called *samizdat* or *tamizdat*.[3] I have now in front of me, as I write these words, several documents that witness to those times: the first clandestine Polish edition of Aleksandr Solzhenitsyn's *One Day in the Life of Ivan Denisovich*, as well as two editions of Vasily Grossman's *Everything Flows*—the famous 1970 Russian edition of Posev Ferlag, and a subsequent Polish edition. Although as young students we were not always able to understand everything these texts had to say, we nevertheless lived with them and the tension and the impatience they articulated. Even today, they still

---

1. Mrówczyński-Van Allen, "Ruskiye myslitieli y Evuropa segodnia [Russian Thinkers and Europe Today]"; Mrówczyński-Van Allen and Montiel, "Aspekty russkoy tradytsiy filosofsko-teologitchevskovo sinteza v postsekularnom kontekste" ["Aspects of the Philosophical-Theological Synthesis of the Russian Tradition in a Post-Secular Context"].

2. Mrówczyński-Van Allen, "Literature and the Totalitarian State."

3. The Russian words *samizdat* and *tamizdat* roughly translate as "self-published" and "published abroad." These words name the reproduction and dissemination of censored publications within and between former Soviet bloc countries. Because such activity was illegal, it was fraught with danger. Those who participated in it or were caught possessing such materials were often harshly punished. —Trans.

speak to us of a totalitarianism that has not yet been converted to the mere past. And so the experiences and memories of those times and places continue to be not just a legacy for which we should feel responsible but also a source of sustenance upon which we continue to draw. I thank those who dared to write, those who had the courage to print what was written, and those who secretly gave us these texts and these spaces of freedom. In my own case, I cannot fail to recall the leader of our circle, Robert Mrówczyński, who was killed in Gdańsk, Poland, by the secret police in 1980.

↬

As I have already suggested, my intention in the present work is simply to point out some aspects of the evolving relationship between the human person and the state that we find in the literary, philosophical, and theological sources mentioned above. What I offer here is therefore a kind of Prolegomenon that marks starting points and traces possible lines of investigation of future work, rather than an exhaustive exploration of all the nuances of this complex subject. I am aware that the relationship between these sources and the totalitarian state opens out onto a terrain explored in the excellent work of Vitali Shentalinski, at the intersection of history and literature.[4] His research, however, reflects an inverse relationship to the one proposed here: Shentalinski's primary concern is the relationship of the totalitarian Soviet state towards literature, whereas my concern is with how literature reflects and resists the totalitarian impulses of the state.

The present work does not attempt to make a philosophical or literary analysis of texts of the authors presented here. Rather, it proposes to look into the world of Russian thought and literature, which, as I hope to show, knew how to address the questions raised for it in its encounter with the totalitarian state. Moreover, because of Russia's specific history, the beginnings of which I outline in chapter 1, Russian thought and literature could, in the first place, be aware of the existence of the questions themselves, which was no small feat. In our own day, this awareness can help us discern the totalitarian features of the idol commonly referred to as the modern state, the idol-state.

As reference points in this reflection on the Russian Idea, then, we will encounter poets, novelists, philosophers, and theologians who are Russian, as well as many others who are not. This fact, I believe, helps us perceive in the heritage of the Russian Idea its character as the continuation of the

---

4. Shentalinski, *Esclavos de la libertad*; Shentalinski, *Denuncia contra Sócrates*; Shentalinski, *Crimen sin castigo*.

best tradition of Russian culture, as well as its universality and perennial relevance.

Although it might seem that Russian philosophy, especially Russian philosophy from a century ago, has nothing to do with our time, the opposite is in fact the case. This is because "our time" is not only heir to that time, but also because the problems that confront human life in contemporary society are in many ways the same, and so the challenges that faced Russian Christian thinkers of the second half of the nineteenth century and the early twentieth century remain alarmingly relevant. Moreover, few, if any, dispute the universal value of the Russian literature of the period under consideration. Nikolai Gogol, Fyodor Dostoevsky, and Leo Tolstoy, to name only the best-known writers, wrote within a concrete context—a context characterized by a vital relationship to a specific tradition. Although the theological-philosophical sources of this tradition are neglected, these sources, like the literature they produced, deserve attention.[5]

The question of the relationship between the separate spheres called religion, science, and politics—or public life in general—has been, in the West, part of the process of the emergence of modernity. In Russia, however, this problem did not undergo the same evolution, and the development of modernity itself, as well as a distinct tradition of Russian thought, did not occur until the eighteenth and nineteenth centuries. In this way, Russian thought began to emerge underground, within the communal, liturgical, and sacramental life of the Orthodox Church and the distinctive approach to metaphysics and anthropology safeguarded by her. Russian thought, therefore, had to confront directly the highly developed modern thought of the West. From the beginning of the seventeenth century, the Kiev Academy, founded by Metropolitan Peter Mohyla—and the rest of the Academies of the Orthodox Church soon followed—taught philosophy, history, logic, natural sciences, and mathematics, including elements of the theories of Copernicus and Galileo, which was unusual for the time.

When the Decree of 1814 took effect, it required minor seminaries to teach philosophy. The Metropolitan of Moscow, Archimandrite Filaret (Drozdov), recommended the practice of Socrates' maieutic method.[6] The Orthodox Church tended, in the spirit of patristic thought, to support philosophical reflection, including critical reflection upon the always-suspect apparatus of imperial power. When, after the Spring of Nations in 1848, the Tsar's government considered philosophy a dangerous discipline and

5. Antonov, *Filosofia religii v russkoy metafizike XIX- nachalo XX veka [Philosophy of religion in Russian metaphysics in the nineteenth century and early twentieth century]*, 35–36.

6. Florovsky, *Ways of Russian Theology.*

ordered the liquidation of the chairs of philosophy at the universities, philosophy continued in the curriculum of the Academies of the Patriarchate.

For centuries, the apophaticism of the Orthodox tradition informed Russian philosophy's sense that, in the words of Gennady Mayorov, "The encounter with God—the Absolute, by reason of the impossibility of complete knowledge of God—occurs not as the result of knowledge, but rather acceptance and recognition by way of faith and love."[7] In other words, Russian philosophy understood itself, above all, in ethical and aesthetical terms. The theology of the icon likewise found a home within Russian philosophy and remained within it until much later, when questions of ontology and anthropology began to emerge. Throughout all this time, Russian thinkers attempted to articulate philosophically and without complexity the experience of the Church as reflected in its tradition and body of doctrine. For instance, Lev Zander contends that in Sergei Bulgakov's *The Unfading Light* we find a distillation of philosophical problems viewed in the light of a religious-philosophical vantage.[8]

In the preface to that work, Bulgakov states in the first sentence, "In these 'miscellanies,' I would like to display in philosophical thought or to incarnate in speculation some religious contemplations connected with a life in Orthodoxy."[9] The book then goes on to analyze religion and its relationship to dogma, miracle, philosophy, apophatic theology, anthropology, history, theocracy, and eschatology. What undoubtedly unites this work is the clear rejection of dualisms between natural and supernatural, immanent and transcendent, and God and creation. Experience not only appears as a crucial category for Bulgakov's philosophical and theological reflection, but, as Leonid Vasilenko explains in *Introduction to Russian Religious Philosophy*, Bulgakov clearly binds his understanding of experience to the Orthodox tradition and to its dogmatic theology.[10]

All this means that, according to Bulgakov, faith needs dogma, since "dogma is the formula of that which is identified by faith as transcendent existence."[11] The continuation of these reflections can be found in the work published in 1921, under the suggestive title *The Tragedy of Philosophy*. The tragedy of philosophy, as Vasilenko helps us see, resides in the deracination of philosophy from its Christian roots. In this work, Bulgakov compares

7. Mayorov, *Filosofia kak isaknie Absoliuta*, 56.

8. Zander, *Bog i mir*, 40.

9. Bulgakov, *Unfading Light*, xxxvii. Many thanks to Eerdmans for providing an advance copy of Bulgakov's text. —Trans.

10. Vasilenko, *Vvedenie v russkuyu religioznuyu filosofiyu*, 193.

11. Bulgakov, *Unfading Light*, 54.

every true philosopher to Icarus, who is compelled to fly, to soar into the sky, but who is always doomed to fall to the hard ground below.[12] The philosopher does not know how to overcome the contradiction that governs philosophy itself: the relationship between experience and rational thought. Even in *The Unfading Light*, Bulgakov indicates that the fundamental themes of philosophy and philosophical systems are not invented or thought (*vydumanye*), but in the first place experienced or intuited. They are of supra-philosophical origin.[13]

Although philosophy begins in experience, it does not end in it. Experience becomes subjected to reasoning. The process of searching for the truth of experience becomes instead the search for theoretical truth, a process that tends to sever theoretical speculation from the indivisible unity of the living truth itself.[14] In this way, reason tends to choose only one aspect of the truth and to create a system on that basis. But this "systemizing spirit" is nothing more than the reduction of the many to the one,[15] and conversely, the elaboration of the many on the basis of the one, which means that all such philosophies are ultimately monist in character. Such philosophical systems, which Bulgakov divides into three main groups—idealist, pan-logical, and realist—are doomed to lead to a false, or at least a partial, understanding of the world. Bulgakov therefore contends that Western philosophy finds itself enclosed in a circle of its own making, a vicious circle of heresy: "In this sense the history of philosophy can be presented and interpreted as religious heresiology."[16]

The way to avoid the trap of philosophy's tragedy—the rupture of the relationship between experience and reason—is to recover and to renew the relationship between philosophy, on the one hand, and the Church's experience on the basis of revelation and tradition and as articulated in her dogmas and creeds, on the other. The path forward therefore involves a return to the experience of the Church of the apostolic age and her subsequent patristic heritage. This is the path Bulgakov takes, which is seen in several articles from 1930 in the journal *Put'*, especially one titled "The Dogma of the Eucharist."[17] From the beginning, Bulgakov studies the relationship of the physical to the metaphysical from within the concrete experience of the participation of the faithful in the Eucharist, in their eating and drinking

12. Bulgakov, "Tragedia filosofii," 314.
13. Bulgakov, *Unfading Light*, 60–66.
14. Ibid., 82.
15. Bulgakov, "Targedia filosofii," 312.
16. Ibid., 317.
17. Bulgakov, "Evharisticheskiy Dogmat."

the body and blood of Jesus Christ. In this essay, Bulgakov bases his whole approach upon a deep knowledge of Scripture as well as patristic sources.

Along similar lines, Father Georges Florovsky likewise indicates that philosophy should be established on the basis of revelation and experience. This affirmation appears as early as his 1931 article published in Munich and titled, "Revelation, Philosophy, and Theology."[18] In this essay, Florovsky writes that faith "is the evidence of experience" and that dogma is its witness. Dogma is the testimony of thought concerning what has been seen and revealed, concerning what has been contemplated in the experience of faith, and this testimony is expressed in concepts and definitions. Dogma is "an intellectual vision." It is, in other words, a logical image, a "logical icon," of divine reality. In promulgating dogma, the Church expresses revelation in the language of Greek philosophy. He then adds, "To put it more correctly: Christian dogma itself is the only true philosophical *system*."[19]

⤺

The unity between philosophy and theology grew extraordinarily rich and profound among Russian philosophers and theologians of the nineteenth and early twentieth centuries. In recent decades, moreover, there are even signs in the West of an attempt by Christian theological reflection to recover precisely this unity between philosophy and theology, between the severed spheres of the "public" and the "religious."

As William T. Cavanaugh demonstrates, religion as a distinct sphere of human activity, one that is separable from culture, politics, and economy, is a modern Western invention.[20] The distinction between the religious and the secular as separate spheres of life, in other words, is a modern myth. It is an ideological distinction proffered as unquestionably true and as necessary to reinforce a particular social organization of power.

When a citizen of Rome said *religio mihi est*, which roughly translates as "this is religion for me," these words alluded to a very serious obligation. Roman *religio*, however, included not only temple ceremonies but also many public oaths and family rites that would be considered secular today. To be religious and yet avowedly atheist—in the modern sense of atheism— was not only possible but was common, even, among certain Roman intellectuals, as perhaps it is today among self-proclaimed secularists. That was certainly the case for Marcus Tullius Cicero, who proposed a sociological

18. Florovsky, "Offenbarung, Philosophic und Theologie."
19. Ibid.
20. Cavanaugh, *Myth of Religious Violence.*

and psychological explanation of the origin of belief in gods in *De natura deorum*, even while he was a priest in the college of augurs of the Roman Republic until his death in 43 BC.

The early Christians did not need the idea of religion. In the Vulgate, the word *religio* appears only six times. In Book X of his famous *De civitate Dei*, Saint Augustine uses *religio* to refer to the worship of one true God, but he goes on to warn of the ambiguity of the word, because, he says, its "ordinary meaning" is really about loyalty in human relationships, especially between family and friends.[21]

From the first lines of his treatise *De vera religione*, written in the year 390, Augustine understands the word *religio* in similar terms. This work also shows the importance of the ontological background of *religio* as constitutive of the relationships that edify the community. Augustine writes, "Every approach to a good and blessed life is to be found in the true religion, which is the worship of the one God, who is acknowledged by the sincerest piety to be the source of all kinds of being, from which the universe derives its origin, in which it finds its completion, by which it is held together."[22] Further along, Augustine writes, "In this way, you see, our faith and teaching have demonstrated (and this is the fundamental principle of human salvation) that there is not one thing called philosophy, that is devotion to wisdom, and another thing called religion, when those whose teaching we do not approve of are not even admitted to share the mysteries with us."[23]

Medieval Christianity never used this concept in its modern sense. Instead, it used *religio* to refer to the status of ordained clergy in monasteries and convents, who were classified as religious to differentiate them from diocesan clergy. In the writings of Saint Thomas Aquinas, *religio* was also the name of a relatively minor virtue, associated with the justice of giving what is due to God in worship, which presupposed the particular context of the Church and a Christian social order.

At the dawn of modernity, Nicolas of Cusa, shocked by the violent fall of Constantinople to the Turks in 1453, wrote a treatise titled *De pace fidei*, an early and serious proposal for an "alliance of civilizations" between the various peoples of the earth and their different forms of worship. In this work, the meaning of the word *religion* becomes broader and its usage different than in the medieval period. Religion becomes a universal genus whose species are distinct faiths: Christianity, Judaism, and Islam, each one characterized by its own systems of abstract truths. In addition, religion

21. Augustine, *City of God against the Pagans*, X.1.

22. Augustine, "True Religion," 1.1.

23. Ibid., 5.8.

becomes associated with an interior impulse that is present in all people, an impulse essentially distinct from the motivations of so-called secular activities, such as politics and economics.

In the writings of John Locke, we find a fully modern division of humanity into two distinct spheres: the secular and the religious. In his *Letter Concerning Toleration*, with its brilliantly ironic calls for the exclusion of Catholics from public life because of their peculiar conception of political power, the English thinker clearly formulates the normative ideal of Western modernity: "To distinguish with precision the tasks of the civil government from the tasks of religion." The state would deal with the "common good"— a public obligation for each individual—and churches would deal with the "interest of souls"—a private matter of choice. The confusion arising from the failure to separate these two spheres leads inexorably to violence, as evidenced, according to Locke, by the so-called Wars of Religion.

This necessarily brief review of the modern concept of religion, among other things, helps us avoid falling into the trap of secular reason in which contemporary political theology is mired—most evident, in my opinion, by the Schmitt-Peterson debate. And it can also help us appreciate the concept of religious experience proposed by Voegelin, for whom post-Enlightenment rationalism, by excluding metaphysics from the scope of reason, restricts reason such that "what Weber, following Comte, understood as modern rationalism should be reinterpreted as modern irrationalism."[24] The irrationality of modern reason—the refusal to recognize the *ratio* of ontology and philosophical anthropology—was fundamental to the birth of civil religion, which today constitutes the ideological space of modern political life. Beginning with the work of Nicholas Berdyaev, attending to this irrationality also permitted the recognition of modern totalitarian systems as fundamentally religious movements. For this reason, Voegelin can conclude: "Some religious experiences would have to be classified as higher, others as lower, by the objective criterion of the degree of rationality which they admit in the interpretation of reality. The religious experiences of the Greek mystic philosophers and of Christianity would rank high because they allow the unfolding of metaphysics; the religious experiences of Comte and Marx would rank low because they prohibit the asking of metaphysical questions."[25]

The practical dimension of the distinctions made by Voegelin in this passage is rooted in the possibility of regarding ontology as constitutive of rational exposition itself and of the existential dimension of human life

24. Voegelin, *New Science of Politics*, 24.

25. Ibid.

within community. It is not a coincidence, therefore, that the "religious experience" of Comte, Marx, or Weber amounts to a rejection of metaphysics. It is also not a coincidence that the consequences of this rejection are atomization and individualization, the final dissolution of community. Soloviev, in his classic work *Russia and the Universal Church*, indicates that the primordial lie of the French Revolution, its *proton pseudos*, is "the conception of the individual man as a being complete in and for himself," the way "this abstract 'Man' was suddenly transformed into the no less abstract 'Citizen,' how the free sovereign individual found himself doomed to be the defenseless slave and victim of the absolute State or 'Nation,' that is to say, of a group of obscure persons borne to the surface of public life by the eddies of revolution and rendered the more ferocious by the consciousness of their own intrinsic nonentity."[26] What prepares a person for totalitarian domination is the disappearance of community, "the fact that loneliness," as Hannah Arendt writes in *The Origins of Totalitarianism*, "has become an everyday experience of the evergrowing masses of our century." Arendt continues: "The merciless process into which totalitarianism drives and organizes the masses looks like a suicidal escape from this reality."[27] Paraphrasing St. Augustine, we might describe the modern state, therefore, as *privatio communitatis*.

Viewed in this light, the creation of the modern state—which is the same process as the sacralization of the state—bears, from the start, the signature of theology. *Corpus mysticum*, from the twelfth century onward, became *corpus juridicum*, extending its meaning to the state, opening for the state the new path of its sacralization, and initiating the development of new foundational ideologies. Gogol, known in Europe as a dramatist, novelist, and short story writer, but almost totally unknown as a Christian thinker, stated that one of the primary features of the history of the West has been the process whereby "the legal and juridical" occupies the "empty places" left by the culture of the Christian community. The author of *Dead Souls* quite rightly points out that the processes that enveloped modern Europe in his own time were the consequence of the void that had appeared in the existential relationships of those who had become individuals and citizens. It was a void that modern Western societies tried to fill with the multiplication of legal systems and legislation that aimed to become the new absolute reference points of the moral. These developments, as Gogol wrote prophetically, will someday bring Europe to "cover itself with blood."[28]

26. Soloviev, *Russia and the Universal Church*, 8.
27. Arendt, *Origins of Totalitarianism*, 478.
28. Zenkovsky, *Russkie mysliteli i Evropa*, 58–59.

The concept of "the legal," along with submission to the judicial system of the state, form the backbone of totalitarian societies, their soteriology. Defendants in the Nuremberg trials were not tried for crimes committed against German law, which was among the most modern and developed legal systems of its time. The Nuremberg Laws were characterized by the same offer of salvation as the Soviet Criminal Code of 1922 or the legal system of the People's Republic of Poland.[29] This offer, however, was not only limited to the conception of law as a repressive instrument. It also established the *legal* possibility—and for that reason the justification—for the expulsion, isolation, and elimination of others, whether Jews, bourgeoisie, kulaks, enemies of the proletariat, enemies of progress, neighbors, brothers, sisters, the elderly or fetuses.

Leszek Kolakowski regards the difference between despotism and totalitarianism as residing in the way the latter is characterized by an inherent tendency to destroy the ties that bind people and to stifle the natural propensity to create communal life.[30] Totalitarianism enacts the definition of tyranny that St. Thomas Aquinas gives in *De regno*, in which the Dominican saint says that tyrants seek to stifle any relationships of friendship among their subjects: "Wherefore they sow discords among the people, foster any that have arisen, and forbid anything which furthers society and co-operation among men, such as marriage, company at table and anything of like character, through which familiarity and confidence are engendered among men."[31]

In *The New Science of Politics*, Voegelin concludes that in order to rebuild the dismembered discipline of political science, "an interpretation of Western history that had grown over centuries would have to be revolutionized; and a revolution of this magnitude would meet the opposition of 'progressives' who would find themselves all of a sudden in the position of retrogressive irrationalists."[32] I do not completely agree with Voegelin's assessment. In the first place, not even the thought of someone as intellectually gifted as Voegelin would be able to convince progressives of the decadence of their thought. The correspondence between Voegelin and Strauss testifies to this. In the second place, the need for a revolution in the interpretation of Western history that had grown over centuries is a peripheral issue. The primary issue, the fundamental issue, consists in rediscovering the identity of the Christian community as a community that possesses a natural po-

29. Kladoczny, *Prawo jako narzędzie represji w Polsce Ludowej.*

30. Kolakowski, "Euro – I Azjakomunizm: jedno czy dwoje?" 375.

31. Aquinas, *On Kingship*, I.27.

32. Voegelin, *New Science of Politics*, 24.

litical dimension, which is the vocation of her members to order life to the common good. And this begins in the Eucharist, which creates and is the creative center of the ecclesial community.

In his rereading of St. Augustine, a rereading liberated from the paradigms imposed by secular political theology, Cavanaugh notes that, in the Augustinian vision of the two cities, the destiny of the *civitas terrena* depends upon the ability of Christians to locate their true membership in a communal body that transcends borders of empire. We are pilgrims on this earth, Cavanaugh writes, following St. Augustine, always aware that our true home is the *civitas Dei*. This communion with our brothers and sisters, both living and dead, is no flight from politics, but rather a radical break from the false politics of the *civitas terrena*.[33] Its politics are false in the sense that the modern state as such is false, because it is only a degraded and banal copy of the body of Christ.[34] Cavanaugh therefore emphasizes that the Church should have no desire for the power of the state. Christian participation in the growth of Christ's body itself questions the false order imposed by the state. Christian participation in the Eucharist disables the false theology and the false anthropology of the self's isolated will. It overcomes individualism and creates an ecclesial community ordered by the movement of *peregrinatio*.[35]

The Church is therefore not sent into the world to be assimilated and diluted by the "open society." The liturgy and the sacraments do not simply generate interior individual principles or "values" (purportedly) necessary to carry out public functions in a (purportedly) neutral and autonomous public space. Much too often, the contemporary search for the so-called "presence of Christians in public life" means, in practice, the abandonment of the public space of the Church, the public space that she is herself. This leads to a situation in which the only alternatives are choices between homologous options offered by the modern state. According to St. Augustine, however, the true *res publica*, the guardian of the public itself, is the Church, not the empire, because the empire forsakes what is most public in its rejection of the justice of God.[36] The event of the Incarnation, renewed at every Eucharist, reminds us of our nature as icons, as sons and daughters of God. It overcomes the alienation in which the idol of the modern state mires us. In the Eucharist, we are given the hypostatic union between reality and sign,

---

33. Cavanaugh, *Theopolitical Imagination*, 14–15.
34. Kantorowicz, *King's Two Bodies*.
35. Cavanaugh, *Theopolitical Imagination*, 50–52.
36. Augustine, *City of God against the Pagans*, X.6.

between *res* and *sacramentum*.[37] The identity that arises from this union is the only guarantee of true philosophy and true politics, the only valid source for communal life, both for those who are Christians and for those who are not. The need for the choice between the idol and the icon continues; it is a daily requirement, common to all.

---

37. Marion, *God Without Being*, 156.

# CHAPTER I

# Apology of a Madman

*The Kingdom of the Beast then also tempted the nations with the same temptation that continues across the centuries: "If you kneel and bow before me, all will be yours" (Luke 4:7). All Russian art was born out of the struggle with this temptation. Russian iconographers responded to it with surprising clarity and power, presenting in images and colors that which filled their souls: the vision of another vital truth and of another meaning of life.*

—Evgeny Trubetskoy

## INTRODUCTION

The nineteenth century, especially its second half, and the early twentieth century represent an especially important epoch in the history of Russian culture. According to the intuitionist and notable Russian philosopher Nicholas Lossky, in order for a particular culture to acquire universal significance, the values developed by it must "hold for humanity as a whole."[1] Russian culture, in the form it took until the Bolshevik Revolution, without a doubt fulfilled that requirement. Russia's cultural significance, not only for the destiny of Russia, but for Europe and the rest of the world as well, was such that it left an immense trove that still remains to be explored, the

1. Lossky, *History of Russian Philosophy*, 9.

1

consequences of which have had, and will continue to have, an enormous influence upon the direction of world history and the fate of the local histories of millions of people.

Of course, those times and those persons are the heirs of the culture and common experience of both Western and Eastern history. Philosophers, Alasdair Macintyre reminds us, do not appear suddenly, out of nowhere. Their contributions cannot be extracted from historical, cultural, and social reality and endowed with a "false independence" in relation to the reality in which they lived and thought.[2] Yet it seems no less true that the second half of the nineteenth and the early decades of the twentieth century represent a unique time. It was a time scarred by the encounter with evil. But it was also a time illuminated by the wonderful moments in which God responded to those who asked, sought, and knocked. These years speak to us in a distinct and unrepeatable manner, and, at the same time, they are part of a much larger historical narrative.

The key to the interpretation of this larger historical narrative, as well as to the mystery of existence and of history more generally, is the human person.[3] The question of the human person must become an eschatological question, otherwise it remains merely ideological. Speaking of the future, we think of all the days of a person's existence. Following the anthropological vision expressed by Stanislaw Grygiel, which is deeply rooted in the Christian tradition and in the thought of Plato, we realize that a way of thinking guides a way of life. But this way of thinking is subordinate to the questions the philosopher formulates "within the perspective of the horizon born from the loving union of Heaven and Earth." Grygiel continues: "In the embrace by which Heaven com-prehends (*com-prende*) the Earth." Within this perspective and in this embrace, "the philosopher glimpses the first principles of being and living, known only by God."[4]

Knowledge of history is much more than just information about the habits and the events of the past; it is a message united to the discovery and the development of human consciousness, which gives history its true value. What matters are not simply the external events but the secret, inner life of history as well. "Each person," writes Nicholas Berdyaev, "represents by virtue of his inner nature a sort of microcosm in which the whole world of reality and all the great historical epochs combine and coexist. The human [person] is not merely a minute fragment of the universe, but rather a world in its own right, a world revealed or hidden according as consciousness is

---

2. MacIntyre, *After Virtue*, 11.

3. Berdyaev, *Destiny of Man*, 16.

4. Grygiel, "Extra Communionem Personarum Nulla Philosophia," 692.

more or less penetrating and extensive. In this development of self-consciousness the whole history of the world is apprehended."[5]

With increasing insistence, experience pushes us to find ourselves before this crucial discovery and to recognize, along with Grygiel, that celes-
tial history determines earthly history, and that the encounter, the intimate
identification of heaven and earth, happens in the depths of history, in its
metaphysics. While history begins in the heavens and in heavenly life, this
does not mean, however, that it is removed from our particular experience.
Rather, it constitutes the deepest center of our lives. In order to appreciate this dynamic, it is necessary to adopt a prophetic relationship with the
past, just as this prophetic relationship interiorly unites the present and the
future. Only such a prophetic relationship fills history with life, restores dynamism and beauty through the spirit's inner fire to history's static death.[6]
Grygiel continues: "The philosopher can do without a good memory for
conceptualized objects, but not without the Memory of the Past and Future
which are greater than time, and at which the *magna quaestio* aims: 'Where
do I come from and where am I going?' . . . Taking place in the time which
separates the Past from the Future, and oriented to both, philosophical
thinking paradoxically travels in one, and not two, directions. There shines
through it the mystery of eternity, in which the Beginning is the End and
the End is the Beginning."[7]

The weight of the ideas that crystallized in those decades at the end
of the nineteenth and at the beginning of the twentieth century in Russia
left a profound imprint on our present. What we are living through today
is in many ways nothing less than a continuation of those times, despite the
attempts to assert the contrary. And with regard to the proper responses to
the problems that have swept us up since those decades, we can see that,
even then, Providence was guiding us.

## Russia in Nineteenth-Century Europe

If we look at a map of Europe in 1853, among the first things we notice is
the sense of a perfect, or near perfect, balance—a balance established by
the Congress of Vienna and maintained by the Holy Alliance. The boundaries of this jigsaw puzzle that, at least in appearance, fit together so well,
were Lisbon in the southwest and Moscow in the northeast. Large patches
of enormous kingdoms and empires, which divided most of the European

---

5. Berdyaev, *Meaning of History*, 22–23.

6. Ibid., 33–35.

7. Grygiel, "Extra Communionem Personarum Nulla Philosophia," 697–98.

continent among themselves, seemed to possess sufficient power to guarantee the status quo for a long time to come. This new Pax Romana was based on two principles: legitimism and balance of power. The year 1853, however, witnessed the beginning of the end of this state of affairs. The Crimean War (1853–1856), which was about to begin, presented the Austro-Hungarian Empire with a difficult decision: whether to support Russia in its contest with Turkey. The decision not to support Russia had weighty consequences. It was, some decades later, the primary cause of the events that led to World War I. The decision was received in St. Petersburg as an act of treason, and it became the beginning of the struggle for influence in the Balkans. The European edifice built with all sorts of Enlightenment "instrumentalisms"—positivisms, evolutionisms, rationalisms, and so on—upon the not-so-distant echoes of the French Revolution and upon the ruins of the Empire of Napoleon Bonaparte, began to crumble. It would collapse precipitously between 1914 and 1919, and it would show the ultimate truth about itself between 1939 and 1945.

⸙

This hoped-for balance was one of the topics of a series of discussions between Prince Charles Maurice Talleyrand and the Emperor of All the Russias, Alexander I, when Alexander I, for two months in the spring of 1814, stayed at the princely palace in a Paris "liberated" by Napoleon Bonaparte. The idea of restoring Europe to the order that had been lost during the French Revolution and the Napoleonic Wars became the main topic of conversation at the highest levels of European diplomacy. Tsar Alexander I, hailed everywhere as the "liberator of Europe," traveled from Paris to England, then to St. Petersburg, and finally, in autumn of that same year, to Vienna. The Congress, which ended in June 1815, brought together representatives from sixteen European countries, including Great Britain (Robert Stewart Castlereagh), Austria (Clemens Wenzel Lothar von Metternich), France (Charles Maurice de Talleyrand), Prussia (Karl August von Hardenberg), and Russia (K. W. Nesselrode). Russia, Austria, and Prussia comprised the central core, the most active founders of the Holy Alliance. The pope did not join the alliance, and Great Britain did not sign the treaty.

The basic doctrine, called legitimism, proclaimed that all sovereigns are anointed by God and that these sovereigns should restore the ancient dynasties. Those who take power without respecting these doctrines are tyrants and cannot be considered legitimate rulers. The second background agreement, which was known as balance of power, was demanded by Britain and applied above all to issues related to conflict and to colonial arrangements. Among other things, the treaty signed on 9 June 1815 established a kind of Union of German States, the restoration of the Kingdom of Poland—a virtual state in which Tsar Alexander I was imposed as king—the declaration of Switzerland's neutrality, the rebirth of the Papal States, the reorganization of various Italian principalities, and the development of diplomatic protocols that remained in effect until the twentieth century. In short, under the leadership of the Russian Tsar—first Alexander I until his death in 1825, and then his brother, Tsar Nicholas I—a new world order was coming into being, and Russia, Austria, and Prussia stood as its defenders.

It is no surprise that, over time, Alexander I lost the nickname "the liberator of Europe" and was given another in its place: "the policeman of Europe." The latter was more in keeping with his actions. The declaration of the constitution of the Holy Alliance, which was filled with invocations of God and the Holy Faith, was a classic example of the political lie. Those who signed it declared that they recognized each other as brothers. Moved by the principles of love, peace, and justice, they committed in all times and places to come to one another's aid.

It did not take long to implement the new doctrine. We see instances of the strictest application of the letter of the agreements in the pacification of Naples in 1821 and Piedmont in 1822—the same year the monarchical order in Spain was restored—as well as in the bloody crackdowns on national uprisings, Poland in 1830 and Hungary in 1848. The Russians were so faithful to their commitment that, although Turkey did not participate in the Treaty, the Russians did not intervene in the famous Greek uprising of 1821. They respected Turkey's right to exterminate the rebels.

Of course, neither in 1815 nor at the beginning of 1853 did anyone expect that the times would change, and that the events of the following decades would drag all of Europe into a war that was, at least then, difficult to imagine. Just as the new world order began in a war on Russian soil with the defeat of Napoleon's army in 1812, the beginning of its end was another war that involved Russia—the Crimean War—and its humiliating defeat by Turkey and its allies, Great Britain and France.

⏤

If we were to look at the 1853 map of Europe, perhaps we would see that Russia was not distant from the rest of Europe, but had already become one of the centers of the most important historical events of the European continent. And perhaps it would not surprise us that its two largest cities, St. Petersburg and Moscow, had already become major European political, intellectual, and artistic hubs. Even more, these cities had become so

significant that many events that began in them acquired worldwide importance. Cultural life in Russia was beginning to bear its best fruit. It is enough
to mention such literary names as Pushkin, Gogol, Turgenev, Tolstoy, and
Dostoevsky—or such names in music as Glinka, Tchaikovsky, Mussorgsky,
and Rimsky-Korsakov—to realize that something important and profound
was happening on the eastern flank of Europe. This cultural development,
understood very broadly to include literature as well as philosophy, is un-
thinkable apart from Christianity, which was the background of all that was
happening in Russia. In the empire of that time, religion had for a long time
belonged to the range of issues that pertained directly to the state, and it also
marked, in a unique way, the lives of its inhabitants.

In the Russia of the Tsars, each person was officially assigned to a confession; the concept of atheism did not exist. Obviously, the vast majority
of Russia's inhabitants belonged to the Russian Orthodox Church, which
was largely controlled by the state. The unitary conception of power, so
characteristic of Russian history, profoundly influenced the relationship between Church and state. Representatives of the Russian Orthodox Church
rarely criticized the tsars explicitly. The story of Ivan the Terrible and the
Metropolitan of Moscow who was appointed by him, Philip Kolychev, was
exemplary in this regard. When Philip condemned publically the atrocities
committed by the Tsar, the Tsar ordered his execution. Later, just before
Ivan died, however, Ivan demanded that he be ordained as a monk, hop-
ing that with this decision he could avoid the final judgment, the vision of
which had begun to torment him. This story shows one of the most characteristic elements of Russian history: the relationship between the Church
and power, where power submits and even exercises institutional control
over Church, but where the Church at the same time safeguards in the
depths of her experience the mystical treasure of her independence. This is
something that no power and no state has been able to control, despite the
deepest desire to do so. It was Tsar Peter I who put things in order for good.
In 1721, he established the Holy Synod, an administrative body subordinate
to the state. The Holy Synod was made up of an ecclesiastical hierarchy, but
the real power, including the power to present hierarchical appointments to
the tsar, resided in the Chief Procurator (*Ober Prokurator*), the official title
of the head of the Holy Synod, a state official directly appointed by the tsar.

Despite this difficult situation, or perhaps because of it, there appears
in early nineteenth-century Russia a revival of interest in Christian experience marked in large measure by the publication in St. Petersburg in 1793 of
*The Philocalia of Nicodemus*, which was translated by a monk from Mount
Athos, St. Paissy Velichkovsky, founder of the Niamets Monastery in Mol-
davia. This book soon became very popular among the intellectual elite.

Not only did it provide access to important patristic texts related to prayer, asceticism, and mysticism; it also symbolized the beginning of a new epoch in the history of Russian culture.[8] Lossky, in his important work *History of Russian Philosophy*, comments: "For persons capable of religious experience it is unquestionable that Orthodoxy in the Russian form of it contains values of exceptionally high order of excellence. . . . It would be strange if so high a culture had produced nothing original in the domain of philosophy."[9] The influence of the Orthodox tradition is well known in Russian literature, but it is often forgotten that this influence reflects a milestone in the development of Russian Orthodox theology, understood in the context of the description of Pavel Florensky, one of the most prestigious Russian Orthodox theologians: "Living religious experience as the sole legitimate way to gain knowledge of the dogmas—that is how I would like to express the general theme of my book. . . . Only by relying on immediate experience can one survey the spiritual treasures of the Church and come to see their value."[10] The conceptual specificity contained in the work of theology was also clearly highlighted by another great master, Paul Evdokimov: "Knowledge of God cannot be treated as a *problem*, because it escapes all philosophical and theological speculation. It belongs to the mystery of Divine revelation, upon which it depends directly. Therefore, it is clear that we will not find a concrete solution, which does not exist anyway, since we are not before a problem but a mystery. Obviously, a mystery cannot be rationalized. But it can be made, in the words of Gabriel Marcel, 'luminous.'"[11]

Among the most prominent pioneers and authors of this revival of Russian Orthodox theology were, without a doubt, St. Seraphim of Sarov, who has been compared to Simeon the New Theologian; Father John of Kronstadt, a famous charismatic preacher and confessor, who is recognized as a saint by the Russian Orthodox Church Abroad; Metropolitan Filaret (Drozdov), probably the best known representative of the Russian Orthodox Church of the nineteenth century;[12] and finally, Archimandrite Feodor (Bukharev), who is considered as precursor of the modern "Russian School" of Orthodox theology.[13]

---

8. Meyendorff, *Orthodox Church*, 104–5.

9. Lossky, *History of Russian Philosophy*, 9.

10. Florensky, *Pillar and Ground of the Truth*, 5.

11. Evdokimov, *El conocimiento de Dios en la Tradición Oriental*.

12. Felmy, *Teología Ortodoxa Actual*, 37.

13. Valliere, *Modern Russian Theology*, 8.

❧

By the year 1853, the city of Moscow barely maintained its ancient structure, which had resembled a giant spider web. On the north bank of the winding Moscow River, the Kremlin stood proudly, surrounded by red walls marked by eighteen towers, signaling the center of the city and the empire. At the bridge, wide avenues opened, like large tentacles, toward the south, north, east, and west. Other streets and avenues expanded in ever-widening circles. The more one moved away from the city center, crossing the line of the old walls that surrounded the city, the more one began to find ruptures in this circular order. Though the city today grows according to new rules, its heart remains raised on Borovitsky Hill and in the Kremlin; its soul spreads out over the roofs and the towers of the Cathedral of the Dormition, the Cathedral of the Annunciation, St. Basil's Cathedral, and also over the small Cathedral of Our Lady of Kazan.

In the middle of the nineteenth century, Moscow experienced huge growth. From some two hundred thousand inhabitants at the beginning of the nineteenth century, it numbered more than a million by the end. The imperial order on the Emancipation of the Peasants from Serfdom (1861) began the peak period of the influx of entire families to the cities that could not purchase or lease any land.

At the same time, a generation of intellectuals had matured, heirs of those educated in the West as a result of initiatives taken by the Tsar Peter the Great. The Tsar, in his openness toward Europe, supported the travel of some of the most promising youth—all of whom came, of course, from higher social classes—to study in Western universities, particularly those in France. The reign of Peter the Great also marked the beginning of the development of the Russian educational system—a significant modernization effort. The level of illiteracy among peasants, however, remained considerable.

❧

Alexander I, influenced by his grandmother, the Empress Catherine II the Great, was educated in the thought of the French Encyclopedists, such as Rousseau, Voltaire, and Diderot. Alexander I spoke fluent French, English, Greek, and Russian. That he spoke Russian, incidentally, is not as obvious as it might seem.

Education began to reach ever widening social circles, especially the children of the ancient nobility of the provinces and the rising bourgeoisie. New universities and public schools were created throughout the empire, even though the nobility traditionally would send their children to private educational institutions.

French became the language of the dance halls of the high aristocracy, the tea meetings of the bourgeoisie, and the gatherings of artists, academics, and students. The language of Balzac was even spoken in the administration. Tsar Nicholas II's Russian was not very good, and he only signed royal decrees if they were written in French, which were then translated back into Russian. Some have seen in this abandonment of the Russian language the reason for the late development of Russian literature.

This was also the epoch of the rise of the Russian intelligentsia, which represented a distinctive social and spiritual phenomenon. It was not a mere social class but was, as Berdyaev argues, an "idealistic class." Its members were educated broadly in and dedicated their lives to the study and discussion of ideas, as well as to action on behalf of them, for the sake of which they were prepared "to face prison, hard labor, and death."[14]

The gulf between the educated elite and the majority of the subjects of the empire was also increasing. The comments of Tsar Nicholas I on the Decembrist Uprising of 1825, which attempted to raise his brother Constantine to the throne and establish a constitutional monarchy, are well-known and significant. When the rebel officers ordered the soldiers to cry, "Long live Constantine!" and "Long live the Constitution!," the Tsar commented that, with the second cry, the people were asking each other, "What is the Constitution, the wife of His Highness the Grand Duke?"

⸊

In 1830, the ban on travel to France imposed by the imperial government influenced the growth of the number of Russian travelers to Germany. Naturally, this situation led to the increase of interest in German culture and thought.

The Orthodox tradition and theology, together with Russian nationalism, on the one hand, and French Enlightenment thought, on the other, formed the field of play; German philosophy provided the first rules of the game; all that remained was to finish arranging the final pieces.

## Western Philosophy in Russia

Since the 1840s, the interest in and presence of philosophy in cultural and social life was already considerable. In Russia, the Hegelian owl of Minerva

14. Berdyaev, *Russian Idea*, 26.

found a favorable environment in which to take flight at dusk. The intelligentsia, which was increasingly influential and difficult to define, became a new social class, though it was prone to creative intellectual and social efforts. During the years of absolute monarchy, the impossibility of exercising the slightest political activity, the practical slavery of peasants, strict censorship, a corrupt bureaucracy, and the increasingly effective work of secret police, led some to make extreme decisions and even sacrifice their lives for the sake of ideas. All political and social persuasions shared a profound sense of nationalism. It would be a mistake to identify such nationalist sentiment exclusively with conservatives or traditionalists. Those who preached the most revolutionary and enlightened social ideas likewise did so in the name of the nation.[15]

Hegel became, as no one else had been until that moment, the omnipresent reference point. His name appeared in the ordinary conversations of intellectuals, artists, and politicians. The same subjects were discussed with equal passion in the capital and in the provinces, in the salons of the aristocracy and the dormitories of students. The Russian intelligentsia discovered very quickly, in Berdyaev's words, an unusual capacity for appreciating the influence of ideas. The passion for philosophy—for Hegel, Saint-Simon, Schelling, Fourier, Feuerbach, Marx, and so on—exceeded the levels of popularity that these figures attained even in their own countries. Russians, as a people, Berdyaev contends, are not very skeptical; they are, rather, "dogmatists," and they do not assimilate well what is relative, such that for them "everything takes on a religious character." When Darwin's theories in the West were treated as a biological hypothesis, they had, for the Russian intelligentsia, "a dogmatic character," as if they concerned "salvation for eternal life." Adherence to materialist premises was considered an act of "religious faith." Any social, political, cultural, and intellectual position was judged with the categories of "orthodoxy and heresy." The unique interest in Hegel, therefore, acquired the character of "a religious influence," and it was even expected that Hegelian philosophy would solve "the question of the faith of the Orthodox Church," the *Cerkiev*. Berdyaev even points out that the young "made love in the language of Schelling's philosophy of nature."[16]

This is how Ivan Kireyevsky, one of the initiators of the Slavophilic current in Russian thought, describes that milieu: "There is almost no man who would not converse in philosophical terms, no youth who would not discuss Hegel, and no book or journal article in which there would be

15. Ibid., 26.
16. Ibid., 26–27.

unnoticeable the influence of German thinking; ten-year old boys speak of concrete objectivity."[17]

Alexander Herzen, one of the greatest exponents of so-called Western ideas, remembers that

> They discussed these subjects [Hegelian philosophy] incessantly; there was not a paragraph in the three parts of the *Logic*, in the two of the *Aesthetic*, the *Encyclopedia*, and so on, which had not been the subject of desperate disputes for several nights together. People who loved each other avoided each other for weeks at a time because they disagreed about the definition of "all-embracing spirit," or had taken as a personal insult an opinion on "the absolute personality and its existence in itself." Every insignificant pamphlet published in Berlin or other provincial or district towns of German philosophy was ordered and read to tatters and smudges, and the leaves fell out in a few days, if only there was a mention of Hegel in it.[18]

In this lively cultural milieu, some among the young intelligentsia predicted future decades especially marked by the irruption of contemporary thought and the rise of a new social consciousness. The direct ancestor of the most clearly defined groups of Russian thought of mid-nineteenth century was known as the Liubomudry Society, or Love of Wisdom Society, an appellation that derived from the Russian for lovers of wisdom (*liubov'* [love], *mudrost'* [wisdom]). Liubomudry was a word, moreover, with something of a mystical character. It was coined by the Society in 1823 and used by them in clear contrast to the word "philosophy."

The problematic tendency to interpret and translate the name of the Society as the "Philosophical Society"[19] contradicts the group's explicit purpose, which was clearly expressed in the name chosen by the promoters of the initiative.[20] The founding of this Society was very significant in the panorama of Russia's still nascent intellectual history. At a time when the tradition of secret societies and spiritualist groups inherited from the French Enlightenment was very much alive and even commonplace, the emergence of German Romanticism led the young idealists to choose an intentionally symbolic and expressive name for themselves. The secret

17. Kireyevsky, "Opyt Nauki Filosofii." Cited in Nahirny, "Russian Intelligentsia," 411.

18. Herzen, *My Past and Thoughts*, 232.

19. We find this line of interpretation, for instance, in Zenkovsky, *A History of Russian Philosophy*.

20. Berdyaev maintains the adjective Liubomudry. See, for instance, Berdyaev, *Russian Idea*, 32–33.

Liubomudry Society was chaired by Prince Vladimir Odoevsky, who, in the German magazine *Mnemosyne* published with the support of the future Decembrist Wilhelm Küchelbecker, wrote: "To this day everyone imagines a philosopher to resemble one of those eighteenth-century French rattles; I wonder whether there are many people capable of understanding the enormous difference between a truly divine philosophy and that of some Voltaire or Helvetius."[21] The Society's substitution of the Slavic term "liubomudry" instead of the word "philosophy" in the name of the Society and its texts articulated the desire for a clear departure from materialist French philosophy, just as it also undoubtedly bore the influence of the new wave of romantic nationalism proclaimed by German idealism. The search for national "distinctiveness" and "authenticity" (*Eigentümlichkeit* or *Echtheit*) inspired the Liubomudry Society to look back toward its own tradition and its own popular sources and to insist on the need for the creation of a culture that was genuinely and distinctively Russian.[22]

⌇

The memories of Alexander Koshelev, a member of the Liubomudry Society, illustrate the Society's attitude and describe the atmosphere of its meetings:

> German philosophy predominated, i.e. Kant, Fichte, Schelling, Oken, Görres, and others. We sometimes read our own philosophical works, but more frequently we discussed the works of the German philosophers we had just read. The chief subject of our discussions was the general principles upon which human knowledge is founded. Christianity seemed to us suitable only for the masses of the people, but not for lovers of wisdom like us. We prized Spinoza particularly highly and put his works far above the New Testament and the rest of Holy Scripture.[23]

We should keep in mind that the creation of the Society was a response to the intellectual and cultural environment of the time, in which the enthusiasm of a few young philosophical novices, who were new employees of the Archives of the Ministry of Foreign Affairs, played a crucial role. One of the founders and presidents of the Liubomudry Society, Vladimir Odoevsky, was twenty years old; the secretary, D. V. Venevitinov, was eighteen; and, probably the youngest of all, the future Slavophile Ivan Kireyevsky, was seventeen. Nicholas Rozalin also participated in meetings along with another

21. Cited in Walicki, *Slavophile Controversy*, 65.
22. Ibid.
23. Koshelov, *Zapiski* [Notes], 11–12.

future Slavophile, Alexander Koshelev. These youthful and energetic philosophers had big plans, among which were to edit a journal, to develop a philosophical dictionary, and to translate all of the classics of philosophy into Russian. They fulfilled their first goal, publishing four volumes of the journal *Mnemosyne*. With regard to the second goal, it seems that they only produced an article for their future philosophical dictionary. And finally, with regard to the third goal, they were even less successful.[24] Not without some irony—and surely with some sympathy as well—Alexander Pushkin labeled them the "archive youth" in his work *Eugene Onegin*.[25]

Perhaps Pushkin's famous reference was an indication of one of the most important phenomena of the emergent Russian culture of the nineteenth and twentieth centuries: the mutual influence and intimate relation between new currents of Russian thought and literature. What at that time was nothing more than a wink from Pushkin—a sympathetic gesture that sought to recognize the efforts of the archive youth in promoting the search for their own spiritual heritage and the union between artistic expression and romantic philosophy—would, decades later, find deep resonances in the encounter between two giants: one of literature and another of philosophy. These two seekers of truth about the human person and about history were Fyodor Dostoevsky and Vladimir Soloviev.

All these young writers, intellectuals, and artists grew up in the same milieu, in the same circles of friends. Indeed, the creation of societies in Russia constituted a true social phenomenon and a fertile cultural nursery. Societies were often promoted by families of high society, and they offered spaces for artists and scientists to gather. Although most of the societies were literary, members debated other topics, such as philosophy, biology, poetry, history, and so on, during meetings as well. The public presentations of sections of the consecutive volumes of Nicholas Karamzin's *History of the Russian State*, an event organized by the Arzamas Literary Society to which Karamzin himself belonged, were especially well attended. This society, founded by D. Dashkov, ran between the years 1815–1817, brought together those who were sympathetic with innovations to the Russian literary language.[26] In 1823, S. E. Raich, who was Odoevsky's professor of literature, sponsored a literary society in Moscow. Among its members were M. Pogodin and S. Shevyriov, both future professors at the University of Moscow. Vladimir Titov, Nicolas Melgunov, and the poet Fyodor Tyutchev were

24. Egorov, *Oblicza Rosji* [Faces of Russia], 121.

25. In *Eugene Onegin* (vii, 49) Pushkin writes, "Viewed by the archive youth who cluster / At any gathering or dance . . ." Pushkin, *Poems, Prose, and Plays*.

26. Bazylow, *Społeczeństwo rosyjskie w pierwszej połowie XIX wieku* [Russian Society in the First Half of the Nineteenth Century], 383–88.

also members of it, in addition to being participants in the meetings of the Liubomudry Society. Although the Liubomudry Society was secret and the Raich Society was public, these societies soon established a close relationship. One of the intellectual bridges that led to this mutual understanding was undoubtedly the thought of Schelling, the German philosopher whose popularity in Russia overshadowed even Hegel.

Schelling's philosophy of art and of nature created common ground for philosophy and literature—especially poetry. His conception of the world—of nature—as a living, spiritual whole, as well as of art as a unity of conscious and unconscious creation, seemed to illuminate for many the most profound essence of the world and of life. The unity of subject and object, conscious and unconscious, spirit and matter—a union expressed in Schelling's and his disciple Oken's concepts of "holism" and of the "absolute"—began to attract the young, who were more than ready to adopt the romantic attitudes then in vogue throughout Europe. The twin challenge of writing poetically about philosophy and creating a poetry capable of participating in philosophical and spiritual conversations was a challenge fit for the times. In the second half of the nineteenth century, it would discover its most notable conquerors.

The Liubomudry Society and the Decembrists established a different kind of relationship. The Decembrists were members of the Northern Society. The Northern Society was based in St. Petersburg and was one of the two societies that arose from the breakup of the Union of Welfare. The other society that arose from the breakup, the Southern Society, was based in Tulchin. It led the revolution, or more precisely, attempted to lead the revolution, after the death of Tsar Alexander I in December 1825. The meetings between the Liubomudry Society and the Decembrists were very numerous, as we have already mentioned. The co-editor of the journal *Mnemosyne* was Küchelbecker, a member of the Northern Society. Vladimir Odoevsky, who chaired the Liubomudry Society, had a close relationship with his cousin Alexander Odoevsky, a renowned Decembrist poet. Discussions between the representatives of the two societies were the order of the day. They professed two concepts of the nation: one associated with the Liubomudry and rooted in German idealism, and another associated with the Decembrists and rooted in Enlightenment rationalism. Moreover, although they agreed on the need for social changes in Russia, they differed with regard to the method of such changes.

The differences between these societies reflected a generational gap, but they also instantiated what distinguished the intellectual atmospheres of Moscow and St. Petersburg. The Liubomudry Society was born in Moscow, while St. Petersburg was the center of the Decembrist movement. Moscow, the former capital of Russia, was distinguished by its semi-patriarchal, historic, and noble character. Likewise, Moscow was the center of the religious, spiritual, and mystical life of Russia, not only with its Christian roots but with its naturalist, spiritualist, and Rosicrucian-Masonic elements as well. Moscow therefore marked the first line of defense in the confrontation with revolutionary or liberal ideas. St. Petersburg, by contrast, was a city without a history. Its eyes were always directed towards Europe, especially France. It was the cradle of liberal, bourgeois-democratic, and socialist ideologies. "For God's sake, escape from the rotten, reeking atmosphere of Moscow," wrote Küchelbecker to Odoevsky.[27]

Odoevsky, a thin man without much in the way of physical appearance who devoted himself to matters of the intellect, was in many ways diametrically opposed to his Decembrist cousin Alexander, who was full of vitality and strength, and who Vladimir used to reproach for an utter lack of interest in the philosophy of Schelling. Somewhat irritated, Alexander replied that he tried to study the thought of the German but found in him absolutely nothing of interest. Vladimir, in response, proceeded to point out the grammatical errors in the French of the letters of his restless cousin.

Not infrequently the discussions between the societies took the nature of public debates—as when, during an afternoon gathering at the home of the future Decembrist Mikhail Naryshkin, Kondraty Ryleyev read his poems. Later, one of the Liubomudry, Alexander Koshelev, related to his fellow-members how impressed he was when he heard the conspirators, calmly and in public, discuss the need to do away with the government ("*d'en finir avec ce gouvernement*").[28]

Despite these ideological disputes, the archive youth had a firm and combative attitude toward their older counterparts. Their secret organization, which sought to generate a revolution against the absolute monarchy of the Romanovs, was the oldest and certainly the first that tried to implement such ideas, though these ideas were not well defined.

One consequence of Napoleon Bonaparte's invasion of Russia in 1812 was the awakening of national sentiment—the identification of Russians with their own national reality. Throughout the war campaign, many young people, including minors from noble families, ran away to join the army, and they often rose to the rank of officers. At that time, the concept of the *fatherland* became for many very concrete, such that the problems that afflicted this still deeply feudal society began to be felt as its own problems. The responsibility for other Russians and the country's future took center

27. Sakulin, *Iz istorii russkogo idealizma*, 304.
28. Walicki, *Slavophile Controversy*, 70.

stage in the consciousness of the generation that had to defend Russia. The idea of the nation began to take a specific imperial shape. When, after the victory, Russian regiments crossed Europe and stayed for many months in France, the young officers encountered another world with different social structures and different administrative and political relationships as a consequence of the French Revolution of 1789. They encountered a world that was *enlightened*, full of dynamism and caught up in a process of transformation.

These soldiers' experience of a modern Europe, combined with an acute sense of their own nation as mired in the past, led to the founding of the first clandestine organizations. This sense of Russia's situation was expressed very pessimistically by Alexander Radishchev in his narrative, *The Journey from Petersburg to Moscow*. During those years, there began an epoch characterized by a growing interest in solving serious social problems, a period of seeking radical solutions.

The organizations of Russian army officers, which were not always political, already existed before 1816. Over time, following the example of the Italian *Carbonari* or the Greek *Heterías*, or even the Prussian *Tugend-bund*, these organizations became increasingly political and clandestine. In 1816, a group of about thirty officers founded the Union of Salvation—a still semi-clandestine organization—that rapidly changed its name to the Society of True and Loyal Sons of the Fatherland. Its members included Captain Nikita Muravyov, Colonel Sergey Muravyov-Apostol, Prince Sergei Trubetskoy, and the most radical of all, Colonel Pavel Pestel.[29] Membership in the organization did not require full ideological unity. The majority thought Russia's future should be based upon a constitutional-monarchical system, although there were also republicans, even those as extreme in their plans as Pestel, who advocated the execution of the imperial family. In the year 1818, the same members created a new and better-structured organization called the Union of Welfare and approved its statutes, which were known as the *Green Book*.

Three years later, as a result of changes in the locations of the deployments of the conspirators' military units, as well as internal differences within the organization itself, the organization split into two: the Northern Society, based in St. Petersburg, and the Southern Society, based in Tulchin and bolstered in 1825 by its union with the Society of United Slavs. Founded in 1823 by group of junior officers, the Society of United Slavs was a revolutionary organization—the most radical of all—which proclaimed the need to unite all Slavic peoples into a single democratic state. In the

29. Bazylow, *Historia Rosji* [History of Russia], 205.

north, the leadership consisted of Captain Nikita Muravyov, Colonel Sergey Muravyov-Apostol, and Prince Sergei Trubetskoy. In the south, Colonel Pavel Pestel, who was the author of the political agenda, led the group.

Pestel's political program, entitled *Russian Truth*, was republican in character. In it, he predicted the overthrow of the Romanov Dynasty; the creation of a strong centralized state; the elimination of the differences between social groups; the liberation of the peasants; the redistribution of the land the peasants cultivated; and the nationalization of the rest of the land, which at that time belonged to the landlords, in order to provide indispensable resources for the realization of the new administrative apparatus. In addition, all males over the age of twenty would be given extensive civil and political rights.

In the north, Nikita Muravyov wrote what would be known as *The Constitution*. It was much less radical than *Russian Truth*, and it proposed keeping the imperial family but limiting its power through the creation of the National Assembly and structuring the state as a federation. It also indicated the need for the liberation of the peasants, although Muravyov's proposal for allocating the land was more moderate than Pestel's.

All these bold plans, however, had no organizational support. The structures of both associations were very weak, and they found limited support among officers. The ordinary soldiers from poorer social classes, who were forced to serve in the army for a term of twenty-five years and who were generally mistreated, had no interest in the things of the lords. It is therefore not surprising that the Northern Society's attempt to begin a revolution upon receiving the news of the death of Tsar Alexander I in December 1825 was doomed to failure from the start.

The hope that the installation of the younger brother of the late Tsar, the Grand Prince Constantine, would be an alternative to the social and political situation under the reign of Alexander I, belonged to the realm of wishful thinking rather than real knowledge of Constantine's actual political convictions. The only thing that differentiated Grand Prince Constantine Romanov from his older brother was the lack of desire to become the next tsar. From Warsaw, where he lived, he sent urgent letters to the youngest of his three brothers, Nicholas, in order to cede to Nicholas the crown of the empire. Nicholas accepted, and therefore became, unexpectedly, Tsar Nicholas I.

The revolutionary officers, despite these developments, organized a desperate propaganda campaign among the soldiers, promising freedom for the peasant farmers, a sensible reduction of military service, and the abolition of censorship. They developed a plan for a *coup d'état*, which consisted in the takeover of government buildings and the Senate's forced proclamation of their manifesto. But when, on the morning of December 26 (O.S. December 14), 1825, more than three thousand soldiers gathered in front of the Senate in St. Petersburg, senators and members of the State Council had already sworn allegiance to Nicholas I. Consequently, the idea to legitimate the *coup d'état* through the use of the imperial administration failed. Prince Sergei Trubetskoy, who had been elected dictator of the uprising, failed to appear in the square due to an apparent change of heart. The revolution had lost its leader.

No decisions were made. Hours passed, and thousands of curious onlookers gathered to observe the rows of soldiers. The soldiers stood firm and motionless, despite the cold. Every moment they grew more aware of the futility of their position, as well as the fact that no one could save them from the punishment that awaited them. But they simply continued to stand on the same site. Nicholas I, equally surprised and disoriented, sent for the governor of St. Petersburg, General Mikhail Miloradovich, with the intention to negotiate. But one of the leaders of the uprising, Pyotr Kakhovsky, in an act of desperation, killed the general. Over the course of the afternoon, the rebels proclaimed Prince Eugene Obolensky the dictator of the uprising, and the rebels exchanged shots with forces loyal to the emperor. Finally, Nicholas I ordered the use of artillery. The first salvo dispersed the rebels: many died in the square, and others drowned trying to cross the frozen Neva River. Most of the survivors ended up being arrested that very night. Some units outside the capital tried to join the uprising. But with the unexpected arrest of Colonel Pavel Pestel and the lack of clear and effective leadership, they were defeated.

The investigation and subsequent trial of the Decembrists lasted only a few months. The Tsar himself was involved in the interrogations. Despite promises to forgive and forget those who confessed, the only act of mercy the Tsar granted to them was to change the death sentence from being drawn and quartered to being hung. On 13 July 1826, Pestel, Ryleyev, Bestuzhev-Ryumin, Kakhovsky, and Muravyov-Apostol were all executed. About six hundred others were condemned to long years of hard labor in Siberia. The legend of the Decembrists was born, and the thirty years of hard autocratic rule under Nicholas I commenced.

The first reactions of the members of the Liubomudry to these events were odd considering their own theoretical commitments: they warmly welcomed the news of the uprising. They forgot philosophy and Schelling, and instead began to take classes in horseback riding and fencing, living now the life of future heroes. But the news of the failure of the revolution quickly dampened the spirits of the archive youth. They suspended the activities of the Society. In the following years and decades, they nevertheless continued to maintain contact with each other, and they participated in cultural life and in philosophical and political debates. Between 1827 and 1830, they published articles in the *Moscow Herald* newspaper, edited by Pogodin.[30]

## THE FIRST CRITIC OF THE MODERN WEST: VLADIMIR ODOEVSKY

In the following years, the members of the archive youth especially emphasized the ideas of Vladimir Odoevsky. The development of his thought on anthropology and historiosophy[31] marked the first attempts to explore the paths down which the Slavophiles would later travel. At this stage, Odoevsky's ideas largely coincided with those of his friend and fellow member of the Liubomudry Society, Ivan Kireyevsky. Odoevsky recognized that his own thought, particularly his thought of the early 1830s, anticipated the proposals of the Slavophiles to some extent. They did so insofar as both were critical of rationalism, as well as materialistic and industrial civilization. They both found in rationalism the source of the separation between subject and object, to which they opposed the integrity of the human spirit. They both saw clear parallels between the rationalism of classical Roman civilization and the modern world. And they both regarded the philosophy of Schelling as the summit of European thought, which the West was no longer able to put into practice.

Despite these commonalities, what differentiated Odoevsky from the Slavophiles was that Odoevsky felt himself to be European. He missed the heritage of Christian Europe and its significance. He had no interest in Russian national and popular culture. On the contrary, he identified with the aristocratic romanticism of the West. He believed in the romantic destiny of the upper classes, and he thought that only the aristocracy was capable of safeguarding England from its total capitulation to the representatives of the modern classes of the industrialized world. He had no pretensions to learn from the people. The desire for Russian excellence concerned Odoevsky. The popular local community, which was so important for the Slavophiles, played no role in Odoevsky's thought.

According to Pavel Sakulin, who in his *History of Russian Idealism: Prince V. F. Odoevsky* compiles Odoevsky's manuscripts from the early 1830s, the thought of the founder of the Liubomudry Society reflects the same shift

---

30. Walicki, *Slavophile Controversy*, 70–71.

31. Historiosophy translates the Russian "istoriosofiya" and means "philosophy of history." It is primarily concerned with the meaning of history, the end of history, etc. See, for instance, Zenkovsky, *History of Russian Philosophy*, 6. —Trans.

found in Schelling.[32] When the German in his Munich lectures began to point to what would later be known as the "philosophy of mythology" and the "philosophy of revelation," Odoevsky was reading mystics and theosophists like Jacob Boehme, John Pordage, Louis Claude de Saint-Martin, and Franz Xaver von Baader. Odoevsky developed a mystical-philosophical idealism upon which he based his historiosophical and anthropological ideas.

The starting point for Odoevsky's anthropology and historiosophy was original sin. The philosopher saw the first humans as free and pure spiritual beings. The fall enslaved humans to nature—a nature that could be reborn only through love and art. Continuous aesthetic development in human history indicated that, one day, humankind would recover its integrity and harmony of spirit, but that renewal would only happen through aesthetics. Art, moreover, fulfilled its vocation only when it was nurtured by religion. The same was also true for science. When art or science separated themselves from poetry and religion, they became egotistical phenomena, leading to the spiritual death of the nation.[33]

According to Odoevsky, England was the best example of a spiritually dead nation. England had been put to death by capitalism, industrialization, greed, and the intstrumentalization of human life and work.[34] Odoevsky saw a parallel between history and the development of philosophical ideas. In this way, human alienation—the process of the conversion of the person to the individual in the England of the Industrial Revolution—reflected, at the level of social praxis, proposals drawn from Anglo-Saxon rationalist and empirical philosophy. This critique, which was characteristically romantic and idealist, led Odoevsky to develop the concept of "instinct" and the human person's "instinctual energies." Instinct, in the vision of this Russian thinker, lacked all biological connotations. Instead, it acquired a kind of mystical dimension as an irrational power that belonged to prelapsarian human nature and made a natural and intimate relationship with God possible. Instinct was a power that, even after the fall, still propelled the creature towards its Creator. The history of humankind, according to Odoevsky, was a succession of epochs dominated either by instinct or rationality. With Roman civilization, rationalism nearly extinguished the spark of God in human beings. Despite everything, rationalism was unable to kill the true nature of human persons. The strength of instinct was necessary in order to return the human to its natural state, to salvation. The appearance of Christianity in world history marked the rebirth of instinct—an instinct

32. Sakulin, *Iz istorii russkogo idealizma*, 324.

33. Ibid., 510–64.

34. Ibid., 577.

even more powerful than before. It was no accident that, in the midst of the appreciation of classical culture in the eighteenth century, an epoch of rationalism would return, and calculation would expel spirit.

Odoevsky had no strong objection to reason. He did preach, however, the need to raise reason toward the level of instinct, as well as the need to achieve a synthesis between empiricism and a philosophical reflection rooted in what was natural to human beings. Getting this balance right in an unbalanced modern world, Odoevsky claimed, was possible through the revitalization of art, because in art we find the power of the spirit that modernity has not completely destroyed.[35] Poetry contained the greatest powers of the human spirit, and the highest genre of poetry was prophetic poetry. Odoevsky noted that a society not steeped in religion and poetry was doomed to degenerate. All human work—art, science, law—would die.

In contrast to the Western world, which, according Odoevsky, was condemned to death, the Russian people received the experience of the ancients but did not stop being like children.[36] It was Odoevsky's vision of Russia, however, that was childish. He idealized the Russian feudal patriarchy over and against European bourgeois society. He did not deny the need for many reforms, yet he was convinced of Russia's unique mission. This sense of Russia's uniqueness found support in Odoevsky's teacher, Schelling, who during a personal meeting with Odoevsky in Berlin in 1842 confirmed that he thought Russia was destined for greatness. Odoevsky, commenting upon his impressions of the meeting, said he felt as though, if Schelling were not so old, he would probably convert to Orthodoxy.[37]

All these thoughts are echoed in the texts Odoevsky began to write from the late 1820s onward. Faithful to his understanding of the union between art and poetry, on the one hand, and his intention to put in practice the holism of Schelling's thought, on the other, Odoevsky created a wide range of texts that varied in form and theme. He wrote about historiosophy, gnoseology, economics, politics, and, of course, art, poetry, and music. On the formal side he presented, with uneven results, a series of dialogues interspersed with short stories and novellas. His intention consisted in teaching the prophetic power of the poet who, through the extreme effort of instinct, had the power to penetrate the world of the secret forces that shaped and unified spiritual and material life.[38]

35. Ibid., 482.
36. Ibid., 591.
37. Ibid., 386.
38. Ibid., 42.

The texts collected under the title *Russian Nights* were published in 1844, and they constituted the first volume of Odoevsky's *Complete Works*. It is noteworthy that, in the dialogues, a character whose name is Faust represents the ideas of Odoevsky himself. The invocation of the protagonist of Goethe's great work illustrates the ties that bind the author to German Romanticism. The invocation, however, is insufficient to save the uneven quality of *Russian Nights*. The dialogues collected in it have more documentary than literary significance—as Odoevsky himself confirms—and they offer a unique and faithful image of the life of the Muscovite intelligentsia of the 1820s and 1830s.[39]

Of the stories that comprised *Russian Nights*, the one titled "A City Without Name" is especially noteworthy. It is a story about the rise and fall of Benthamia, a city founded on the teaching of Jeremy Bentham—an obvious symbol of the utilitarianism that characterized, according to Odoevsky, England at the beginning of the eighteenth century.

Bentham's ideas and those developed by his disciple John Stuart Mill are known as utilitarianism, which is as much a theory about human welfare as about what is right. As a welfare theory, utilitarianism holds that the good is that which maximizes utility, and it understands utility as pleasure, preference-satisfaction, or an objective list of values. As a theory about what is right, utilitarianism considers the consequences of an action, and it claims that right action is that which provides the greatest happiness for the greatest number."[40] In *A Fragment on Government*, Bentham writes that a "fundamental axiom" in the moral world, which has yet to be developed, is that "*it is the greatest happiness of the greatest number that is the measure of right and wrong.*"[41] Along similar lines, Mill begins "What Is Utilitarianism?," the second chapter of his programmatic book *Utilitarianism*, in the following manner:

> The creed which accepts as the foundation of morals, Utility, or the Greatest Happiness Principle, holds that actions are right in proportion as they tend to promote happiness, wrong as they tend to produce the reverse of happiness. By happiness is intended pleasure, and the absence of pain; by unhappiness, pain, and the privation of pleasure. To give a clear view of the moral standard set up by the theory, much more requires to be said; in particular, what things it includes in the ideas of pain and

39. See the 1844 introduction to Odoevsky, *Russkie nochi*, 50. All additional citations are from Odoevsky, "A City Without Name," in *Russian Nights*. —Trans.

40. Bentham, "Defense of Usury," 163.

41. Bentham, *Fragment on Government*, 93. Bentham's italics.

pleasure; and to what extent this is left an open question. But these supplementary explanations do not affect the theory of life on which this theory of morality is grounded—namely, that pleasure, and freedom from pain, are the only things desirable as ends; and that all desirable things (which are as numerous in the utilitarian as in any other scheme) are desirable either for the pleasure inherent in themselves, or as means to the promotion of pleasure and the prevention of pain.[42]

The thought of Bentham and Mill sought to indicate to humankind the road toward happiness—a happiness that, in their opinion, was attainable by means of adequate legislation and education.[43]

There is no doubt that, as Andrzej Walicki emphasizes, Odoevsky's narrative resembles Weber's spirit of capitalism—the systematic planning, the calculation, and so on—which eventually subordinates all aspects of individual and communal life.[44] But "A City Without Name" more broadly reflects Odoevsky's position in a debate that, during the nineteenth century, permeated and absorbed all of Western civilization and made it a new social, economic, and political reality: modernity. The modern world is a world in which philosophy in the service of the useful becomes an ideology. In Odoevsky's text, we find allusions both to the economic liberalism of Adam Smith and the evolution and radicalization of that liberalism in the thought of Bentham and Mill. Presumably, the Russian thinker knew the thought of Smith and its development by Bentham, which regarded the Church as among the major obstacles to the advancement of economic freedom. Classic liberal socio-economic thinking proclaimed the need for the liberation of the market from all interference, whether political, moral, theological, or even familial.[45] This liberationist line of thinking was common, to greater or lesser extent, to all modern thought, both for the idealist hermeneutics of Weber, as well as for the positivism initiated by Auguste Comte and continued in the thought of Karl Marx and Emile Durkheim. As Alasdair MacIntyre points out, utilitarianism unites the eighteenth-century project of the justification of morality with the emotivism of the twentieth century. Utilitarianism and its repercussions, over the course of nearly two centuries, marked many social processes and institutions, and remained "as

---

42. Mill, "Utilitarianism," 126.
43. Berlin, *Four Essays on Liberty*.
44. Walicki, *Slavophile Controvers*, 77.
45. Long, *Divine Economy*, 193.

an inheritance long after utilitarianism had lost the philosophical importance which John Stuart Mill's exposition had conferred upon it."[46]

In his short story, Odoevsky not only describes a vision of a world built upon these modern ideologies, but he also announces its decline and fall. The citizens of this new city, the city of Benthamia, are immigrants from the Old World, and they create, on a distant island land, a new civilization. The citizens decide that their god is self-interest, and so, in the central square of the city, they build "a colossal statue of Bentham," and on its pedestal they inscribe "in gold letters: SELF-INTEREST."[47] Likewise, after some disagreement, they decide to build a church and a theater: the church so that the citizens always remember that self-interest forms the foundation of their ethics, and the theatre to strengthen their belief that self-interest is the source of happiness and of progress, while altruism always leads to failure.

> The colony prospered. Common activity surpassed all belief. All classes of inhabitants were up from early morning, afraid to lose even the smallest part of their time—and everyone went about his business: one was busy building a machine, another tilled new land, a third invested money—they hardly had time to eat. Social conversation considered only the question of what one could extract benefit from. Many books on the subject appeared. What am I saying? That was the only kind of book that was published. A girl would read a treatise about a weaving factory instead of a novel; a boy of twelve would begin saving money for capital to be used for mercantile operations. Families had no knowledge of useless fun, nor of useless pastime—each minute of the day was scheduled, each step was weighted, and nothing was lost to no purpose. We did not have a moment's repose; we did not have a minute of what other people called self-enjoyment—life incessantly moved forward, whirling and crackling.[48]

Meanwhile, on a neighboring island, people found another colony, consisting of a peaceful village of simple peasants who lived from day to day. Benthamia's citizens immediately recognize a perfect opportunity to benefit themselves. They establish the concept of exploitation, and immediately establish trade relations with the new colony. As they discuss whether

46. MacIntyre, *After Virtue*, 65.

47. Odoevsky, "A City Without Name," 104. For the sake of clarity, I have altered Olga Koshansky-Olienikov and Ralph Matlaw's translation slightly. Following Walicki, I use "self-interest" rather than "benefit." —Trans.

48. Ibid., 105.

it would be beneficial to acquire permanently the land of their neighbors, they carefully calculate the benefits and costs of a war. When their attempt to purchase the land is refused, they decide that invasion would lead to a net benefit, and so they conquer and occupy the neighboring island. In this way, there begins a dynamic of exploitation, trade relations, and, ultimately, conquest directed against other colonies both near and far.

This policy makes Benthamia strong and dangerous but also increasingly internally unbalanced. The merchants, serving the god of self-interest, establish monopolies, applying techniques to control both markets and the freedom of the other inhabitants, because the entire project of obtaining profit justifies any economic behavior. Not all participate in the success, however, and the differences between rich and poor become increasingly clear. More and more, the various groups that comprise the new oligarchy fight amongst themselves for the reins of power. Finally, the merchants succeed and impose their understanding of self-interest upon all spheres of life, enriching themselves on bankruptcies, stocking up on goods that are in demand only to sell them later at higher prices, engaging in stock market speculation, and establishing monopolies under the banner of free trade. In the end, religion turns out to be useless, for the new ethic consists in the fundamental ability to extract profit, and intellectual activity centers upon strategizing such extraction. Accounting replaces poetry, and the monotonous sound of machines replaces music.

During the merchants' reign, a prophet appears, but no one heeds his warnings about the impending disaster. Instead, they lock him in an asylum. A series of *coups d'état* follow: first the artisans take power, then the farmers. Each group, each in the same way, cares only for its own self-interest, which accelerates the fall of the city. Then there begins the reign of a new kind of chaos and destruction. The once flourishing colony becomes a desolate landscape. The citizens, decimated by famine, brutalized by war, and organized into increasingly savage and hostile bands, forget their own past. They even forget the name of their city, hence, the title, "A City Without Name." They give superstitious and primitive worship to a stone, without even knowing that this stone—the stone upon which the statue of Bentham once stood, which was erected in honor of self-interest—is the only thing that remains of the past. In the end, war, starvation, earthquakes, disease, and wild animals eventually erase the last traces of the prideful city.

For a contemporary reader, Odoevsky's narration of the city of Benthamia evokes the world described by Alasdair MacIntyre in "A Disquieting Suggestion," the first chapter of the now classic book *After Virtue*.[49] In

49. MacIntyre, *After Virtue*, 1–5.

both cases, the image of a "fictitious" civilization serves as a starting point for a reflection on the world in which the philosopher actually lives. The central thesis of the exercise coincides in both cases and is summarized in MacIntyre's conclusion that "we have—very largely, if not entirely—lost our comprehension, both theoretical and practical, of morality."[50]

But to this image of modern Western civilization condemned to violence, and, ultimately, to death, Odoevsky opposes a vision of a young Russian nation, uncontaminated by the "moral preaching" of Franklin and the liberal economic theories of Smith, and the creative potential of a culture elevated upon the foundations of the Catholic tradition.[51] Such a rejection of an enlightened, positivist world, which would later return in the Slavophiles, tended to rely upon a highly idealized conception of Russia. In the first half of the nineteenth century, the idea that Russia had a unique and universal mission became increasingly popular. But not everyone agreed with the view that the Russians—through their elites, of course—were prepared to take the lead role in the history of Europe, or even in the history of their nation's own destiny. In fact, we cannot understand the ideas of Odoevsky if we do not understand him as one voice—and not even the most well-known voice—among his contemporaries. His was a voice immersed in a debate that, in contrast to the debates at the meetings of the archive youth in the 1830s, and despite the particularly harsh dictatorship of Tsar Nicholas I, soon became public.

## "The Shot" of Peter Chaadayev

In 1836, the magazine *The Telescope*, edited by N. I. Nadezhdin, published, probably without the consent of the author, the first of Peter Chaadayev's *Philosophical Letters*. The letter was written seven years earlier, and had since ceased to be fully representative of Chaadayev's thought. Nevertheless, as Alexander Herzen describes the publication of the letter: "The letter was in a sense the last word, the limit. It was a shot that rang out in the dark night; whether it was something foundering that proclaimed its own wreck, whether it was a signal, a cry for help, whether it was news of the dawn or news that there would not be one—it was all the same: one had to wake up."[52] The publication of the first of Chaadayev's *Philosophical Letters* represents one of those rare moments in the history of thought that emphatically shows the way words possess a precious power. In this case, words were

50. Ibid., 2.

51. Walicki, *Slavophile Controversy*, 79–80.

52. Herzen, *My Past and Thoughts*, 292–93.

not only capable of causing a huge scandal but they also catalyzed a debate that transcended its local context and permitted the articulation of ideas of worldwide import.

↬

Herzen was right: one had to wake up. But this awakening was not pleasant for everyone. The founder of the Liubomudry Society indignantly wrote to a friend: "What Chaadayev said about Russia, I say about Europe and vice versa."[53] In the Russia of Nicholas I, with its "Triad" of Official Nationality proposed by Minister of Education Sergey Uvarov and embraced by the Tsar—orthodoxy, autocracy, and nation[54]—the consequences of the publication of a letter that so blatantly contradicted the official line that the West was breaking down and that only Russia could offer a flourishing future to all humankind was much more than an ordinary social scandal. At the public and political level, the magazine that published the letter was shut down, the editor was exiled to Siberia, the censor responsible for checking the contents of the magazine was fired, and following the Tsar's personal instructions, Chaadayev was declared mentally ill and confined to house arrest.

The most important consequence of the dissemination of the letter in print—the letter had circulated for years in copied manuscripts without raising suspicions—lay in the unusual debate it provoked. The debate held academic societies, the political world, and the nascent intelligentsia on tenterhooks, but it also translated into a far-reaching intellectual and social event in the Russia of the second half of the nineteenth century and the early part of the twentieth. The vision of Russia and its relationship with Europe articulated in Chaadayev's letter triggered a storm of philosophical statements, reflections, and studies that progressively reflected the division of opinions expressed in two opposing definitions of what came to be called, a few decades later, the *Russkaya ideya*, the Russian Idea.

53. Koyré, *Etudes sur l'histoire de la pensée philosophique en Russie*, 29–30.

54. The first two terms of this triad do not leave the least doubt as to their meaning. The third term, however, is more difficult to interpret. The Russian word *narodnost* can be understood to mean "nation" or "people." It might seem that this ambiguity in the so-called Triad of Official Nationality is intentional. Sergey Uvarov, the creator of the Triad, was at that time Minister of Education. It is probable that he wanted to underscore the unity and harmony of the relationships between state and people, opposing the Russian national reality—*narodnost* understood as nation—to the reality of the rest of Europe, and, at the same time, emphasizing the specifically Russian consciousness of popular unity—*narodnost* understood as people—in contrast to Western republican tendencies.

⌐

Awakened by Chaadayev's "shot," two great currents of Russian thought were born, the Slavophiles and the Westerners. These names arose very early as a consequence of that debate, and each had a pejorative connotation, which is not surprising given that each term was coined by its ideological opponent: "Westernizer" was imposed by the Slavophiles, and "Slavophiles" was imposed by the Westernizers.

This division led to a simplified interpretation of what these two groups actually shared in common, relegating the debate to a reductionist, and therefore misleading, contest between European and Slavic, Western and Eastern, which only permitted the two groups to offer simplistic sketches of the complex, underlying controversy. At its heart, this was a debate about three intimately related issues: (i) the definition of the human person, or anthropology; (ii) the kind of society that people create or should create, or historiosophy; and, finally, (iii) the account of universality, whether ecclesiological or national, that framed both the anthropology and the historiosophy. The debate about the Russian Idea was a debate about the idea of Europe, the idea of humanity, because it was also a debate about the human person and what it meant for human persons to relate to the reality that surrounds them and to the history in which they participated.

In this debate, God and the Church clearly acquired a leading role. Any attempt to interpret the debate initiated by the letter of Chaadayev that ignores this background demonstrates either an unjustifiable tendentiousness or a disturbing ignorance of the profound unity between Christian tradition and experience in the social and historical context of nineteenth-century Russian philosophy.[55] Berdyaev, in his *Russian Idea*, puts it this way in his description and analysis of Russian thought and culture of the nineteenth century: "The question of socialism, the Russian question of the organization of mankind in terms of a new personnel, is a religious question; it is a question of God and immortality. In Russia the social theme remains a religious theme, even given atheistic thought."[56] In Berdyaev's words, we once again perceive the three intimately related issues noted above in the birth and the development of the Russian Idea: a vertical ontological unity always articulates and grounds the tripartition of anthropology, historiography, and ecclesiology.

---

55. Antonov, *Filosofia religii v russkoy metafizike XIX- nachalo XX veka* [Philosophy of religion in Russian metaphysics in the nineteenth century and early twentieth century], 37–38.

56. Berdyaev, *Russian Idea*, 123.

Any philosophical reflection always has an intrinsically and primarily ontological self-definition, and therefore, an anthropological self-definition. As Berdyaev writes, "The ethical ideas of the Russians are very different from the ethical ideas of Western peoples, and they are more Christian ideas. Russia's moral values are defined by an attitude towards man, and not towards abstract principles of property or of the State, nor towards good in the abstract."[57] Isaiah Berlin confirms Berdyaev's claim: "The central issue of Russian society was not political but social and moral. The intelligent and awakened Russian wanted above all to be told what to do, how to live as an individual, as a private person. Turgenev testifies that never were people more interested in the problems of life, and never less in those of pure aesthetic theory, than in the 1840s and 50s."[58]

The historiosophical aspect consisted not only in the reference points that appeared over the course of the debate about the history of Europe in general and Russian history in particular, but especially in the very purpose of the debate itself, which centered upon Russia's fate in its own history and in the history of humankind. As Berdyaev writes, "There are two prevailing myths which are capable of becoming dynamic in the chorus of the peoples—the myth of the beginning and the myth of the end. Among Russians, it was the second myth, the eschatological myth, which prevailed."[59] Berdyaev continues:

> Russian nineteenth-century thought was mainly preoccupied with problems of the philosophy of history which, indeed, laid the foundations of our national consciousness. It is no accident that our spiritual interests were centered upon the disputes of the slavophiles and westerners about Russia and Europe, the East and West. Chaadayev and the slavophiles had helped to turn Russian speculation towards these problems, for, to them, the enigma of Russia and her historical destiny was synonymous with that of the philosophy of history. Thus the elaboration of a religious philosophy of history would appear to be the specific mission of Russian philosophical thought, which has always had a predilection for the eschatological problem and apocalypticism. This is what distinguishes it from Western thought and also gives it a religious character.[60]

57. Ibid., 267.
58. Berlin, *Russian Thinkers*, 174.
59. Berdyaev, *Russian Idea*, 32.
60. Berdyaev, *Meaning of History*, xxv.

The ecclesiological aspect consisted in the thought and practice of the Church, which explained and displayed the answers to the debates about anthropology and historiosophy. Human persons cannot define or understand themselves without looking beyond themselves; they cannot survive the amputation of their supernatural dimension. Such an understanding, however, also requires that the history and the social reality people fashion likewise reflect this looking-beyond-itself, this transcendence. As Berdyaev writes, "The Russian people, in accordance with its eternal Idea, has no love for the ordering of this earthly city and struggles toward a city that is to come, towards the New Jerusalem. But the New Jerusalem is not to be torn away from the vast Russian land. The New Jerusalem is linked with it, and it, the soil, leads to the New Jerusalem."[61]

The Christian interpretation of anthropology and historiosophy culminated in the rediscovery of the Church, while the opposing, post-Enlightenment interpretation led to the construction of a state-church. Slavophile positions became for their opponents a reference point that in large measure defined the lines of thought of Westernizers themselves. Recall that Herzen, in his debates with Khomyakov, one of the forerunners of Slavophile ideas, provided the reader of the many volumes of the history of the Church a study of the events of the ecumenical councils.[62] This feature of the debate on the Russian Idea also clearly related to the great ideological struggle between positivism and the Counter-Enlightenment, a struggle that the Russian Idea largely had as its background and that it at times managed to transcend. In *Theology and Social Theory: Beyond Secular Reason*, John Milbank affirms the influence of Christian thinkers, Catholics in this case—De Maistre, who lived and was very popular in Russia, as well as De Bonald—on the positivist philosopher Auguste Comte and the precursor of socialism, Claude-Henri De Rouvroy, Count of Saint-Simon.[63] The Count of Saint-Simon used to identify God with gravity and desired the birth of the science of religion, a "new Christendom."[64] Milbank also observes that, in the same way that for Marx the constant philosophical reference point was Hegel, for Comte it was De Bonald.[65] Later, Durkheim, through the

61. Berdyaev, *Russian Idea*, 255.

62. Anniekov, *Literaturnyie wspominaniya* [Literary Memories], 293.

63. Milbank, *Theology and Social Theory*, 55.

64. de Saint-Simon, *Nouveau Christianisme*, 59–85, 141–85. See also Milbank, *Theology and Social Theory*, 60.

65. Milbank, *Theology and Social Theory*, 60. See also Gouhier, *La jeunesse d'Auguste Comte et la formation du positivisme*; Spaemann, *Der Ursprung der Soziologie aus dem Geist der Restauration*, 199–201.

mediation of Comte, absorbed the influence of the metaphysics of the social fact (*fait sociale*) originally developed by De Bonald.

The clear exposition of Durkheim's political program, where the new secular "sociology" appeared as the axis of the interpretation and development of modern society, was paradigmatic for all post-Enlightenment positivist thought. As Milbank points out, "since only the Nation State embodies and guarantees the new totemism, which is the cult of the sacrality of individual freedom and choice, there can be no opting out of state institutions, including its secular education, where 'sociology' will be found on the curriculum. As Charles Péguy well understood, this was still the voice of the positivist new papacy, the secular transformation-through-disguise of a new and perverse theology."[66] Undoubtedly, the debate over the Russian Idea reflected the same process: "Here also, the reversal leaves intact the metaphysical framework within which the reversal occurs."[67]

The story that began with a conception of the human person that turns away from God (the anthropological narrative of the Westernizers), which led to the idea of a secular society destined to progress, driven by human intelligence and will, and capable of transforming human history (the historiosophical narrative of the Westernizers), and to the establishment of a socioeconomic system capable of ensuring human happiness (the ecclesiological narrative of the Westernizers), was a story that originated in the same aspirations of the Slavophiles. It is a story, however, with very different results. From the beginning, the great debate over the Russian Idea was part of a worldwide debate. As for the rest of Europe, the issue of the nature of the human person and of history had everything to do with the social question. This too, as Berdyaev describes it, had a religious character, even in the atheistic perception of socialists or anarchists. Dostoevsky understood this well, and he reflected upon it profoundly in his writings. For this reason, it is Dostoevsky who is usually credited for crowning the great debate and creating the concept of the Russian Idea—an idea that, according to Dostoevsky, belonged to all humankind, and synthesized all the ideas to which Europe had given birth.[68] But it is without a doubt Soloviev who played the greatest role in popularizing the Russian Idea. On 25 May 1888, in the Parisian salon of Princess Sayn-Wittgenstein, Soloviev gave a famous lecture, which, that same year, became a book published in French under the title *L'Idee russe*.[69] It was Soloviev who definitively honed the concept

66. Milbank, *Theology and Social Theory*, 68. See also Rolland, *Péguy*, 137–39, 309.

67. Milbank, *Theology and Social Theory*, 60.

68. Gulyga, *Rosyjska idea i yego* tvorcy [Russian Idea and Its Creators], 12.

69. Solovyov, *Życie i ewolucja twórcza Włodzimierza Solowiowa* [Life and Creative

and masterfully demonstrated its significance. He located it both soteriologically and historiosophically, and he showed that it carried no nationalistic baggage but represented a new aspect of the Christian idea as such, a sketch of the fullness of life.[70] Soloviev also clearly allowed us to understand the basis of the Russian Idea: the question of evil, which he treats not only socially and politically but above all as an ontic or existential problem. Soloviev's interest was in "evil and the militant and peaceful methods of combating it," which had to conclude with "a definite statement of the last, most extreme manifestation of evil in history, the picture of its short-lived triumph and its final destruction."[71] The issue of where to find assistance in this fight against evil became the innermost axis of the Russian Idea. It was an issue that belonged to the culture and religious consciousness of Russia, full of existential tension and an ongoing and profound moral debate, which Dostoyevsky calls the *damn problem*. On this basis, in what follows we will try to provide a sketch of the Russian Idea, which, after Soloviev, continued to develop in the thought of Bulgakov, Berdyaev, and the brother-princes, Fr. Trubeckoy and P. Florensky.

Thanks to this approach, the significance of the discourse of faith and reason to the debate about the Russian Idea will also be evident. We see this discourse not only in the ideas of the Slavophiles but also in the ideas of the Westernizers as well. Here I follow Herzen's statement that both streams are two sides of the same god, Janus,[72] a Slavic pagan deity represented by a human figure with a head with two faces. In an obituary of one of the most prominent Slavophiles, Konstantin Aksakov, Herzen writes: "Yes, we were their opponents, but very strange opponents: we had *one love* but *not an identical one*. Both they and we conceived from early years one powerful, unaccountable, physiological, passionate feeling, which they took to be a recollection, and we, a prophecy, the feeling of boundless, all-encompassing love for the Russian people, Russian life, the Russian turn of mind. Like Janus, or like a two-headed eagle, we were looking in different directions, while *a single heart was beating in us*."[73]

This kind of philosophical debate obviously was not the exclusive property of the history of Russian thought, but, unfortunately, it is as little

---

Evolution of Vladimir Soloviev], 274–75.

70. Soloviev, "Historia i budushchnost' teokratiy" [History and Future of Theocracy], 243.

71. Soloviev, *War, Progress, and the End of History*, 21.

72. Herzen, *Rzeczy minione i rozmyślania*, 300. Cited in Berdyaev, *Russian Idea*, 39.

73. Herzen, *Pisma filozoficzne* [Philosophical Works], 476. Cited in Riasanovsky, *Russia and the West*, 89.

known in the West as its importance is great.[74] Just as Odoevsky with his vision of the city of Bentham reflected the way that Western philosophical currents left a profound impression upon the young intellectuals of Russia, Chaadayev's "Letter One" represents the first and most obvious attempt to provide answers. Both Odoevsky and Chaadayev entered the same European philosophical conversation only to trigger a distinctively Russian debate. The debate about the Russian Idea was the first attempt to reflect on the basis of a common cultural experience that was European and Christian, as well as Russian. Within this debate, we can locate two modes of communication: one that is internal and Russian, and another that is external, between Eastern and Western Europe. Both dialogues were intertwined and complementary. Their difference is that, while the development of the internal dialogue was dependent upon and submerged within the great dialogue between East and West, the dialogue between East and West was not, until now a dialogue, because it lacked one of the interlocutors. The Western intellectuals did not pay much attention to the cultural and philosophical developments that arose out of the debate on the Russian Idea and were not able, therefore, to assess its importance or to enjoy the richness of thought that this debate generated. Perhaps now is the time to recover this heritage.

---

74. It is not a coincidence that in the encyclical *Fides et ratio*, Pope John Paul II, in the chapter titled, "The Interaction Between Theology and Philosophy," writes:

> The fruitfulness of this relationship is confirmed by the experience of great Christian theologians who also distinguished themselves as great philosophers, bequeathing to us writings of such high speculative value as to warrant comparison with the masters of ancient philosophy. This is true of both the Fathers of the Church, among whom at least Saint Gregory of Nazianzus and Saint Augustine should be mentioned, and the Medieval Doctors with the great triad of Saint Anselm, Saint Bonaventure and Saint Thomas Aquinas. We see the same fruitful relationship between philosophy and the word of God in the courageous research pursued by more recent thinkers, among whom I gladly mention, in a Western context, figures such as John Henry Newman, Antonio Rosmini, Jacques Maritain, Étienne Gilson and Edith Stein and, in an Eastern context, eminent scholars such as Vladimir S. Soloviev, Pavel A. Florensky, Petr Chaadaev and Vladimir N. Lossky. Obviously other names could be cited; and in referring to these I intend not to endorse every aspect of their thought, but simply to offer significant examples of a process of philosophical enquiry which was enriched by engaging the data of faith. One thing is certain: attention to the spiritual journey of these masters can only give greater momentum to both the search for truth and the effort to apply the results of that search to the service of humanity. It is to be hoped that now and in the future there will be those who continue to cultivate this great philosophical and theological tradition for the good of both the Church and humanity. (§74)

## The Birth of Self-Consciousness

The internal dialogue arose as a consequence of the vision of Russian society as viewed through the prism of Western European thought, and from the perception of Russia's image both in the philosophy of the Enlightenment and in the philosophy that opposed it. This phenomenon, as we have already discussed, took place because, at that moment, Russian national consciousness was born. This national consciousness needed to create its own foundations. It began to do so, especially at the beginning of the eighteenth century, when a group of historians dedicated to the study of Russian history emerged. Early researchers of Russian historical sources were German scholars, such as Gottfried S. Bayer, Gerhard F. Müller, August L. Schlözer and Johann Philipp G. Ewers. But they were accompanied by the first generation of Russian historians, such as Vasily Tatishchev, Mikhail Lomonosov, Mikhail Shcherbatov, Ivan Boltin, Nicholas Novikov, and Nicholas Karamzin.

The investigation of historical materials and their subsequent publication led naturally to historical analysis and the growth of interest in it. History as viewed through the prism of the Enlightenment led researchers to look for concepts such as natural law or social contract, which made their work a basic instrument for reflection on power and the state.[75] The works that opened and closed this first period of the science of Russian history, which belong to so-called noble historiography, were Vasily Nikitich Tatishchev's *Russian History Since Ancient Times* and the aforementioned *The History of the Russian State* by Karamzin. The hundred years or so between these works witnessed remarkable progress in methodology and historical research. The emergence and development of Russian literature, the growing number of the educated, and, above all, the birth of national sentiment, contributed to the great success of the work of Karamzin. The first edition of the eight volume *History of the Russian State* appeared in February 1818, with an exceptional run of three thousand copies, all of which sold within the first month. In order to appreciate this fact, we should keep in mind that until that moment, work dedicated to history had a maximum print run of six hundred copies, which is no surprise, considering that at the beginning of the century the number of subscriptions for books on history numbered exactly five-hundred and twenty-nine.[76] What was exceptional about the

75. Kuzimin, "Politicheskiye i pravoviye vzgliady V. N. Tatashchieva" [Political and Legal Ideas of V. N. Tatishchev].

76. Kozlov, "Status istorii v rossii v konce VXIII- pervoy chetvierti XIX v." [Status of Russian History at the end of the Seventeenth Century to the First Quarter of the Nineteenth Century], 218. Cited in Blachowska, *Narodziny Imperium* [Birth of the

Karamzin phenomenon was that the readers of his work not only included the bourgeoisie, aristocracy, and nobles with education, but also traders, even "peasants and soldiers"—a surprising fact that Karamzin himself pointed out in a letter.[77] Karamzin's work was even supported by the Tsar. When on 16 March 1816, Karamzin presented to Alexander I the first eight volumes of his work, the Tsar, fully aware of the importance of Karamzin's work, honored him with the distinction of the Order of St. Anne first class and named him Minister of State (*statskovo sovietnika*). It is also true that— and this was unusual for that time—the printing run was subsidized by the Tsar, who assigned sixty thousand rubles to finance the first edition.[78] Despite this, the social response was still surprising. As Pushkin wrote, "Everyone, even fashionable ladies, hurried to read the history of their native land, a history previously unknown to them. Ancient Russia seemed to have been discovered by Karamzin like America was by Columbus."[79]

Without a doubt, one of the factors that helped the success of the *History of the Russian State* was its living and simple language, the type of informative narrative that until then was uncommon in Russia. As Karamzin wrote years earlier, "It grieves me to say this, but in fairness it must be said that till now we have had no good history of Russia, that is, one written with philosophical understanding, a critical spirit, and noble eloquence. Tacitus, Hume, Robertson, and Gibbon—these are models! It is said that our history in itself is less interesting than others. I do not think so. All that one needs is intelligence, taste, and talent."[80]

Karamzin's formal success was not all that made his work an early nineteenth-century best seller, which was rapidly translated into French, German, Polish, Italian, and even Chinese. History itself created the fundamental conditions of Karamzin's success. The times created readers of history, and so there appeared writers of history.[81]

This was the historical moment when Russia began to look at itself and was ready to start asking questions about its own identity and destiny. At the beginning of *The History of the Russian State*, Karamzin writes: "History is in a certain sense the sacred book of the nations, their most important and indispensable book, the mirror of their being and activities, the tables

---

Empire], 42.

77. Letter to V. N. Karazin, 27 February 1818. Cited in Karamzin, *Istoria gasudarstva Rossiyskego*, 520.

78. Blachowska, *Narodziny Imperium* [Birth of the Empire], 41.

79. Pushkin, *Polnoye sobranyie sochineniy* [Collected Works], 1429. Quoted in Vernadsky, *Russian Historiography*, 53.

80. Karamzin, *Letters of a Russian Traveler*, 218.

81. Eydelman, *Pushkin*, 24.

of their revelation and of their laws, the injunction of the ancestors to their posterity, the complement, the exposition of the present, and the example of the future."[82] Early nineteenth-century Russia witnessed the encounter between a new kind of historical investigation and an emergent Russian philosophy. The emergence of this new experience encouraged the historical analysis of the specific situation in Russia. It enabled a sense of the challenges ahead, as well as the need to ask difficult questions and to search for the right answers to them. It was at this point that Chaadayev posed the challenging questions to his contemporaries: "Well, I ask you, where are our wise men, where are our thinkers? Who has ever thought for us? Who thinks for us now?"[83]

## "WELL, I ASK YOU, WHERE ARE OUR WISE MEN, WHERE ARE OUR THINKERS?"

The young poet A. Pushkin was not mistaken when in 1818 he saw in Chaadayev the incarnation of his romantic ideas of a providential figure marked by destiny, called to change the history of Russia. In "To Chaadayev," he writes:

> . . . Comrade, believe: joy's star will leap
> Upon our sight, a radiant token;
> Russia will rouse from her long sleep;
> And where autocracy lies, broken,
> Our names shall yet be graven deep.[84]

In another poem, "Towards a Portrait of Chaadayev," Pushkin writes:

> . . . By heaven's high will
> He was born to the shackles of the Tsar's service,
> He would have been Brutus in Rome, in Athens Pericles,
> But here he is a Hussar officer.[85]

Pushkin's intuition did not deceive him, for Chaadayev truly was the architect of a great movement of liberation—the liberation of thought. Chaadayev, who in Pushkin's eyes reflected the figure of a classical hero, had a personality that made his contemporaries treat him with almost religious reverence. The Russian historian V. Zenkovsky compared him to St. Isaac

---

82. Wiener, *Anthology of Russian Literature*, 37.
83. Chaadayev, *Philosophical Letters and Apology of a Madman*, 41.
84. Pushkin, *Poems, Prose, and Plays*, 50–51.
85. Quoted in Zenkovsky, *History of Russian Philosophy*, 152.

the Syrian, one of the greatest mystics of the Christian East, stressing that both were able to feel deeply "the flame of things," to perceive the mystical profundity of the world, and to experience the history that transcends an impoverished materialistic interpretation of it.[86]

Chaadayev was a figure so emblematic of his time that subsequent generations have found it nearly impossible to classify him. Without a doubt his life escapes stereotypes, including those operative among the young Russian intelligentsia of the nineteenth century. Similarly, his thought refuses to surrender to those who use the labels imposed by the methodological myopia characteristic of modern historical research. Andrzej Walicki is probably correct when he concludes that those determined to apply to Chaadayev's life and work completely extraneous criteria—and therefore criteria foreign to the living experience of Chaadayev—only serve to make these criteria seem abstract and unhistorical. Those so determined typically come to the conclusion that the author of the *Philosophical Letters* "contradicts himself and betrays inconsistencies at every step."[87] Such conclusions, however, only "represent an admission of defeat on the investigator's part and indicate certain methodological inadequacies."[88]

Chaadayev, without a doubt, was a child of his time—a privileged child, capable of surpassing the limits of his time and provoking an explosion of revolutionary ideas, but he did not let these ideas imprison him. He both fulfilled and transcended his time. Like John the Baptist, he prepared the way for another, even greater than he.

From childhood he was raised in the cultured environment of the high bourgeoisie and Russian aristocracy. After the early death of his parents, he was raised by his uncles, the princes Shcherbatov. He was formed in the French-cosmopolitan spirit, surrounded by the circle of friends of his uncle, Prince Mikhail, a great ideological opponent of the policy of the Empress Catherine. The cultural environment of Russia, which under the reign of Alexander I was permeated by Enlightenment ideas—and especially in the Tsar's last years, mystical and universal ideas—prepared the ground for a large group of young intellectuals. The war against Napoleon not only triggered a process of national self-assertion but also permitted the winners to know the social reality of the West firsthand. Within this framework the biography of Chaadayev begins.

From a young age Chaadayev was known for his great intelligence. In the year 1809, he began his studies at Moscow University when he was only

86. Ibid., 155.
87. Cited in Walicki, *Slavophile Controversy*, 83.
88. Ibid.

fifteen, but he did not finish them. In 1812, after the French invasion, he enlisted, like many other youths of his generation, as a volunteer in the army of the Tsar. He eventually attained the rank of officer in the elite unit of the Hussars of the Imperial Guard. At that time, it was common for some of the most talented Russian thinkers to have had a military experience.

The great twentieth-century philosopher Jean Guitton, who analyzed the conditions of intellectual labor just as he appreciated the specific features of distinct nations ("Every nation is characterized by what its people most readily rebuild, when they must, from scratch: for the English it is a club; for the Poles it is an army, or the kernel of an army; or the Russians it is a community . . ."[89]), realized the unique value of this military experience. As Guitton observes, recalling Descartes and Renan, many intellectuals completely lack a sense of responsibility. Not only do their mistakes not affect them directly; their mistakes sometimes even give them glory. By contrast, in the army, every officer directly and personally bears the responsibility of the consequences of their orders. In making decisions, the honor and even life itself is at stake. Moreover, Guitton insists, the lives of soldiers develop within a framework particularly favorable for intellectual work:

> An army is a school of collective, efficient thought. And yet, paradoxical as it may seem, no profession is more favorable to thought than soldering, because it alternates the most intense action and absolute leisure, forces one to confront danger and the unforeseeable, as well as pure chance, and imposes on one a wide range of tasks. It is a very free life where the imagination, which discipline usually curbs at so many points, may expand in a variety of dreams, in which serious thoughts find nourishment in carefree ones; this is the freedom enjoyed by the man who does not know what tomorrow will bring but who has made up his mind what the worst can be, and does not doubt that it will come to pass. In this the military profession is a mirror of the intellectual office: the secret, I think, is to make yourself carry out very precise plans but at the same time to leave yourself a wide margin of liberty; to establish some very clear directions for your activity but to allow for a measure of chance; not to know exactly where you will arrive but to know nonetheless that you will get there.[90]

It was surely in the Tsar's army where these soldier-intellectuals perceived with special intensity the currents of the mystical interpretation of

89. Guitton, *Student's Guide to Intellectual Work*, 3.
90. Ibid., 10.

history that marked Tsar Alexander I's reign after the year 1812, staged with particular pomp and clarity in the creation of the Holy Alliance.[91] During the war against Napoleon, both liberal and radical thought also increasingly developed and defined themselves. They were influenced by German Romanticism, and, in time, by German philosophy more generally. Despite the increasingly close relations with liberal societies, Chaadayev felt more attracted to the search for spiritual answers, to the universal Christianity so championed by Alexander. In 1815, during his stay in Krakow, Chaadayev even joined the Freemasons, a fraternity that promoted such universalism.[92] This fact, however, only illustrated Chaadayev's attempt to find his own way, for at the same time he was intellectually close to future Decembrists.[93] Indeed, he was so close that when he met the young student and poet Alexander Pushkin in 1816, Pushkin saw in him one of the most illustrious representatives of liberal ideas.[94] In "To Chaadayev," the poet writes:

> . . . We are impatiently discerning;
> In hope, in torment, we are turning
> Toward freedom, waiting her command . . .[95]

The Decembrists themselves thought so much of Chaadayev that, in early 1821, they decided during a clandestine meeting in Moscow to send a member of their group, Ivan Yakushkin, to meet the young philosopher and to offer Chaadayev a formal invitation to join them. But the invitation arrived late. In December of the previous year, Chaadayev had filed for permission to end his service in the imperial army. In February 1821, he was discharged from his duties.[96]

The reasons Chaadayev left the military are not fully understood. They are related to the encounter between the young Hussar officer and the Tsar, which took place some months before in Opava.[97] Whatever triggered Chaadayev's decision to abandon a promising military career was an undoubtedly complex and profound process. Apart from the two streams we have already identified that weighed upon his intellectual and spiritual

91. Zenkovsky, *History of Russian Philosophy*, 131, 51.

92. Kamieniskiy, "Paradoksy Chadayeva" [Paradoxes of Chaadayev], 12. Cited by Walicki, *Rosja, katolicyzm i sprawa polska* [Russia, Catholicism, and the Polish Question], 38.

93. Zenkovsky, *History of Russian Philosophy*, 152.

94. Walicki, *Slavophile Controversy*, 84.

95. Pushkin, *Poems, Prose, and Plays*, 51.

96. Grigorian, *Czaadayev i yego filosofitskaya sistema* [Chaadayev and His Philosophical System]. Cited in Walicki, *Slavophile Controversy*, 83–85.

97. Lossky, *History of Russian Philosophy*, 48.

development—the idea of universal Christianity promoted by Alexander I and the liberal thought that was increasingly influential among young Russian intellectuals—we cannot overlook, as some have tended to do, the influence of French traditionalist Catholic philosophers. It is an influence seen especially in Chaadayev's *Philosophical Letters*. Without proper appreciation of this influence, the correct interpretation of *Philosophical Letters* is impossible. It is no coincidence that Chaadayev defines Russia not by what it is but rather by what it is not, taking as a definitive point of reference Western Catholicism and the Catholic West.

## THE WESTERNIZATION OF RUSSIA

Catholicism at the time of Alexander I was very popular among the Russian aristocracy, and it is probable that Chaadayev come to know De Maistre personally when he resided from 1803–1818 in St. Petersburg as ambassador of Sardinia.[98] The Tsar's sympathies for the Catholic Church were rather circumstantial and marked by his own vision of a universal Christianity, which was a-confessional and had occult and Masonic tendencies. It was, moreover, an *enlightened* Christianity. But the special attraction to Catholicism and to the unification of the Church was nothing new. Already in 1800, Tsar Paul I said that "I am Catholic at heart (*Je suis catholique de coeur*)" and offered Pope Pius VII asylum in Saint Petersburg and ecclesial union.[99] A few decades later, in 1825, Alexander I sent Michaud de Sabaudia on a confidential trip to Rome. During an audience with Pope Leo XII, he knelt and announced that the desire of the Tsar of Russia was to receive the Catholic faith and bring his people to union with the Vatican. To this end, he requested that the Pope send a trustworthy priest to receive the Tsar's solemn proclamation of faith. Leo XII accepted and first decided to send Fr. Cappellari, who would be the future Pope Gregory XVI, but Cappellari said no. The mission was finally given to Fr. Orioli, but when he was ready for the trip the news of the Tsar's sudden death arrived.[100]

Perhaps these facts would not be more than anecdotes if they did not illustrate an important part of the complex process of the Westernization of Russia. Despite their significance, in most studies on the subject they are superficially analyzed or simply omitted altogether. This is one reason that

98. Quénet, *Tchaadaev et les Lettres Philosophiques*, 157.

99. Boudou, *Le Saint-Siège et la Russie*, 19–20.

100. Ibid., 135–36. There is a much more extensive discussion in Pierling, *L'Empereur Alexandre I est-il mort catholique?* See also Gagarin, *Le archives russes et la conversion d'Alexandre I, Empereur de Russie*.

the contemporary perception of the process of intellectual and spiritual ex-
change between Russia and Western Europe is dominated by an incomplete
picture that focuses upon the birth of a new, enlightened, and secularized
Russian intellectual class—a class principally dedicated to the service of an
enlightened autocracy, which later became an independent and revolutionary intelligentsia. But this is a stereotypical image that is far from the truth,
as M. Raeff quite rightly demonstrates.[101] The process of Westernization or
Europeanization of the Romanov Empire—or the development of relations
between Europe, both Western and Central, and Russia—was not limited
to the creation of a new, Europeanized, enlightened, and secular force for
social progress within Russian society, a force which resulted in one of the
most horrific dictatorships in the history of humankind. This process also
had a profoundly religious and ecclesiastical character.

This was a phenomenon of such depth and significance that even the
Russian Orthodox Church found herself at its epicenter and largely medi-
ated the dialogue between the intellectual and cultural life of the Catholic
West and that of the Orthodox East. Perhaps the Slavophiles should receive
the most credit in creating the legend of the Russian Orthodox Church as
the bastion of the ancient tradition in opposition to the influence of the
decadent Catholic West. This is a relatively fragile myth, which does not
do justice to history. According to Meyendorff, Russia, more than other
European nations, has been portrayed in the light of generalized theories.
The schema of influences divided among Byzantium, the Mongols, and the
West is well known.[102] Obviously, the tendency to oversimplify complex historical and cultural processes is dangerous. The problem with this particular
schema resides in the considerable imbalances it generates in the interpretation of the component parts, particularly the influence of the Western
European part. Therefore, Meyendorff quite rightly emphasizes not only the
development of Ukraine as a separate cultural model but also the strong
Polish influences that also form an important part of the realities of Russian
history.[103]

The *Rus'* of Kiev—the historical embryo of Russian culture and the future Russian Empire—received its formal baptism in the epoch of the unity
of the Church. The Baptism of Russia, which took place between 988 and
989, was given visible expression in the marriage of Prince Vladimir and the
sister of the Byzantine emperor Basil II, Anna. Even in the years after 1054,
the relations between the bishops of Rome and the young Russia did not

---

101. Raeff, *Origins of the Russian Intelligentsia.*
102. Meyendorff, *Byzantium and the Rise of Russia*, 261.
103. Ibid.

change drastically, as the Church of Kiev became independent of Constantinople in 1051. It is important to note, therefore, that the separation of the Russian Orthodox Church from Rome was not a direct result of the decision of the prince of the Kievan *Rus'*, Vladimir, to convert. Rather, it was the result of a long process carried out by a totally different state, Muscovite Russia. In 1075, Prince Iziaslav I of Kiev requested the patronage of St. Peter, which was fulfilled by Pope Gregory VII when he sent Iziaslav a crown. In the twelfth century, the Latin monk St. Anthony built the convent of Novgorod, and Metropolitan John II of Novgorod wrote a letter to Pope Clement II confirming that the Church of Kiev agreed with Rome on all matters of doctrine. The marriages between the reigning Rurikovich Dynasty and the Polish, German, Hungarian, and French princely families of the Latin rite multiplied. These relationships were maintained relatively closely until the dire consequences of the passage of the Crusaders through Constantinople in 1204. Later, Moscow became the capital of Russia, and, after rejecting the agreement of the Union of Florence (1438–1439), proclaimed its autonomy from the Russian Orthodox Church. The fall of Constantinople in 1453 by the hands of Mohammed II gave Moscow the opportunity to proclaim itself, in the words of its first Patriarch Gennadios Scholarios, the sole bulwark of Orthodoxy.

In Rome, these events only further strengthened the idea of attracting Russia to the fight against the Muslims. They also revived the spirit of ecclesial unity. The marriage of Sophia Paleologue—who had taken refuge in Rome and who was the niece of the last emperor of Byzantium, Constantine XI, Thomas Paleologue—to the Grand Prince Ivan III, seemed to offer the opportunity of the unification so desired by Rome. For the Prince, the wedding, celebrated *per procura* on 1 June 1472 in Rome, was an opportunity for Moscow to assume the legacy of the Constantinian Empire and raise the Byzantine coat of arms, emblazoned with a double-headed eagle, above Russia. Russia, however, did not join the Crusades, but, instead, continued its westward expansion, which led to continual conflict with its Catholic neighbors—a fact that led to tensions. Pope Sixtus IV's promise to deliver the imperial crown to Prince Ivan therefore lost its appeal. Ivan had already received from Rome, thanks to his marriage to the beloved daughter of the Church of Rome—Cardinal Bessarion educated the Uniate Princess Sophia in Italy—all that was needed to turn Moscow into the Third Rome. The Vatican idea of the *translatio imperii*—to hand over to Russia imperial dignity as heir to the traditions of Rome and Byzantium—would help legitimate the new Russian autocracy. Despite the clearly pragmatic and purely political sense that motivated Ivan, the fact that the inheritance and the legitimacy derived from Rome could not be minimized. It was significant, as Meyendorff observes, that the *translatio* was suggested in letters from the Venetian senate but not the senate of some Russian or Byzantine city.[104] Belonging to the same culture, civilization, and faith made the Prince aware of the importance of assuming the imperial title, and led to his desire to create a Third Rome rather than, for instance, a Second Constantinople.[105] The West, moreover, perceived this as something to be welcomed. Though the idea of the Third Rome was never formally confirmed, it did provide one of the ideological foundations for the development of the history of the Russian Empire. There was another attempt to make it a reality in 1588, when the Patriarch of Constantinople, Jeremias II, visited Moscow. Boris Godunov, the Prime Minister of Tsar Theodore Ivanovich, tried to convince him to remain permanently in Moscow. If he had succeeded, no doubt, he would have immediately formally proclaimed Moscow as the Third Rome.[106] Though the attempt to proclaim Jeremias II the Patriarch of Moscow failed, the idea that, in Meyendorff's words, Russia was part of "a wider, universal community"[107] took root.

The importance of those events, which was more than symbolic, led Fr. Florovsky, one of the greatest Orthodox theologians of the twentieth century, to define them as "the beginning of Russian westernism." According to Florovsky, the "marriage of our tsar in the Vatican"—the marriage between Princess Sophia and Prince Ivan—symbolized the union between Moscow and Rome. "The marriage quickly drew Moscow closer to the orbit of contemporary Italy and did not signify any awakened awareness for Byzantine traditions and memories."[108] The fact that the heart of the Russian Empire, the Kremlin, was built by the Italian architects Marco Friazin and Pietro Antonio Solari, who, along with Aleviz Friazin, also participated in the construction of the cathedral of Milan, illustrates the degree of this closeness. It was an encounter that caused important changes. The replacement of Byzantine political ideas, which Moscow now found partly obsolete, by those brought by the Italian-educated Princess Sophia—ideas symbolized by the new buildings of the Kremlin[109]—did not contradict the idea of the Third Rome, as Meyendorff points out, but rather reinforced it and complemented it.[110] This new political vision, as well as the ideological-religious frame-

---

104. Ibid., 274.
105. Ibid., 275.
106. Ibid.
107. Ibid., 273.
108. Florovsky, *Ways of Russian Theology*.
109. Meyendorff, *Byzantium and the Rise of Russia*, 274.
110. Ibid.

work of the Third Rome, was from the West. Its roots once united Rome and Constantinople. Since then, it had started to unite Rome and Moscow, Western and Eastern Europe.

↫

The importance of the intimate relationship between the Church and the society in which she grows undoubtedly finds its confirmation in the history of Russian culture. What we call, culturally speaking, a process of "Westernization," is often called, ecclesiologically speaking, a process of "Latinization." Neither the Church's influence on the cultural development of European peoples nor her influence in Russia between the fifteenth and nineteenth centuries can be denied. For this reason, the claims of Florovsky on the deep and lengthy process of Latinization of the Russian Orthodox Church relate to the phenomenon of social and cultural Westernization.

Where this process acquired special strength and became the starting point for a new stage of the Latinization of the Russian Orthodox Church was in the territories of the Polish-Lithuanian kingdom, as well as in the western part of the Russian Empire, especially after the Union of Brest in 1596. At that time, the Orthodox engaged in direct debate with Catholic theologians, and they did so by employing the same methods and the same scholastic modes of argumentation. Interestingly, what became the bastion of the resistance against the Union, the Kiev Theological Academy, which was founded by the Metropolitan Peter Mohyla, became the first and most important center of Latinization—the Latinization that "absorbed not only the language, theology, and morals, but even the religious psychology [of Russian Orthodoxy]."[111]

One of the moments that most clearly illustrated the depth of this process and the considerable tensions it created was the *Raskol*, the split or schism of the Russian Orthodox Church into an official church and that of the so-called Old Believers. The cause of this division was the Orthodox clergy's opposition to the Latinization of the *Cerkiev*. The direct trigger of the *Raskol* was Patriarch Nikon's 1653 reforms. These reforms, which were primarily liturgical, led to violence, which caused profound wounds within the Russian Orthodox Church. The defining moment of this confrontation was the Council of Moscow, which took place from 1666 to 1667. Representatives of the *Cerkiev*, who were supporters of Nikon, declared the need for a new translation of sacred texts and the need for urgent liturgical reforms. Those who did not agree would be declared excommunicated. Within the

111. Florovsky, "Western Influences in Russian Theology," 162–63.

broader eschatological and messianic context, where the idea of the Third Rome was also an important point of discussion, the issue of language itself was one of the principal topics of debate. Boris Uspensky quite rightly explicates what was at stake:

> The ancient Slavic liturgical language was not understood only and simply as one possible system for the transfer of information, but, above all, as a symbolic system of representation of the Orthodox confession, and, in this way, as an icon of orthodoxy. The theological motivation of this perception was a theory of language elaborated in the Orthodox *Cerkiev* on the basis of Greek and then widely diffused throughout Russia. According to this theory, soul, word, and reason form an indivisible unity, identified as one of the manifestations of the Trinity. The word has a double origin: it first arose in the soul in an unknowable manner; it then arose in the body, materializing through the human body in a similar way to how God the Son was born in the incomprehensible beginning of God the Father and then was born materially through the human body of the Virgin Mary. In the same way, the correct faith defines a proper way of expressing itself.[112]

Obviously, this conception of language influenced the perception of other languages, especially those associated with different confessions, such as Latin in the Roman Catholic Church.

⟜

The Orthodox attempt to deal with Catholic scholastic theology ultimately meant the degeneration and dilution of the spirituality of the Eastern Christian churches as they attempted to move from symbol to logical argument, from synthetic perception to conceptual analysis. In trying to create its own scholasticism, Orthodoxy ultimately lost its very essence.[113] In the Eastern tradition, there is no sharp distinction between mysticism and theology, between personal experience of the divine mystery and dogmatics. There is no clear separation between the theology taught by the Church and a widely understood religious philosophy.[114] This process ultimately resulted in the transformation of the Eastern mysticism-existentialism on the model of the rationalism-juridicism dominant in the West.

112. Uspienski, *Religia i semiotyka*, 77.
113. Congar, *After Nine Hundred Years*, 40–41.
114. Lossky, *Mystical Theology of the Eastern Church*, 8–9.

This phenomenon spread throughout Russia as a result of the reforms of Peter the Great, who was a great supporter of Lutheranism. Once he removed the Patriarchate and made the Russian Orthodox Church subordinate to the secular institution of the Synod, he sought to impose an educational system modeled on Protestantism. His two collaborators, Teofan Prokopovich, student of the Kiev Theological Academy, and Bishop Stephan Javorsky, who were both formed in the culture of Kiev, were able to convince him, however, to implement a Latin system instead. As a consequence, the educational system of the Orthodox Church up to that point was almost entirely transformed. The Orthodox theological academies established an educational model imported from Kiev. All classes, including theology classes, were offered in Latin. The books used were often the same as those in Catholic seminaries.[115] As Florovsky points out, though people continued to pray in Slavic, they thought in Latin.[116] It is unsurprising, therefore, that a deep rift began to appear between clergy trained in seminaries, on the one hand, and the monks enclosed in increasingly isolated monasteries, who turned their backs on "the things of this world,"[117] on the other. Tsar Peter's intention to modernize Russia meant he had to neutralize the opposition: the "Europhobic" Muscovite Orthodox. To this end, he began a process of substituting the Orthodoxy of Moscow with that of Kiev. Upon arriving and assuming ecclesiastical positions of responsibility, the new priests that had been trained in seminaries of Kiev began to change the liturgical books, and in this way, they displaced the ancient Russian-Slavic liturgical language with a Ukrainian variant. This process of Latinization lasted nearly a century, and as late as the early nineteenth century Latin still dominated the Orthodox schools. Vladimir Soloviev's family guarded its Latin Bible, marked by the seal of his grandfather—*Ex libris Michael Soloviovus*—as they would a treasure.[118]

The Latinization of the Orthodox Church entailed the Westernization of Russian culture and society. As for the ecclesial experience, I largely share the opinion of Florovsky that this ended up as a pseudomorphosis,[119]

---

115. Florovsky, "Orthodox Church and the Ecumenical Movement Prior to 1910," 186.

116. Ibid., 167.

117. Florovsky, *Ways of Russian Theology*, 97.

118. Solovyov, *Zycie i ewolucja twórcza Wlodzimierza Solowjowa* [Life and Creative Evolution of Vladimir Soloviev], 23.

119. Florovsky, "Orthodox Church and the Ecumenical Movement Prior to 1910," 181. Florovsky draws the concept of pseudomorphosis from Oswald Spengler, who, in *The Decline of the West*, uses it to explain what are, to his mind, cultures that are incompletely developed. The term is used in mineralogy to describe the way one mineral can

although now it is easier to see that theology and Latin scholastic culture more generally were unprepared to assume the great riches of the Russian Orthodox Christian heritage, and that there was no dialogue on terms that were acceptable to and understandable by both parties. In our own time, such a dialogue still needs much time to develop. There also needs to be a rediscovery of common roots, so that, instead of a relationship of opposition, there instead appears a natural sense of communion. But surely we can also find good fruit amidst the bad; in fact, such good fruit has become, over time, increasingly visible. Russia's sense of belonging to a broader cultural entity, of belonging to a European and Christian civilization, certainly started with the Baptism of Russia and the Vatican Marriage, and it has been strengthened by the process of Westernization and the correlative process of Latinization. We should therefore see Latinization as a long and still unfinished search for a common language, a clear expression of the profound need for a Church immersed within an increasingly shared cultural space to communicate. This sense, which finds expression in the two aforementioned processes, enabled the flowering of nineteenth-century Russian culture and thought. Whatever the philosophical or ideological positions of the Russian thinkers of the time, all reflected a common denominator: being deeply rooted in Russian culture and history, they had at the same time grown and developed their work within a European and Christian culture. None of them created in the abstract, outside of this European and Christian civilization, even though some indeed tried to contradict what they understood as European or Christian, Western or Catholic. Moreover, it was the evolution of this Latinized consciousness, this Westernized thinking, that led some Russians and Europeans to see the precious value of Eastern Christian spirituality, others to find answers in the Catholic Church, and still others to discover what was most valuable of all: the real and profound unity of the Church as the heart of the history of Christian civilization. There is no denying that the process whose history I have been describing played a large part in the flowering of philosophical thought and literature, as well as in the Orthodox theological revival, of nineteenth century Russian culture, at least in the same measure as the cultural heritage of the Byzantine East. The failure to appreciate this is a failure to appreciate the full splendor of Russian Slavic history and culture. It is a failure to understand the message that the greatest exponents of this history and culture have handed down to us all.

---

have the characteristic outward form of another. Florovsky uses it here to address the inability of Orthodox Christian theology to break out of the mold of Western thought. —Trans.

〜

With this approach, we more accurately approximate the complex world of the young Peter Chaadayev. It enables us to understand the *Philosophical Letters* in its rich cultural, historical, and spiritual context. We more clearly see that if the debate about the Russian Idea was polarized into two distinct groups, it had to do with their divergent relationships to Christianity in general and Orthodoxy in particular. We better appreciate the significant fact that the two most illustrious exponents Russian philosophy of the nineteenth century, Chaadayev and Soloviev, were ardent Catholophiles, and that their knowledge of and appreciation for Catholicism was not superficial but had deep roots in the history and culture of the Russia of their time.

The reign of Alexander I was very important for the increasingly tense relationship between Western and Eastern Europe. The atmosphere of European unity and the desire to establish a common ideological framework led to increasing interest in Catholicism as the religion that reflected Western unity. Conversions to Catholicism among the Russian aristocracy became quite remarkable: Colonel Michael Lunin, Assistant to the Grand Prince Constantine, then a Decembrist condemned to exile in Siberia; Prince Dmitry Golitsyn, missionary in Pennsylvania; Prince Pyotr Kozlovsky, a descendant of the Rurikovich Dynasty; Sofía Swetchine, a woman of exceptional influence in European cultural circles, who was the daughter of the secretary of the Empress Catherine II. Sophia's nephew, Prince Ivan Gagarin, also achieved great notoriety. He was attracted to Catholicism largely through the writings of Chaadayev and became a tireless promoter of the idea of Russia's conversion to Catholicism. He authored the very significant book, *Is Russia Catholic?* (*La Russie sera-t-elle catholique?*), and anticipated the ecumenical and theocratic thought of Vladimir Soloviev.

According to Vladimir Soloviev, there were three distinct phases in the process of Westernization from the early nineteenth century: (i) theocratic and pro-Catholic, (ii) humanist, rational, and liberal; and (iii) naturalist, positivist, and socio-economic.[120] The representative of the first phase, according to Soloviev, was, of course, Chaadayev, which only serves to confirm the image of Russia in the early decades of the nineteenth century as a country where Catholicism was an unexceptional spiritual and social option, well-known and respectable among aristocracy, bourgeoisie, and intellectuals alike. With the coronation of Tsar Alexander I, the hopes that were born within these classes, which awaited the arrival of the constitutional monarchy, found support in the universal spirit of Catholic Europe. We can

---

120. Soloviev, "Zapadniki y y zapdnichestvo," 583.

see the direct influence of this idea in the memorandum prepared for the emperor by the German Catholic Franz von Baader, which reflected the doctrine of the Holy Alliance: "Über das durch die Französische Revolution herbeigeführte Bedürfniss einer der neuen innigeren Verbindung Religion mit der Politik (On the need, provoked by the French Revolution, for a new and more intimate connection of religion with politics)."[121] The influence exercised by De Maistre was undoubtedly very important, but the presence of the Jesuits, who were hosted by the Empress Catherine II in 1773, was very important and crucial in Russian cultural and social circles as well. The ability to establish intellectual frameworks for dogmatic debates was for many a testament to the common threads between Catholicism and Orthodoxy, which could be defended with reason and contribute to the intellectual life of a rationalist Europe. The university founded by the Jesuits in St. Petersburg for the sons of aristocratic families achieved enormous popularity. In fact, it was closed because of the number of students that converted to Catholicism, despite the opposition of the Jesuit Fathers, who had pledged to avoid any kind of proselytism. One of the most influential theological academies, also founded by Jesuits, was that of Poland, whose level of teaching far exceeded that of the Orthodox schools. It was not by accident that, at the beginning of the century, Russian foreign policy was directed by a Polish Catholic, Prince Adam Czartoryski. When the Ministry of Religious Affairs and Enlightenment was created in 1817, A. N. Golicyn, within whose family there were many converts to Catholicism, became its director. Nevertheless, the ambiguity of the Tsar's ideas led to a complicated situation. One of the symbols of the official idea of the empire, universal Christianity, was Christ the Savior Cathedral, which was designed that same year by A. L. Witberg in such a way that it could be used both for Orthodox and universal Christian worship. The regulations imposed by Minister Golicyn pointed in the same direction. In the name of love and of Christian unity, these regulations banned religious debates.[122]

Of course, the Catholic Church distanced herself from the initiatives of Alexander I and this kind of post-Enlightenment syncretism. She finally expressed her position in the clearest way possible by refusing to participate in the Holy Alliance. The Tsar's first reaction was considerable anger. But, over time, and due to the Church's firmness, he began to identify his vision of universal Christianity with Rome and with Catholicism as its most traditional and best institutionalized examples. This shift was reflected in the

---

121. Baader, "Über Das Durch Die Französische Revolution Herbeigeführte Bedürfniss Einer Neuen Innigeren Verbindung Der Religion Mit Der Politik," 157–58.

122. Florovsky, *Ways of Russian Theology*, 134.

somewhat odd decision to ban "the existence of clandestine organizations of whatever confession" in 1822, and, two years later, to dismiss minister Goli-cyn.[123] The extent to which the Tsar actually understood Catholic dogma is debatable, but, certainly in the last years of his life, as Andrzej Walicki em-phasizes, Alexander I increasingly inclined towards the idea of conversion and the marriage of the Orthodox and Catholic Churches. This no doubt reflects the exceptional status of Catholicism in Russia in the early decades of the nineteenth century.[124]

⤶

This rich spiritual and intellectual milieu was an impetus for Chaadayev to pursue the study of religion, with a special interest in the mystics and the writings of Jung Stilling.[125] According to Mikhail Osipovich Gershen-zon—the first scholar of the work of Chaadayev and author of the study, *Peter Chaadaev: Life and Thought*—Chaadayev's conversion and discovery of the Christian faith had already taken place in 1820, and he lived into it in a profound manner.[126] In 1821, he separated himself from the social life of the salons of Moscow, and he immersed himself in intense spiritual warfare. These long months of complete isolation, coupled with enormous intellectual exertion, exhausted Chaadayev to such an extent that he was forced to set aside his studies and rest. He decided to travel throughout Eu-rope, and during this time, he had the opportunity to meet the representa-tives of the French traditionalist school. While in Paris, he grew to know Sofía Swetchine, who made a deep impression upon him. A few years later he wrote to A. I. Turgenev: "You cannot begin to understand the extent to which everything about this woman interests me."[127] The unique personality of Madame Swetchine stood out within French loyalist and conservative circles. A student and friend of Joseph de Maistre, she was considered "the most prominent Russian of her time."[128] Her path to conversion to Catholi-cism was by way of a thorough study of Catholic history and theology. She read Russian, French, Greek, Latin, Hebrew, German, English, and Ital-ian. When she began to consider the possibility of conversion, she delved into an exhaustive study of the twenty volumes of Claude Fleury's *Histoire*

123. Walicki, *Rosja, katolicyzm i sprawa polska*, 28.

124. Ibid., 30.

125. Zenkovsky, *History of Russian Philosophy*, 154.

126. Ibid., 148–49.

127. Chaadayev, *Polnoye sobranyie sochinieniy* [Complete Works], 101.

128. Journel, *Une russe catholique*, 114, 132–35.

*ecclésiastique* before making a final decision. Although she received an excellent education in the spirit of the French Enlightenment, her decision to convert was by no means merely an intellectual one.

When she arrived at court in 1797 as a friend of the Empress Maria Feodorovna and was soon obliged by her father to marry the much older Nicolas Svechin, she came to know many in the Orthodox Church. Through this grew her friendship with Roksana Sturdza, the principal point of connection between the court of Alexander I and von Baader. Although Swetchine increasingly established friendships with French Catholics and although the Jesuit priest Rozavena became her spiritual director, she remained Orthodox. She even wrote to her friend Roksana that Rozavena's arguments only confirmed her convictions.[129] Finally, in 1815, she publically converted to Catholicism and moved to Paris a year later. Her house immediately became a meeting center for French Catholic intellectuals and a site of intellectual exchanges between ultramontanists and liberals. J. B. Lacordaire, Father Xavier de Ravignan, Bishop Felix Dupanloup, Charles Montalembert, and Alexis de Tocqueville all passed through the doors of Sofía Swieczina's salon. De Tocqueville considered her his most intelligent reader. Of course, Russian intellectuals and aristocrats passing through the City of Lights likewise arrived at her salon.[130] For some of these visitors, Swieczina's private chapel was the location of their conversion to Catholicism. This was not the case with Chaadayev, however, who forcefully protested when Turgenev called him Catholic. Chaadayev's close friend, Prince Gagarin—one of the most celebrated Russian Catholic converts—recalled that the philosopher frequently participated in Orthodox liturgical celebrations and partook of the sacraments.[131] Zenkovsky is therefore right when he states that "the inner wholeness of Chaadayev's religious world had very deep roots; it did not spring from intellectual needs alone."[132] The well-known phrase written by Chaadayev in 1823 is emblematic: "There is only one way to be a Christian, and that is to be one *completely*."[133]

During Chaadayev's trip to Europe, Russia's internal situation changed profoundly. Alexander I died; there was the outbreak and defeat of the uprising of 1825; and Nicholas I unexpectedly received the throne of the empire. But we must realize that freedom in imperial Russia was only relative. Catholic evangelization, for instance, was prohibited by law, and there were

129. Ibid., 98–99.

130. Walicki, *Rosja, katolicyzm i sprawa polska*, 28, 36.

131. Zenkovsky, *History of Russian Philosophy*, 155.

132. Ibid., 154.

133. Chaadayev, *Polnoye sobranyie sochinieniy* [Complete Works], 236.

adverse social pressures upon the converted. But if Alexander I's reign was a time of relative freedom, that of Tsar Nicholas I could be described, in Herzen's words, as "an amazing time of outward slavery and inner liberation."[134]

## Chaadayev's "Inner Liberation"

When Chaadayev returned to Russia in the year 1826, he immediately personified Herzen's phrase. He locked himself in his house and began to live a life of "inner liberation." Having accumulated the experience of three years in Western Europe, he continued to study. A thorough study of German philosophy complemented the strong French influence of De Maistre, Bonald, and Chateaubriand on Chaadayev's thought. In 1825, he had become personally acquainted with Schelling, with whom he continued to correspond once he returned to Russia. Chaadayev was one of the first in Russia who studied Hegel. At the same time, he carefully read Kant's *Critique of Pure Reason*. It is significant that, upon finishing it, Chaadayev crossed out the title on the cover and wrote beneath it, *Apologoete adamitischer Vernunft* (*The Apology of the Reason of Adam*).[135] The philosophical structure that began to crystalize in those years synthesized French traditionalism with German Romanticism, and, despite its strong Catholic background, refused to reject Orthodoxy. As Chaadayev writes in "Letter Three," "Christianity wholly depends on the principle of the possible and necessary rebirth of our being, and all our efforts should tend toward this," which means that "our former nature dissolve[s] and the new, Christ-made man begin[s] to appear within us."[136]

Work on the *Philosophical Letters* started between 1825–1826. In eight letters, written in French and probably directed to Mrs. Panov, who was their official recipient, Chaadayev reflected upon all these years of study and spiritual experience. The letters end in 1831, but "Letter One" was not published until1836. The consequences of this publication, some which have already been mentioned, meant that this was the only one of the letters to be published in Chaadayev's lifetime.[137]

134. Herzen, "Rosja i stary swiat" [Russia and the Ancient World]. Cited in Karpovich, *Imperial Russia*, 28.

135. Lossky, *History of Russian Philosophy*, 49.

136. Chaadayev, *Philosophical Letters and Apology of a Madman*, 68.

137. Chaadayev's "Letter One," along with the two letters that follow it, were edited six years after his death, in the year 1862, by Chaadayev's disciple, Ivan Gagarin, in *Philosophical Works of Peter Chaadayev*. These were the same letters that were compiled in 1906 in *Vaporsy filosofiy i psiclogiy*, and then, in 1913, by Gershenzon in *P. J. Chaadayev: Zhyzn' i musleniye*. We have the other letters thanks to their discovery by

The starting point for Chaadayev's philosophical reflection was Russia and the Russian Idea. But in order to elaborate his proposal and arrive at concrete conclusions, he first needed to develop an account of philosophical anthropology and historiosophy. To this end, he drew support, on the one hand, from the religious philosophy of Schelling, and the other hand, and even more strongly, from De Maistre, Bonald, and Lamennais. The influence of Christian Neo-Platonism, clearly present in Orthodox mysticism, was also notable. All this meant, however, that he increasingly distanced himself from German Romanticism and felt attracted to Catholic traditionalists, who sought to articulate an understanding of the alliance of tradition and reason, opposed to the uncontrolled irrational forces that were destructive of social order and that led to revolution and terror.[138]

Against Enlightenment individualism and rationality, Chaadayev's philosophy acquired a holistic character, which was part and parcel of his belief that all reality participated in a structured and hierarchically-organized unity sustained and transcended by God. God was the principle of universal consciousness—the spirit of the world, identified with the supra-individual human consciousness. Beneath universal human consciousness was empirical individual consciousness, which is especially characteristic of those who have lost unity with the totality of all that exists. According to the philosopher, universal human consciousness, the spirit of the world, developed within history. All human activity was directed from the outside by a higher power. The search for the autonomy of reason therefore became the source of the difficulty of knowing the truth. Individual reason received its strength from its union with universal reason; human persons bore its indelible mark, the prelapsarian memory of the divine word addressed to them. In Chaadayev's opinion, those who proclaimed the autonomy of human reason repeated the original sin. They tried over and over again to reach the apple from the Tree of Good and Evil. Chaadayev therefore discovered the impotence of isolated Kantian reason, the absurdity of the moral autonomy of the person. The moral law, just like truth, was not *within*

---

Prince D. Shakhovskoy. Letters II, III, IV, V, and VIII were translated into Russian in the year 1935 and appeared in *Literaturnoye nasledstvo*. Letters VI and VII were not included, probably due to the simple reason that, as M. Lossky intuits, the authorities were uncomfortable with their profound message centered upon the salvific value of the Church. The first edition of all the letters in the original French appeared in Paris in 1970, thanks to the work of the Jesuit François Rouleau, under the title, *Pierre Tchaadaev: Lettres philosophiques adressées à une dame*. The bilingual edition, which gathers all of the eight letters in French, along with their Russian translation, is *Polnoye sobranyie sochinieniy i izbranyie pisma*, published in Moscow in 1991.

138. Gershenzon, *P. J. Chaadayev*.

us, as Kant said, but *external* to us.[139] Chaadayev was convinced that, left to ourselves, we were doomed to destruction. Only exceptional people, led by mysterious impulses, had no need of being subordinate to an inherited tradition. The victory over individualism—over the "I"—which meant life in total harmony with higher law, returned us to the figure of Adam prior to the expulsion from paradise.[140]

⌒

In this context, the historiosophy of Chaadayev was nothing more than the search for God in history, the attempt to sanctify the history secularized by the Enlightenment. According to Chaadayev, this search for God in history was the center of philosophical discourse. It is likely that the invocation *Adveniat regnum tuum* at the beginning "Letter One" sought to reflect this approach.

Chaadayev's philosophical discourse in "Letter One" begins with a personal description, a historiosophical analysis. There is a clear anthropological introduction. Chaadayev uses a description of the spiritual and emotional state of the addressee of the letter to sketch his conception of human persons as spiritual beings—beings that, thanks to the discovery of their religious dimension, perceive the world around them in a new way. This approach allows Chaadayev, in turn, to describe himself and his own experience. He asks, "First, whence comes this intellectual disturbance which so troubles you, which wearies you, you say, to the point of affecting your health? Here is the sad result of our conversations."[141] Reading Chaadayev's question, it is hard not to recall the years of effort that he dedicated to his studies. He has no doubt that there are "conversations" that search for truth in such a way that, instead of "calm and peace," they bring only "anguish, qualms, almost remorse."[142] But Chaadayev is not surprised at this result of the encounter between the birth pangs of a new consciousness and the world that, with different eyes, begins to be discovered: "It is the natural result of that baneful state of things which, among us, invades all hearts and souls. You merely yielded to the action of those forces which here shift everything about, from the highest ranks of society to the slave who exists only for the pleasure of his master. Besides, how could you have resisted it?"[143]

139. Chaadayev, *Philosophical Letters and Apology of a Madman*, 67–69.
140. Ibid., 76.
141. Ibid., 31.
142. Ibid.
143. Ibid.

He is convinced of his interlocutor's vocation: "But those clouds which today darken your sky will one day, I hope, be dissipated into a salutary dew which will bring fertility to the seed cast into your heart; the effect which a few worthless words have had on you is to me a guarantee of the greater effect which the work of your own intelligence will surely produce in the future."[144]

Once Chaadayev has marked his conception of the human person—his point of departure—he then analyzes the surrounding world with a significant focus upon the function of the Church as the bearer of truth within it: "As for external matters, it is sufficient for you today to know that the doctrine founded on the supreme principle of unity, and of the direct transmission of truth through an uninterrupted succession of its ministers, cannot but be that which best corresponds to the true spirit of religion, for it is wholly contained in the idea of the fusion of all the moral forces in the world into a single thought, a single feeling, and in the progressive establishment of a social system or church which will make truth reign among men."[145]

He addresses, moreover, how the faithful live their union with the Church: "I believe I told you, one day, that the best way to keep religious feeling alive is to observe all the practices prescribed by the Church. This exercise in humility contains more than is usually recognized; the greatest minds have deliberately and thoughtfully practiced it; it is a true worship of God. Nothing so strengthens the spirit in its beliefs as the strict performance of all obligations attached to them. Moreover, most of the Christian rituals, inspired by the Supreme Reason, possess real efficacy for anyone who can be permeated by the truths they express."[146]

Chaadayev does not doubt the transcendent value of tradition and ritual practice, above all in the context of the community of believers. But then there characteristically appears in Chaadayev's text the Promethean romantic element, which attributes to exceptional people alone the right of prophetic and mystical leadership over the people: "There is but one exception to this rule, otherwise perfectly general, and that is when one finds in oneself beliefs of a superior order, which elevate the soul to the very source whence flows all our certitude, and which yet do not contradict popular beliefs, but rather reinforce them; then and only then it is permissible to neglect external observance in order the better to devote oneself to more important labors."[147]

144. Ibid., 31–32.
145. Ibid., 32.
146. Ibid., 33.
147. Ibid.

According to Chaadayev, universal consciousness—the spirit of the world—develops historically, while, contrary to Enlightenment ideals, individual actions have no value in relation to this progress. They cannot contribute anything because they are always governed more or less consciously by selfishness.[148] Only chosen spirits, conscious of the mystery of human destiny, participate in the creative power of history that transcends the limited, secular view of the Enlightenment. This awareness of service to the masses belongs, according to Chaadayev, to the Christian tradition, which provides the only way to understand the language of the times, whose beginning, like all language and all time, is in God.[149] Thus, Chaadayev, who understands individualism as an evil in itself, sees figures like Moses or David, because of their exceptional and providential power, as able to feel the fire of history and so become instruments in God's hands. In a similar fashion, Christians are called to guide other nations because they understand their calling in terms of Christ's transformation and fulfillment of history. History becomes the privileged place for the study of human nature, which can only be understood from the perspective of the path it has traveled.[150] It is not strange, then, that, like Pascal, Chaadayev sees in the passage of generations the development of a single person, who exists across time and whose final destination is the union of all people and nations.[151] In this way, Chaadayev sees an intimate relationship between the spiritual and the material, between the personal and the communal, and the importance of the development of each: "There is a mode of behavior imposed on the soul just as there is on the body: man must learn to submit to it. This is an old truth, I know; but it seems to me that in our country it still has the value of novelty."[152] And this view of the lack of balance in the growth of a people leads him to describe Russia in the following way:

> One of the worst features of our unique civilization is that we have not yet discovered truths that have elsewhere become truisms, even among nations that in many respects are far less advanced than we are. It is the result of our never having walked side by side with other nations; we belong to none of the great families of mankind; we are neither of the West nor of the East, and we possess the traditions of neither. Somehow divorced

148. Ibid., 60.

149. Ibid., 64.

150. Ibid., 109–10.

151. Ibid., 135, cf. 95. The text Chaadayev quotes is: "That the whole succession of men is but one man who abides always." Cf. Zenkovsky, *History of Russian Philosophy*, 162.

152. Ibid., 34.

from time, we have not been touched by the universal education of mankind. That wonderful interconnection of human ideas in the succession of the centuries, that history of the human mind which brought man to the state in which he is today in the rest of the world, has no influence upon us. That which elsewhere has long constituted the foundation of society and life is still for us but theory and speculation.[153]

According to Chaadayev, Russia's isolation from world history—"that history of the human mind which brought man to the state in which he is today in the rest of the world"—is of utmost significance. A nation that separates itself from the growth of all humanity is doomed to failure, because it cannot know the continuity of tradition or the basis of social organization. Its history becomes merely an accumulation of coincidences, of disordered fragments. It cannot find the place Providence has prepared for it:

> Look about you. Don't you think that we are very restless? We all resemble travelers. Nobody has a definite sphere of existence; we have no proper habits; there are no rules, there is no home life, there is nothing to which we could be attached, nothing that would awaken our sympathy or affection—nothing durable, nothing lasting; everything flows, everything passes, leaving no traces either outside or within you. In our houses we seem to be camping; in our families we look like strangers; in our cities we look like nomads, even more than the nomads who tend their herds on our steppes, for they are more attached to their wastelands than we to our cities. And do not think that this is not important. Poor souls that we are, let us not add to our other afflictions that of not understanding ourselves, let us not aspire to the existence of pure intelligences; let us learn to live sensibly within our given reality.[154]

The philosopher describes the profound uprooting of the Russian people. Despite centuries of history, they live like campers in their houses, strangers in their families, and nomads in their cities. The cause of this situation is that Russia did not participate in the "adolescence" of peoples. While other peoples experienced times of "great passions, strong emotions, great national undertakings"[155]—and in so doing created their own distinctive traditions, "their most vivid memories, their legends, their poetry, their

---

153. Ibid.
154. Ibid., 34–35.
155. Ibid., 35.

greatest and most productive ideas,"[156] which became the basis for their societies—Russia, in contrast, remained isolated. This isolation, which was full of terror, brutality, and marked in a very significant way by Mongol domination—whose spirit, Chaadayev points out, persists in Russian authoritarianism and nationalism—did not allow Russia to join in the moral growth of the peoples of Europe:

> But we Russians, we are devoid of all this. At first brutal barbarism, then crude superstition, then cruel and humiliating foreign domination, the spirit of which was later inherited by our national rulers—such is the sad history of our youth. We had none of that period of exuberant activity, of the fervent turmoil of the moral forces of nations. Our period of social life which corresponds to this age was filled with a dull and gloomy existence, lacking in force and energy, with nothing to brighten it but crime, nothing to mitigate it but servitude. There are no charming remembrances, no graceful images in the people's memory; our national tradition is devoid of any powerful teaching. Cast a look upon the many centuries in our past, upon the expanse of soil we inhabit, and you will find no endearing reminiscence, no venerable memorial, to speak to you powerfully of the past, and to reproduce it for you in a vivid and colorful manner. We live only in the narrowest of presents, without past and without future, in the midst of a flat calm. And if we happen to bestir ourselves from time to time, it is not in the hope, nor in the desire, of some common good, but in the childish frivolousness of the infant, who raises himself and stretches his hands toward the rattle which his nurse presents to him.[157]

Chaadayev later concludes: "Our first years, spent in immobile brutishness, have left no traces on our minds; we have nothing that is ours on which to base our thinking; isolated by a strange fate from the universal development of humanity, we have also absorbed none of mankind's ideas of traditional transmission. Yet it is on those ideas that the life of nations; it is from those ideas that their future develops and that their moral growth derives."[158]

Chaadayev is not alone in noting the situation in which Russia finds itself. He believes that it is necessary and possible to recover lost time. He simply asks his contemporaries to adopt the attitude of civilized peoples, and to attempt to take advantage of the heritage of other peoples. He is convinced that "nations are moral beings in the same way that individuals

156. Ibid.
157. Ibid., 35–36.
158. Ibid., 36.

are. As years make the education of persons, so centuries make theirs."[159] This experience of historical education can be shared, since it belongs to a supranational community that is Christianity itself:

> The peoples of Europe have a common aspect, a family resemblance. In spite of the general division of these peoples into Latin and Teutonic branches, into southern and northern, there is a common link which unites them into a fasces,[160] clear to anyone who has studied their general history. You know that even recently all Europe was called Christendom, and that this word has its place in public law. In addition to this general character, each of these peoples has a particular character, which, however, consists of no more than history and tradition. It is what makes up the hereditary intellectual patrimony of these peoples. Every individual has a right to it; each assimilates during his lifetime, without fatigue or labor, these notions scattered in his society, and profits by them.[161]

Chaadayev, however, is fully aware of the extreme difficulty of this challenge. Once Russia separates from common history, once it rejects God's providential plan for its people, it is condemned to rely on itself alone:

> And yet, situated between the two great divisions of the world, between East and West, with one elbow leaning on China and the other on Germany, we should have combined in us the two great principles of intelligent nature, imagination and reason, and have united in our civilization the past of the entire world. But this is not the part which Providence has assigned to us. Far from it, she seems wholly to have neglected our destiny. Suspending, where we were concerned, her beneficial action on the human mind, she left us completely to ourselves, she wished to have nothing to do with us, she wished to teach us nothing. Historical experience does not exist for us. To behold us it would seem that the general law of mankind has not been revoked in our case. Isolated in the world, we have given nothing to the world, we have taken nothing from the world; we have not added a single idea to the masses of human ideas; we have contributed nothing to the progress of the human spirit. And we have disfigured everything we touched of that progress. From the very first moment of social existence, nothing has emanated

159. Ibid., 37.

160. A fasces is a bound bundle of wooden rods, often including an axe with its blade exposed.

161. Ibid., 38.

from us for the common good of men; not one useful thought has sprouted in the sterile soil of our country; not a single great truth has sprung from our midst; we did not bother to invent anything, while from the inventions of others we borrowed only the deceptive appearances and the useless luxuries.[162]

Chaadayev is aware of the great risks involved in such a situation. Tsar Peter the Great tried to bring to Russia the ideas of the West. The last and final step in this regard was taken by Emperor Alexander I. But, as Chaadayev writes, "we brought back nothing but evil ideas and baneful errors, which resulted in an immense calamity that set us back half a century. We have something in our blood which drives out all true progress."[163] The philosopher warns his contemporaries about the danger of taking as their own the "disfigured idea of human passion," which had already meant a great loss for Russia:

What were we doing at the time when, from the midst of the struggle between the energetic barbarism of the northern peoples and the high idea of religion, the edifice of modern civilization was being built up? Driving by a baneful fate, we turned to Byzantium, wretched and despised by those nations, for a moral code that was to become the basis of our education. Only a moment earlier an ambitious mind had removed this household from the universal brotherhood: what we got was thus the idea as it had been disfigured by human passion. At the time, in Europe everything was animated by the vivifying principle of unity. All emanated from it and converged upon it. The whole intellectual movement of those times tended to build up the unity of human thought, and all incentive had its source in this powerful need to arrive at a universal idea which is the genius of modern times. Strangers to this marvelous principle, we became the prey of conquerors, and when, freed from foreign yoke, we could, had we not been separated from the common family, have profited from the ideas which had blossomed during this time among our Western brothers, we fell instead into an even harsher servitude, sanctified as it was by the fact of our deliverance.[164]

Chaadayev had no doubt that Russia's separation from the West was an enormous disaster:

162. Ibid., 41.
163. Ibid., 88.
164. Ibid., 42–43.

Many glowing rays were already then illuminating Europe, flashing out from the apparent darkness with which it was covered. The greater part of the knowledge in which man prides himself today was already anticipated by individual minds; society already had assumed a definite character; and, by turning back to pagan Antiquity, the Christian world had found the forms of beauty which it lacked up to then. But we locked ourselves up in our religious separatism, and nothing reached us of what was happening in Europe. We had no dealings with the great project of the world. The outstanding qualities with which religion had endowed modern peoples and which, in the opinion of a healthy mind, raises them as much above the Ancients as they in turn were above the Hottentots and the Lapps; these new forces with which it had enriched the human mind; these customs which submission to a disarmed authority rendered as gentle as they had at first been brutal, none of this had taken place among us.[165]

He is also convinced that Christianity is the axis of the development of peoples because Christianity is the force that transforms the history of peoples. This belief enables Chaadayev to define his vision of the root of the problem:

While the Christian world marched on majestically along the road marked out for it by its divine Creator, carrying along generations, we, although called Christians, stuck to our place. The entire world was being rebuilt, while we built nothing: as before, we hibernated in our hovels built of logs and straw. In a word, the new destiny of mankind was not being fulfilled in our country. We were Christians, but the fruits of Christianity were not ripening for us.

I ask you, is it not absurd to suppose, as is generally done in our country, that we can appropriate in one stroke this progress of the peoples of Europe, made so slowly through the direct and evident action of a unique moral force, and to suppose that we can do this without even trying to find out how it developed?

Nothing is understood of Christianity if it is not seen that Christianity has a purely historical side which is so essentially part of dogma that it contains in a way all the philosophy of Christianity, for it demonstrates what that religion has done for man and what it will do for him in the future. Thus, the Christian religion is seen not only as a moral system conceived in the perishable formulae of the human intellect, but also as a divine, eternal power acting universally in the material world

165. Ibid., 43.

and whose visible action should be a perpetual teaching to us. This is the true meaning of the dogma expressed symbolically in the belief of a Universal Church.[166]

The discovery that Christianity's power derives from a very specific source—"Wherever the name of Christ is pronounced, that name alone captivates men, whatever they may try to do about it"[167]—enables Chaadayev to locate the true center of the history of humankind in the one who is its beginning and end:

> But the influence of Christianity on society as a whole is still more remarkable. Picture to yourself the entire evolution of the new society, and you will see how Christianity transforms every human interest into its own, everywhere replacing material necessity with a moral one and stimulating in the domain of thought those great disputes unknown to the history of any other age or to any society, those fearful collisions of ideas, when the whole life of peoples became but one great idea and one boundless feeling; you will see how it absorbs everything: private and public life, family and fatherland, science and poetry, reason and imagination, memory and hope, joys and sorrows.[168]

Was Chaadayev right in his description of Russia's reality? How far does his vision extend? To what depth of the mystery of time has the philosopher, and perhaps also the mystic, been able to delve? These questions are still the basis of what will probably be an endless dispute. For many, Chaadayev's writings offer interesting and valuable insight into "the theurgical understanding and perception of history," as V. Zenkovsky puts it.[169] For others, who interpret Chaadayev through the lens of a geometric, three-dimensional perspective of history, both "Letter One" and the seven other letters amount to an attempt, doomed in advance, to cross the Red Sea. Undoubtedly, the work of Chaadayev will always appear as a challenge, an opportunity to wake up, a clear sign of the beginning of the adult life of Russian philosophy. The author was aware of this power of his words; indeed, he even knew from whence this power derived: "What I have said about our country must seem full of bitterness to you, yet I have spoken but the truth, and not even the whole truth. Moreover, Christian consciousness

166. Ibid., 43–44.
167. Ibid., 48.
168. Ibid., 49–50.
169. Zenkovsky, *History of Russian Philosophy*, 155.

tolerates no blindness, least of all that of national prejudice, since it most of all divides men."[170]

The letter ends with the promise that the philosopher will return to these reflections the following day, and he closes it with the expression, "Necropolis, 1829, 1 December." Over the course of the following months, Chaadayev wrote the other seven letters. These other letters were not fully edited until many years later, so they did not influence the development of Russian thought in the same way as "Letter One" did.

## The Apology of a Madman

Toward the end of the last of his philosophical letters, "Letter Eight," Chaadayev offers a vision of the end of history and the creation of the Kingdom of God on earth, a grand unification of the world's souls and moral powers—a unification that is "the whole mission of Christianity." This event will fulfill the destiny of humankind, and there will appear "the resolution (*dénouement*) of the drama of the universe, the great apocalyptic synthesis."[171] The importance of the publication of "Letter One" in 1836 often prevents us from realizing that it was the conclusion of a particular stage of life of the thinker, the starting point for an even broader philosophical reflection. After firing the shot that started the debate about the Russian Idea, Chaadayev actively participated in the conversation his letter generated. In fact, at the time "Letter One" appeared in *The Telescope*, the author had already distanced himself from some of the ideas expressed in it. But the public reaction to the pessimistic and very unfavorable view of Russia, which Chaadayev went so far as to compare to a cemetery—a view he offered precisely at the moment of the historic apogee of Russia's power—was so explosive that Chaadayev had little room for fine tuning.

Some friends tried to support Chaadayev even though at many points they did not agree with him. This was the case, for instance, with Odoevsky, who apparently also managed to influence the evolution of some of Chaadayev's ideas.[172] Pushkin wrote Chaadayev a long and loving letter in which he said he shared Chaadayev's negative view of social life in Russia. But Pushkin strongly distanced himself from the views of the philosopher regarding Russia's history. The poet praised the attitude of the Orthodox Church because "she was never stained with the vileness of popery," and

170. Chaadayev, *Philosophical Letters and Apology of a Madman*, 50.

171. Ibid., 160.

172. Lossky, *History of Russian Philosophy*, 50.

he stated firmly that he would never desire another homeland.[173] Others, like Herzen, who were enthusiastic because of the awakening provoked by Chaadayev's shot, were able to discern in the letter only an intimation of a revolutionary message. Herzen was aware that Chaadayev's "neo-Catholicism," as Herzen described it, was intimately related to conservative French Catholicism, as well as to Chaadayev's relationship to the Polish messianists, Z. Krasinski and A. Mickiewicz.[174] But Herzen was never able to see the fullness of the Chaadayev's philosophical vision.

The truth of the matter is that the overwhelming majority did not even try to see Chaadayev's vision. The general opinion was that philosopher was a traitor to Russia, "a proud slave to everything that is strange," committed to kissing the shoes of the popes.[175] Metropolitan Seraphim, in the name of the Russian Orthodox Church, sent Count Benckendorff, the chief of the imperial police, an official letter of protest against the publication of "criminal libel about the nation, the faith, and the government."[176] Benckendorff also issued a final opinion on the ideas contained in "Letter One": "Russia's past was amazing, its modern history is more than excellent and in regard to its future, this surpasses even the most daring imaginations."[177]

Given the huge wave of public outrage, the Count seemed to fail to remember the letter Chaadayev presented to him in July 1833, requesting that he pass it along to Nicholas I. The letter proposed a profound reform of the education system, which would eliminate all Western influences and which would be the basis of Russia's separation from the West. Benckendorff considered the attempt to advise the Tsar an enormous act of arrogance, and he refused to act as an intermediary.[178] What may seem surprising in Chaadayev's proposal is nothing more than the evolution of his ideas. Since December 1829, the year he wrote "Letter One," until the letter's publication in 1836, Chaadayev continued to revise his ideas such that the letter that Nadezhdin ended up publishing in *The Telescope* was no longer completely representative of his thought. The tipping point for Chaadayev was the outbreak of the July Revolution of 1830 and its effects. Following the French traditionalists, Chaadayev's faith that France and Europe more generally would recover from the wounds inflicted by the 1789 Revolution and the Enlightenment capitulated before a shocking reality. The Three Glorious

173. Ermichev and Zlatopolskaya, *P. J. Chaadayev*, 74–75.

174. Herzen, *My Past and Thoughts*, 298–300.

175. Lebiediev, *Chaadayev*, 171–72.

176. Ermichev and Zlatopolskaya, *P. J. Chaadayev*, 80–81.

177. Lebiediev, *Chaadayev*, 35.

178. Chaadayev, *Polnoye sobranyie sochinieniy i izbranyie pisma*, 82–84, 315.

Days (*Les Trois Glorieuses*), from 27 to 29 July 1830, dealt a blow to all who wanted to see the Congress of Vienna as the great panacea to the social and political problems that plagued Europe. The Holy Alliance has sometimes been considered an instrument of political repression, ready to maintain at all costs the principles of the Old Regime. But it never really worked in political practice. Moreover, the name "Holy Alliance" itself never appeared in any diplomatic document of the time. The Holy Alliance failed because it appealed to the old notion of the unity of Christianity, which presupposed the existence of a community of states and legitimate monarchies based on the same principles. King of France, Charles X of Bourbon, represented the kind of monarch convinced of the necessity and legitimacy of absolutist governments. "I would rather chop wood," he proudly declared on one occasion, "than be king under the conditions of the king of England" and share power with parliament.

When liberal deputies asked for the right to control the actions of government ministers, who had until then been solely responsible to the king, Charles X responded by dissolving the Chamber of Deputies. In addition, he tightened press censorship and limited electoral law. The next day the Revolution of 1839 broke out, lasting three days. Seeing the danger that the Revolution could come under the control of Republicans, the liberal deputies decided to take matters into their own hands. The grave disturbances forced the last Bourbon on the throne of France to abdicate and leave the country. In August of that same year, the interim government, backed by liberals such as M.J. Lafayette, A. Thiers, F. Mignet, and J. Laffitte, proclaimed the Prince of Orleans, Louis Philippe, "King of the French by the grace of God and the desire of the nation." More significant than the dynastic change on the French throne, these July days of 1830 marked a major triumph of the French bourgeoisie. The striking speed of events shook the whole of Europe and was a stimulus for liberal and nationalist movements. One of the most immediate effects of the July Revolution was the common victory of liberal and nationalist ideas in the struggle for independence in Belgium.

In the Polish territories controlled by the Russian Empire, republican and liberal organizations proclaimed the Warsaw uprising on 29 November 1830, which began at the Academy of Cadets. Tsar Nicholas I, the Grand Duke Constantine, fled Warsaw with his troops. Poland was declared independent and the country awaited the arrival of Western aid. But the only army that entered Polish territory was sent by Nicholas I. The numerical superiority of the imperial army and the uprising's lack of organization led to the Tsar's victory in a war that lasted from January to September 1831. The Kingdom of Poland was annexed to the Russian Empire as a conquered province, and the country was occupied by the Tsar's army, which began an epoch of cruel and continuous pacification of Poland. Nicholas I abolished the liberal constitution granted by Alexander I in 1815. Because the intellectual class had been the soul of the revolt, the Faculty of Law of University of Warsaw was closed and the rich collections of the National Library were transferred to Moscow. Liberal governments of France and England protested the atrocities of the Russian army in its occupation of Poland, but neither nation decided to intervene.

The liberal revolution in France, the victory of the liberal and nationalist revolution in Belgium, and the nationalist insurrection in the Russian-occupied part of Poland, must have impressed Chaadayev sufficiently that he began to question some of his ideas about Europe. In an 18 September 1831 letter to Pushkin, Chaadayev writes:

> Quite recently, about a year ago, the world lived in perfect confidence about its present and future and studied in silence its past, learning from it. The intellect was being regenerated in peace, man's memory was being renewed, opinions were becoming reconciled to one another, passion was being repressed, anger was deprived of sustenance, and vanity found satisfaction in good works; all human needs were gradually becoming confined to the realm of mental activity and all the interests of man were gradually being subsumed by the interest of the progress of the universal intelligence. For me this was an article of absolute faith, a source of boundless belief.[179]

And suddenly, because of the "absurd stupidity" of one man, Charles X, "all this became naught": "Tears fill my eyes," Chaadayev writes, "when I see the vast calamity that has befallen that ancient, my ancient, society; this general catastrophe, which befell Europe in such an unforeseen manner, has doubled my own unhappiness."[180] In this situation, the only possible response is to search for the "stamp of Providence." But he does not know where to find it. "I am not the only one to retain hope that reason will revert to being reasonable. But how and when will this reversion take place? Will it be achieved by some powerful spirit sent by Providence on a unique mission, or will this be the result of a sequence of events brought about by Providence for the instruction of mankind? I do not know."[181]

These surprising events forced Chaadayev to revise his ideas, and he started to see the advantages of Russia's separation from the West. Such separation protected Russia against outside threats, allowing Russia to fulfill

---

179. Chaadayev, *Philosophical Works of Peter Chaadaev*, 151.
180. Ibid.
181. Ibid.

the great destiny Providence had prepared for it. In this way, Chaadayev made sense of Russia's own lack of history: Russia did not participate in the development of Western civilization because it was safely waiting for its moment in world history. Chaadayev did not doubt that this role would further unite Russia to the Catholic Church, though, at the same time, he began to view the Orthodox Church in a different light. In his 10 April 1833 letter to Turgenev, Chaadayev proclaims Rome as the spiritual capital of humanity and the symbol of its future union. Rome is "the link between ancient and modern times," as well as the embodiment of "all the memories of humanity."[182] Two years later, even before the publication of "Letter One" of the *Philosophical Letters*, he writes in another letter to Turgenev: "You know that, in my opinion, Russia was called upon to furnish some immense intellectual development: Russia was one day supposed to provide the solution to all the questions which are debated in Europe. Placed beyond the rapid movement which carries along the spirits there, being able to consider with calm and with a perfect impartiality, all that agitates and impassions the souls in Europe, Russia was invested, in my opinion, with the task of explaining the human enigma one day."[183] And in another letter from the same year, 1835, he writes:

> It's Europe, on the contrary, which we are destined to teach about an infinity of things which Europe could not understand alone. Don't laugh! You know that this is my intimate conviction. A day will come on which we will place ourselves amid intellectual Europe, as we are already placed amid political Europe, then we will be more powerful by our intelligence than we are today by our material power. This will be the logical result of our long solitude: great things have always come from the desert. The powerful voice which is resounding in the world, will singularly serve to hasten the accomplishment of our destinies. Struck with stupor and surprise, Europe has pushed us away with hatred; the fatal page of history written by the hand of Peter the Great is torn up; thank God, we no longer belong to Europe: since this day then, our universal mission has begun.[184]

The evolution of Chaadayev's historiosophical vision did not itself change. As Zenkovsky highlights, the philosopher continued to emphasize a "theurgical" conception of history, which clearly appeared along with the idea of Moscow as the Third Rome. The trope of Russian idiosyncrasy, of the

182. Ibid., 156.
183. Ibid., 158.
184. Ibid., 162.

transfiguration of Russia through "the strength of piety" into "Holy Russia," into the Kingdom of God, did not disappear with the decline of the ecclesiastical consciousness in modern secular society, but it was transformed. "Eighteenth- and nineteenth-century Russian humanism—in its moral or aestheticizing form—grew from this *theurgical* root, from the religious need to 'serve the ideal of justice.' This same theurgical motif found expression in the occult searchings of the Russian freemasons, and in the mystical flurry of various spiritual movements during the reign of Alexander I; it was also expressed with exceptional force in Chaadayev."[185]

In the year and a half following the publication of "Letter One," Chaadayev, who was declared mentally ill and subjected to house arrest by a direct order of Tsar Nicholas I, did not have many occasions to explain his position. He tried to do so in a letter he wrote on 8 November 1836 to Count S. Stroganov explaining that the text published in *The Telescope* did not cohere with his current thinking.[186] Probably because he was overwhelmed by events, in 1837 he began to write his last and unfinished work, whose title, significantly, was *Apology of a Madman* (*Apologie d'un fou*). Later, once the restrictions upon him were lifted, Chaadayev reappeared in the Muscovite salons. Despite the scandal caused by his letter, he was extremely well-received and widely respected, even becoming something of a cult figure in the capital. The courage and depth of his ideas even earned him the respect and admiration of his opponents. "At a time when thought seemed buried in a deep and involuntary sleep," Khomyakov wrote years later, "he was especially valuable, both in keeping watch himself and in awakening others. . . . Perhaps he was most valued by those who considered themselves his opponents."[187] Herzen remembers him in the following way:

> Chaadayev's melancholia and peculiar figure stood out sharply like a mournful reproach against the faded and dreary background of Moscow "high life." I liked looking at him among the tawdry aristocracy, feather-brained Senators, grey-headed scapegraces, and venerable nonentities. However dense the crowd, the eye found him at once. The years did not mar his graceful figure; he was very scrupulous in his dress, his pale, delicate face was completely motionless when he was silent, as though made of wax or marble—"a forehead like a bare skull"— his grey-blue eyes were melancholy and at the same time there was something kindly in them, though his thin lips smiled

185. Zenkovsky, *History of Russian Philosophy*, 155–56.

186. Chaadayev, *Polnoye sobranyie sochinieniy i izbranyie pisma*, 112–14.

187. Quoted in Zenkovsky, *History of Russian Philosophy*, 151.

ironically. For ten years he stood with folded arms, by a column, by a tree on the boulevard, in drawing-rooms and theatres, at the club and, an embodied veto, a living protest, gazed at the vortex of faces senselessly whirling round him. He became whimsical and eccentric, held himself aloof from society, yet could not leave it altogether, then uttered his message, which he had quietly concealed, just as in his features he concealed passion under a skin of ice. Then he was silent again, again showed himself whimsical, dissatisfied, irritated; again he was an oppressive influence in Moscow society, and again he could not leave it. Old and young alike were awkward and ill at ease with him; they were abashed, God knows why, by his immobile face, his direct gaze, his mournful mockery, his malignant con-descension. What made them receive him, invite him . . . still more, visit him? It is a very difficult question.[188]

It is unclear to what extent Chaadayev's solitude fed on the feeling of being misunderstood, especially in moments like the ones Herzen describes. But what seems clear is that this feeling of being misunderstood did not leave him indifferent. Chaadayev's love-hate relationship with Muscovite society, reflected very suggestively by Herzen's description, pushed Chaadayev to try to explain the direction of his thinking, despite his awareness that very few people would understand it. How does a philosopher perceive his relation-ship with the world around him if he names his masterpiece, *Apology of a Madman*? Moreover, who judges madness in reality? And more importantly still: What are the symptoms of madness? When do they first appear?

Chaadayev seemed to have experienced a conflict between two loves: love of homeland and love of truth. It was an encounter that was often pain-ful, especially when the one who takes exclusive possession of the power to determine patriotism is the one who governs. When "the Triad" of Official Nationality—orthodoxy, autocracy, and nationality—seemed to conflate love of homeland and love of truth, speaking against this conflation in the way Chaadayev did could certainly look like madness. The Tsar's reaction demonstrated the weight and importance of Chaadayev's text. But it also potentially evidences another phenomenon: fear of the truth. A liar or a criminal is jailed; a prophet is proclaimed mad, because the teachers of the lie know that the most dangerous weapon against the truth is discrediting truth-tellers. When prophets are condemned, they become martyrs, and martyrs are especially dangerous. Throughout its history, Russia's rulers, like the rulers of many other nations, have often made use of this method in the treatment of their most uncomfortable critics. We do not know to

188. Herzen, *My Past and Thoughts*, 295–96.

what extent Chaadayev wanted to become a martyr, or if he foresaw the consequences of the publication of his work, or even if he cared about the consequences. However, we can surmise that, for Chaadayev, the ability to voice his ideas, even if they no longer fully represented his views, must have seemed to be no more than a simple act of coherence, of integrity. Perhaps for this reason, he never objected, as far as we know, to the publication of "Letter One." He may have never objected because his interpretation of history had not changed: he remained convinced that history's ultimate end was the birth of God's Kingdom.

## THE LOVE OF THE TRUTH

Despite a year and a half of being imprisoned in his home under police and medical control, and despite the explicit prohibition against taking up his pen, Chaadayev took the most courageous step a person in his position could take: to write what he thought. The words that we find at the beginning of *Apology of a Madman* permit us to peek into the drama of the philosopher: "I love my country more than anyone does, believe me; I am eager for its glory; but it is true that the patriotic feeling which animates me is not exactly like that of the men whose shouts upset my obscure existence and cast back onto their sea of misery my ship, which had run aground at the foot of the Cross. It is true that I have not learned to love my country with my eyes shut, my head bowed, my mouth closed."[189] Yet he remains convinced that as beautiful as "love of country" is, "there is a [finer thing], namely, love of truth. . . . It is not by patriotism but by means of truth that the ascent to Heaven is accomplished."[190] Despite the extreme difficulty of his position, he demonstrated intellectual integrity by acknowledging that his ideas, at least in some important respects, had changed. The Revolution of 1830 in France was a turning point. With it, Chaadayev's vision of Europe, as well as Russia, changed. He still maintained his basic thesis that Russia had no history and did not develop through its own internal effort. But he also admitted that the public criticism of him had been extremely hard to bear.

The change appeared in Chaadayev's new thesis: the idea that Russia's lack of history was not necessarily a disadvantage, an omission of Providence. Russia's isolation was a rare opportunity, a chance to inscribe itself into the history of humankind, to construct its own destiny in accordance with divine designs. The nations of Europe, bound by their own history and

189. Chaadayev, *Philosophical Letters and Apology of a Madman*, 173.
190. Ibid., 164.

their own traditions, were in reality prisoners of their past. But Russia, according to Chaadayev, could benefit from its experience so as not to repeat their mistakes; it had been given the opportunity to construct the future without looking back. The idea of the *tabula rasa* allowed Chaadayev to reassess Russia's mission and discern the sources of its future without conditioning them by relations with the West. Chaadayev therefore introduced into his historiosophy the concept of the *tabula rasa*, which for him reflected Russia's status as a consequence of having failed to obey the designs of Providence. But Chaadayev used the idea of the *tabula rasa* without its implications of a supra-individual capacity for the transmission of tradition. For, as Chaadayev saw it, human freedom entailed the capacity to oppose the plans of God. The opposition came from the action of an individual agent, an "I" dragged downward by the terrible weight of sin. But this very same freedom allowed the "I" to shed its egotism and offer its destiny to Providence. The image of Russia as a blank page ready to be written was not new. For instance, Leibniz used it to describe the reforms introduced by Tsar Peter the Great. Diderot used it as well in commenting on the reforms of Empress Catherine II. But Locke's understanding of the *tabula rasa* had no place in Chaadayev's thought. The implication of Lockean philosophical principles, which Chaadayev rejected, led to the following Burkean reflection:

> If man is given us at birth packed full of innate principles, inexorable instincts, inborn traditions, it is obvious that little fresh can be made of him; he will live and die precisely as his fathers lived and died, and any attempt to alter or improve his lot is doomed to disappointment. Sweeping away the whole accepted theory of man at a blow, Locke presents us with an entirely different situation, in which man's mind when he is born is no more than a sheet of blank paper whereon we may write what we will. No more revolutionary doctrine has ever been put forward, for by it most obviously education and environment become lord and master of man, and it is possible to change the whole face of society in a single generation.[191]

Years later, Herzen picked up Locke's interpretation of the *tabula rasa* and proclaimed the possibility of the creation of a new society based on Russian socialism.[192] It is worth remembering, however, that Herzen himself was well aware of the limits of the ideas he proclaimed: "Socialism will be developed in all its phases even to its uttermost consequence, the absurd. Then, once

191. Cobban, *Edmund Burke and the Revolt against the Eighteenth Century,* 24.

192. Herzen, *Izbraniye filosofskiye proizwiedieniya* [Anthology of Philosophical Texts], 148, 296–98.

again, there will come forth the cry of negation from the titanic breast of the revolutionary minority; once more the mortal struggle will commence, a struggle in which Socialism will take the place of present Conservatism, to be conquered in its turn by a revolution to us unknown."[193] The root of the difference between Locke and Chaadayev, then, was this: for the Russian philosopher, God, not human beings or their surroundings, had the power to write on the blank page of Russia—and not just Russia as a collection of individuals but on Russia *as a people*. And for the author of the *Apology of a Madman*, the means God used for this purpose was the Church.

In his change of opinion about the Russian Orthodox Church, Chaadayev's vision of the Russian *tabula rasa* still responded to his perception of the flame of history. His understanding of Russia's future as a space open to the intervention of God's will was deeply rooted, as Zenkovsky emphasizes, in a "Christocentric conception of history."[194] The experience of the Revolution of 1830 showed him that the Western social order based on the Catholic tradition did not offer the guarantees he thought it did. This forced him to look for other solutions. Russia's readiness to create a new society, and Russia's embrace of autocracy for effective execution of the plans of Providence, led Chaadayev to a new perspective: "History is no longer ours, granted, but knowledge is ours; we cannot repeat all the achievements of the human spirit, but we can take part in its future achievements. The past is no longer in our power, but the future is ours."[195] And he continued to write, affirming Russia's call "to resolve the greater part of the social problems, to perfect the greater part of the ideas which have arisen in older societies, to pronounce judgment on the most serious questions which trouble the human race."[196]

Crucial to Chaadayev's new approach was that he began to identify Russia's mission with the mission of the Orthodox Church. "However, I am anxious to say it [what I said in "Letter One"] and happy that I was induced to make this confession . . . there was exaggeration in not giving its due to that church, so humble, at times so heroic."[197] Having held the view that the schism had excluded the Eastern Church from world history, Chaadayev now appreciated the positive side of the schism: Christianity had been forced to survive on its own strength, taking root in the desert without the burdens of historical commitments, growing in an interior fashion. Chaadayev saw the Catholic Church in terms of her call to create history. She was

---

193. Ibid., 102–3.

194. Zenkovsky, *History of Russian Philosophy*, 157.

195. Chaadayev, *Philosophical Letters and Apology of a Madman*, 174–75.

196. Ibid., 174.

197. Ibid., 176.

ambitious, intolerant, and interested in the goods of this world, but, despite all this, nevertheless able to carry on a high social mission in the service of humankind. Chaadayev described the vocation of the Orthodox Church differently: living in solitude imposed by the barbarians, she safeguarded the contemplative-ascetic dimension of Christianity. Thanks to this past, in which she was a stranger to any secular ambitions—which were contradictory to her own innermost nature—the Orthodox Church appeared as the other pole of the same absolute truth that builds up both Catholicism and Orthodoxy alike. In this way, Chaadayev concluded that Catholicism and Orthodoxy were complementary strands of the same gospel truth: on the one side, the historical and social activity of Catholicism, and on the other side, the contemplation and asceticism of Orthodoxy. Thus, the philosopher thought the Russian people found its vocation in its deep union with the Orthodox Church. The author of *Apology of a Madman* concluded his reflection in this suggestive way: "[T]hat church, so humble, at times so heroic, which alone attenuates the emptiness of our chronicles, on which devolves the honor of our ancestors' every act of courage, every great sacrifice. Her vocation has been to give to the world this teaching: a great nation completely impregnated by faith in Christ; this is an interesting phenomenon, which we offer to serious minds for the purposes of study."[198]

This new way of interpreting Russia's lack of history, along with the incorporation of the Orthodox Church into his vision, is perhaps unsurprising if we keep in mind that the Church played a key role in the work of Chaadayev from the beginning, and that he himself never felt estranged from Orthodoxy. The Church was always the key to the discovery and subsequent interpretation of the meaning of history. In a time that witnessed the fall of Western traditionalism, Chaadayev's gaze turned toward Russia and toward the Orthodox Church. The disaster of the year 1830 was not a defeat of the Church; it was the failure of a society that, marked by the weight of its own history, did not know how to discover the mystery of time. That Chaadayev never became Catholic, which for some was a sign of his incoherence as a philosopher, acquires its meaning in the light of the development of his thinking. But for almost all of his contemporaries, the development of Chaadayev's ideas remained unknown. Chaadayev's letter to the Tsar in which Chaadayev advocated a profound reform of the Latinized

198. Ibid. There seem to be some divergences in the various manuscripts of Chaadayev's *Apology of a Madman*. While the sentence, "Her vocation has been to give to the world this teaching: a great nation completely impregnated by faith in Christ; this is an interesting phenomenon, which we offer to serious minds for the purposes of study," does not appear in the English translation of Mary-Barbara Zeldin with which I work, it does appear in the Russian and Polish text with which the author works. —Trans.

educational system signaled that Chaadayev assumed Orthodoxy's own experience of history had the same value as Catholicism's. When Chaadayev discovered that the experiences of both churches are two poles of the same truth, there is no longer any justification for the attempt to replace one by the other. The difference invited Orthodoxy and Catholicism to learn from one another's history rather than impose those histories upon one another. Chaadayev's "new" line of thought was simply a continuation of the same line of thought he had pursued from the beginning: the Kingdom of God realized in history of the world, with the Church as its historical incarnation. Chaadayev continued to see Russia as a place prepared for the Church to fulfill its historic vocation. He simply now allowed Russia to do the same.[199] The historical identification between the destinies of the Orthodox Church and the Russian Empire nourished Chaadayev's Russian Idea. But if we add to this the higher idea of a universal unity—a unity that Chaadayev never abandoned—it is difficult to deny that the evolution of his thinking leads to the conclusion that the future lies in the unity of Orthodoxy and Catholicism[200]—a unity based upon equality of rights, as well as respect for Orthodoxy's and Catholicism's different historical experiences and vocations.[201] This new epoch in Chaadayev's life, despite the consequences of the publication of "Letter One," reflected a certain amount of optimism about the possibilities for Russia to take the leading role in its own history and its fulfillment of Providence. Even enlightenment principles espoused by the Russian autocracy, principles that spoke of following the "voice of an enlightened reason, of a deliberative will,"[202] seemed to be in service of higher designs.

Chaadayev could even interpret positively the appearance of the first Slavophiles, "our fanatical Slavists,"[203] who researched in the libraries and desired to find evidence to contradict those who described the Russian people as incapable of owning its own story. He understood the importance of the birth of the Slavophile movement, "the first act of our nation's emancipated intellect."[204] But he was also concerned about the movement. "No man who seriously loves his country can remain anything but gravely affected by this apostasy on the part of our nation's most enlightened minds

---

199. Zenkovsky, *History of Russian Philosophy*, 166–67.

200. Chaadayev continued to maintain a very negative view of Protestantism.

201. Walicki, *Rosja, katolicyzm i sprawa polska*, 47.

202. Chaadayev, *Philosophical Letters and Apology of a Madman*, 175.

203. Ibid., 168.

204. Ibid., 171.

toward what until now was the cause of our glory and our honor."[205] This perception of the dangers that lurked behind the Slavophiles' "anti-Western passions" is visible in the letter that, in the year 1824, Chaadayev wrote to Schelling trying to get him to condemn the Slavophile movement.[206]

Chaadayev's vision was not based on the exclusion of the Western heritage for that of the Eastern but on their complementarity. His attempt to understand history in a "theurgical"—even Christocentric—fashion, led him to understand the relationship between West and East in terms of mutual dependence and interrelationship—a relationship articulated by the respective experiences of Catholicism and Russian Orthodoxy. This position was very clearly expressed in Chaadayev's correspondence with Count Adolphe de Circourt. In a letter dated 15 January 1845, Chaadayev writes: "Our Church is essentially ascetic just as yours is essentially social . . . These are the two poles of the Christian sphere turning on the axis of its absolute truth, of its real truth."[207]

These disagreements marked the relationship between Chaadayev and the Slavophiles from the beginning. But just as Chaadayev's "Letter One" played an important role in the awakening of Slavophile ideas, Slavophile ideas influenced Chaadayev's thought as well. While Chaadayev's dialogue with Slavophiles was largely limited to personal meetings and correspondence, the increasingly popular and elaborate position of the Slavophiles, which occupied an important place in public debate, began to be reflected in Chaadayev's thought. He himself recognized, in 1846, that he had made some concessions to the "new school."[208] These concessions consisted in, above all, his change of mind regarding the Orthodox Church, even recognizing that Christian dogmas had been saved with more zeal and faithfulness by the Orthodox.

In the debate on the interpretation of Russian history, Chaadayev thought the Slavophiles tended to justify and glorify Russian history too easily. According to Chaadayev, in order to begin to create its own history and offer its experience to other nations, Russia had to face the errors of the past. As Chaadayev writes to the Count of Circourt: "The epoch of our genuine emancipation from the influence of foreign ideas will only date from the day when we perfectly understand the roads travelled by us, when the confession of all the faults of our past life will escape from our lips despite ourselves, when the cry of repentance and of sorrow will become

---

205. Ibid.

206. Chaadayev, *Polnoye sobranyie sochinieniy i izbranyie pisma*, 1:232.

207. Chaadayev, *Philosophical Works of Peter Chaadaev*, 192.

208. Ibid., 204.

heard from the depths of our souls. Then we shall naturally take our place among people destined to figure in humanity, not only as battering rams or as a club, but also as ideas."[209] Khomyakov's criticism of Ivan the Terrible brought Chaadayev great joy. Chaadayev expressed hope that future research would lead to the conclusion that "that monster could only exist in the country where he appeared."[210] At that time, despite all the differences between them, Chaadayev saw the activity of the Slavophiles as a sign of hope, an effort in the right direction. "For at the very heart of this new school," Chaadayev writes to Count Circourt, "which claims to lead us back to an imaginary past, more than one lucid mind, more than one sincere soul, has already been led to admit to the sins of our fathers."[211] Today, we know that the Slavophile movement largely opted to glorify Russian history rather than to analyze it critically.

What Chaadayev nevertheless accepted from the Slavophiles was the thesis concerning the historical role of the simple Russian people, although Chaadayev's interpretation differed from the most popular theories of the Slavophiles themselves. Chaadayev affirmed that the Russian people became Christian at a time when the social character of the Church had not yet appeared. Though the Christianity that came to the ancient *Rus'* permeated intimate family life, it had no influence on the establishment of social relations at more complex levels, such as the state. "One could not deny," writes Chaadayev, "the fact that the religious system of the West was much more favorable to the social development of the people than that which fell to our lot."[212] Chaadayev reversed the Slavophile thesis about the negative influence of Rome and its consequence, the Great Schism, by recalling that, in the period before the Schism, the capital of the Roman Empire was Constantinople, not Rome. Though these developments strengthened the independence of the Western Church and removed her from the center of imperial power, they contributed to the increased subordination of the Eastern Church to the emperors. As a consequence, the Orthodox Church inherited obedience to the emperors and was unable to "'socialize' Christianity or 'Christianize' the social system."[213]

The next event of European history that forced Chaadayev to change his mind was the Spring of Nations. The revolutions of 1848 definitively extinguished his hopes centered upon the figure of the tsar. Russia played

209. Ibid.
210. Gershenzon, *Sochineniya i pisma P. Ia. Chaadaeva*, 248–49.
211. Ibid., 204.
212. Ibid., 202.
213. Walicki, *Slavophile Controversy*, 111.

a key role in repressing independence movements. The armies of Tsar Nicholas I managed to "restore order" in Moldova in 1848, and the following year, in 1849, they intervened in Hungary. The Russian expeditionary force, under the command of General Paskievitch, served as a valuable aid to the Austrians and showed its great experience in the brutal pacification of national uprisings. At that time, Chaadayev's discovery of the culture of the Russian people, which he characterized in terms similar to the Slavophiles, became very important. He particularly disapproved of the servitude of the peasants, which he compared to the institution of slavery in the West. However, he noted—and this differentiated him from the Slavophiles—that while slavery in the West resulted from conquests, in Russia the condition of the peasantry was the consequence of a state that, from its inception, had been driven by the desire to enslave not only human beings but freedom of thought as well. Chaadayev's views on this topic were reflected in an extraordinary manner in some notes found in one of the books in his library. In language stylized in the language of peasants, Chaadayev advises the "Russian Orthodox people" that Christian peoples and nations have rebelled against the "Tsars-lords" and "have moved like an ocean wave" against them. It ends very significantly: "We do not want any king except the King of Heaven."[214]

Over the years, Chaadayev's pessimism gained strength. In an increasingly critical manner, he thought the authoritarian power of the tsars would not bring Russia closer to a society called to fulfill the designs of Providence. After the Spring of Nations, Russia experienced the worst years of the "realm of brutal fact and ritual," as he put it in a note written on one of Khomyakov's theological texts.[215] The Crimean War, which broke out in 1853, became definitive in this process. Chaadayev was convinced that the responsibility for this shameful war was shared as much as by Russian nationalism—the official doctrine of the state—as by nationalist Slavophile ideas. Both these nationalisms "claimed to be national," but their "unpatriotic dreams" were in fact articulated in "the customary banal idiom."[216]

In the midst of these events that overwhelmed him, Chaadayev recognized that he did not know how to define his world or recognize himself in it. At the beginning of the Crimean War, he wrote another letter, "Letter from an Unknown Man to an Unknown Woman." The unknown man is

---

214. Shakhovskoy, "Niizdanyi proyekt proklamacyi P. J. Chaadayeva 1848 g." [Unedited Project of a Proclamation of P. Chaadayev, 1848], 679–82. Cited in Lossky, *History of Russian Philosophy*, 50.

215. Chaadayev, "Zamiecheniya na broshuru A. S. Khomiakova (1854)" [Notes in S. Khomiakov's Notebook (1854)], 304–6.

216. Chaadayev, *Philosophical Works of Peter Chaadaev*, 244–45.

obviously Chaadayev. But who is the unknown woman? Would it be too much to assume that it is Russia? Or even Europe? In this letter, Chaadayev writes the following words:

> No, a thousand times no, this is not the way that we loved our country in our youth. We wished her well-being, we desired some good institutions for her, we even sometimes went so far as to wish her a little liberty if that were possible, We thought of her as great and powerful, full of future, but we did not think either that she was the most powerful country in the world, or that she was the most fortunate. We were far from imagining that Russia might stand for some sort of abstract principle containing the definitive solution of the social problem or that Russia constituted in herself an entire separate world, a direct and legitimate inheritor of the glorious eastern empire with its titles and virtues. Nor did we believe that Russia had a special mission to absorb in herself all Slavic people and thereby to bring about the regeneration of the human species. We especially did not think that Europe was on the point of receding into barbarism and that we had been charged with saving civilization with some scraps of that same civilization which had served once to snatch us from our ancient torpor.
>
> We treated Europe with civility, even sometimes with respect; for we know that Europe had taught us many things, among others, its own history. When it happened by chance for us to triumph over her, as Peter the Great did, we said it is to you Gentlemen that we owe it.[217]

Chaadayev never abandoned this pessimism. It seems that the historical events that marked his time demonstrated to him that the idea of the Kingdom of God, as the definitive fulfillment of human history, was still distant. Moreover, these events totally banished from Chaadayev's mind the vision of Russia as a center of such designs. Nicholas I's reign of repression left no space for hope. In one of his last texts, an article written in 1854 for the French press, Chaadayev writes: "When we speak of Russia, often she is treated like a state that is equal to others, but the reality is totally different. Russia is a world apart, obedient to the will, whim, and fancy of one sole person—regardless if he is called Peter or Ivan. In each case, he is the epitome of an arbitrary will. Contrary to all the laws of human society, Russia is headed in a single direction: towards its own enslavement and toward the enslavement of all its neighbors."[218]

217. Ibid., 244.
218. Chaadayev, "Nieopublikovannaya satiya" [Unedited Article], 365.

EPILOGUE

According to Chaadayev, the European aristocracy, which was created by Enlightenment thought and conservative reaction to it, collapsed. The aristocracy soon became the scene of a struggle between bourgeois liberalism, radical democratic movements, and socialism; and between independence-nationalist currents and the policies of repression and expansion of great empires. The Catholic Church in the West stopped playing the role Chaadayev attributed to it, and the Russian Orthodox Church never even tried to play it. The empire of the tsars, which became a conservative stronghold sustained by harsh repression, offered no alternative. Apparently Chaadayev left us with no clear response to this situation at the conclusion of his thought. His works, except for "Letter One," were unknown to his contemporaries. But his personality and freedom of thought were sufficient to mark profoundly the beginning of an extremely rich intellectual and cultural epoch.

Chaadayev's courage, his lack of fear in asking difficult questions, was the basis of his significance. He did not yield to the easy answers often shared by the majority. Of course, the price of such an attitude was the very lack of answers and the close companionship of solitude. The great lesson Chaadayev taught us was the gift of asking difficult questions, even if, consequently, it becomes difficult to find the right answers, even if we end up making mistakes. "Letter One" had a great question mark as its background, and the whole life of Chaadayev himself was a profound expression of astonishment—of astonishment before the God who creates human creatures; who rules history and invites human creatures into it so that they might learn, in liberty, to participate in it; who incarnates this invitation in Christ and continues to offer it in the Church. It is for this reason that Zenkovsky affirms: "Chaadayev's basic theological idea was that of the Kingdom of God, understood not in *isolation from earthly life* but, in its *historical incarnation*, as the *Church*."[219]

Perhaps what made Chaadayev most attractive to his contemporaries was that he embodied the idea of the philosopher. In contrast to the "eighteenth-century French rattles" so ridiculed by the Lubomudzhy, Chaadayev's commitment to his own ideas helped recover the image of a classical philosopher. We should remember that the classic understanding of philosophy was very different from the modern understanding. Classical

219. Zenkovsky, *History of Russian Philosophy*, 156. Zenkovsky's italics. He continues: "[T]he Kingdom of God is being created on earth. Hence Christianity is essentially historical; it cannot be understood in 'other-worldly' terms. . . . [F]or Chaadayev the religious unity of history *presupposes* the *unity of the Church*" (165).

philosophers did not see themselves so much as theoretical researchers but as those dedicated to a vital moral and intellectual experience that served to perfect themselves and the world around them. Some early Christian theologians identified themselves as philosophers, for instance, Tertullian. In his *Homilies on St. Matthew*, St. John Chrysostom used the term *philosophia* in different contexts to denote a wide range of matters: virtue, perfect virtue, wisdom, humility, perfection, rationality, and self-control. Viewed in this light, this affirmation by Chaadayev is illuminating: "I am, thank Heaven, neither a theologian, nor one learned in the law of the Church, but simply a Christian philosopher."[220]

The questions raised by Chaadayev, both in his writings and especially in his life, were a challenge. They were a sign that gave birth to a profound series of reflections, which Dostoyevsky would later call the Russian Idea. These reflections represented the essence of Russian philosophy. Although they are largely unknown in the West, they belong to the most valuable heritage of human thought. It is a heritage to which Soloviev, Bulgakov, Berdyaev, Florensky, among others, would later contribute—a heritage that still offers answers to many of the questions before which Western philosophy remains powerless.

220. Gershenzon, *P. J. Chaadayev*, 104.

# CHAPTER II

# The Russian Idea and Its Interpretation

*The analysis of the icon leads us to the idea of all ideas, to humankind.*
*The icon does not represent but reveals; it is presence and community.*

—Sergei Bulgakov

## INTRODUCTION

This chapter neither is nor purports to be a systematic analysis of Russian religious thought, even within the framework of what came to be known as the Russian Idea. With the works and authors chosen and discussed below, I have only tried to illumine an event that is, to my mind, of paramount importance for contemporary European thought and that is a natural extension of the tradition of Odoevsky and Chaadayev traced in chapter 1. It is an event, however, that is generally unknown in the West, and so its consequences have not yet been sufficiently studied and assessed. My hope is that it could still be a source of inspiration.

As I have sought to suggest in the prologue, though it might seem that Russian philosophy, especially Russian philosophy of more than a century ago, has nothing to do with our time, this view is entirely mistaken. It is mistaken because "our time" is heir to that time. The problems that continue to mark human life and contemporary society, in many ways, remain the same. For these reasons, the challenges facing Russian Christian thinkers of the second half of the nineteenth and early twentieth centuries are still alarmingly relevant. While in recent decades there are signs in Western Christian thought of an effort to return to a union between theology and philosophy, such a union was already articulated richly and deeply among Russian philosophers and theologians of the nineteenth and early twentieth centuries, to which we do well to attend.

⤹

My choice of authors and works referenced indicates the dynamic development of Russian Christian thought. This development had as an indispensable referent and recipient the thought and culture of Western Europe. The fact that Soloviev delivered his lecture, "The Russian Idea," in Paris and in French, was not mere coincidence. As I mentioned in chapter 1, the philosopher delivered the famous lecture, which became a book that same year, published in French under the title *L'Idee russe*,[1] on 25 May 1888, at the Parisian salon of the princess Sayn-Wittgenstein. As Soloviev himself indicates, the Russian Idea was born in a particular place in history: "between the petrification of the East" and the "disintegration of the West."[2] The Russian Idea certainly shines with the splendor of a universal vocation, because it represents "an aspect of the same Christian idea."[3]

The choice of authors and works for this study also reflects the belief that the Russian Idea, while beginning with Chaadayev's insights, was not fully defined by him. It reached its fullest expression in the thought of Soloviev and then later in the rich contributions of Berdyaev.

## The New Human Person

As we have already seen in chapter 1, the alignment between East and West marked the Russian intellectual world to such an extent that it became the axis of debates that have lasted from the nineteenth century to the present. The now classic controversy between the Slavophiles and the Westernizers reflects the importance of the binomial Russia-Europe.

The Slavophiles glorified Russia's past, claiming that the centuries of isolation and backwardness that Russian civilization inherited was an opportunity for Russia to create a new model of society uncorrupted by the

1. Solovyov, *Vladimir Solovyov*, 323.
2. Ibid., 101.
3. Gulyga, *Ruskaya idea i yego tvorcy* [Russian Idea and Its Creators], 12.

exalted rationality, as well as the ubiquitous utilitarianism and individualism, of the West. For those of the Russian intelligentsia who identified with the Slavophiles, the beginning of any interpretation of social reality, political or religious, was marked by the clash between the Catholic and Protestant West, on the one hand, and the Orthodox East, on the other. After this there typically followed a critique of Western culture and praise for what was born of the Russian tradition, or relatedly, the damage sustained from not attending to the Russian tradition. The Westerners, in contrast, placed special emphasis on the promise of Russia's future, proclaiming that, through the creative perception of the values appearing in the West, Russia was beginning a period of flowering.

Neither the Slavophiles nor the Westerners foresaw the *coup d'état* and the Bolshevik Revolution of 1917, which made Russia a paradigmatic example of the modern state of the twentieth century. The Russian state appeared as an unexpected outcome of the debate between the Slavophiles and Westerners. It was totalitarian in character, promoting a scientific understanding of the human person and of history. Sustained by an ideology that was fundamentally religious—with its cult of the party, its leadership, and the rites of an elaborate state liturgy—it enslaved and exterminated its own citizens.

"The state," however, is not just an abstract concept but an incarnate reality. "The state" was real people who carried "the state" within themselves. The socialist-communist state, as well as the national-socialist or national-liberal state, did not emerge from nothing: it did not spring from a socio-historical vacuum. They all resulted from and responded to a historical process and a concrete social situation. And they belong to one and the same tradition. They are human creations, made in the image and likeness of humans. Moreover, as a consequence of the transcendental dimension of humans, these state creations come with their own messiahs and redeemers.

This is the process by which the modern Turkish state was built on the Armenian holocaust, by which German National Socialist specialists traveled to the liberal United States to study the most advanced methods of eugenics, by which the Frenchman Maréchal Pétain sent his Jewish compatriots to National Socialist death camps. It is exactly the same process by which a single company—although under a different name, of course—produced Zyklon-B for the gas chambers of Auschwitz and now manufactures RU486, the abortion pill that is available at pharmacies throughout the world.

In a similar manner, the thought of Karl Marx, which originated within the Western tradition, attracted many Russians, both Westernized and Slavophiles. As Berdyaev comments in *The Russian Revolution*:

> Marx is not the only thinker who has insisted on the over-
> whelming importance of economics, that is, of the degree of
> mastery over the elemental forces of Nature which socially orga-
> nized man has reached; other historians and Utopian Socialists
> did so before him—Saint Simon, for example, who anticipated
> Marx in many respects. But Marx made the idea into a system
> of universal economic metaphysics, and he combined his eco-
> nomic metaphysics or ontology (i. e., his teaching on the nature
> of being, on the ultimate reality) with the doctrine of the class
> struggle, which is the special "discovery," or rather "revelation,"
> of his own genius. This last had also been spoken of before him
> by a more modest science, history; but the idea of the prole-
> tariat's messianic vocation belongs to Marx alone.[4]

Berdyaev then continues:

> But the most important aspect of Marx's teaching concerning
> the proletariat's messianic vocation is the fact that he applied
> to the proletariat the characteristics of God's chosen people. . . .
> [F]or him the proletariat is a new Israel, God's chosen people,
> the liberator and builder of an earthly kingdom that is to come.
> His proletarian Communism is a secularized form of the ancient
> Jewish chiliasm. A Chosen Class takes the place of the chosen
> people. . . . It was not in the name of man that Marx raised the
> standard of revolt, but in the name of the mightiness of a new
> deity, the social collectivity. He is not so much moved by pity
> for the suffering humiliated proletariat, longing to alleviate its
> sufferings and liberate it from humiliation, as by the idea of the
> coming might and power of the proletariat, the future messiah
> destined to organize an earthly empire.[5]

At the outset of *The Russian Revolution*, Berdyaev asks a series of important questions: "How was it possible for Holy Russia to be turned into an
arsenal of militant atheism? How is it that a people who are religious by their
very structure and live exclusively by faith have proved to be such a fruitful
field for anti-religious propaganda?" And he then responds to his own questions: "To explain that, to understand Russian *anti-religious* psychology, one
must have an insight into the *religious* psychology of the Russian people.

4. Berdyaev, *Russian Revolution*, 60.
5. Ibid., 69.

. . . The nineteenth century saw the advent of an original type of Russian . . . and it is this type which gives us the key to the militant atheism of the Russian Revolution."[6] We cannot understand this militant atheism without first having understood its internal religious structure.

In the early 1950s, the philosopher Alasdair MacIntyre observed the same dependence: Marxism does not face Christianity in a posture of antagonism. Rather, Marxism represents a transformation of Hegel's secularized version of Christian theology. It is not so much an atheist doctrine as a Christian heresy.[7] The religious nature of Marxism was even more pronounced in the interpretation and practice of "orthodox Marxism," as Berdyaev calls it, the mythological-religious-mystical version of Marxism developed by Lenin, which eventually adapted very well to historical and cultural conditions of Russia. Lenin stressed the original and national[8] character of the Russian Revolution. He repeated that the Russian Revolution will not be as the dogmatic Marxists imagined it would be. "Bolshevism is much more traditional than is commonly supposed," argues Berdyaev. "It agreed with the distinctive character of the Russian historical process. There had taken place a Russification and orientalizing of Marxism."[9]

In effect, Marxism was for the Bolsheviks a philosophy and a religion, not just a struggle to change the socio-political aspects of life. It was a phenomenon that neither Marx nor Western Marxists foresaw—a profound and intimate union of two messiahs: Russian national messianism and the messianism of the proletarian class. [10] In this way, the Third Rome of the monk Filofei became the Third International of Lenin, where Marxists also raised as high as possible the banner of truth; but for them, "truth is only a weapon of war exuding hate; a truth appertaining not to Eternity, but to the Five-Year Plan."[11]

Following Berdyaev's line of thought, it is easy to see how reason, science, democracy, nation, and even human beings themselves can be "messianized." From this vantage, we can also better understand why Chaadayev,

6. Ibid., 1.

7. MacIntyre, *Marxism and Christianity*, 12–13.

8. "The Russian revolution was universal in its principles as is every great revolution. It was brought about under the flag of internationalism, but for all that it was profoundly national and became more and more national in its results. The difficulty of forming a judgment about communism is due precisely to this twofold character that it has—it is both Russian and international." Berdyaev, *Origin of Russian Communism*, 114.

9. Ibid., 106.

10. Berdyaev, *Russian Revolution*, 71.

11. Berdyaev, *End of Our Time*, 258.

Soloviev, and Berdyaev cannot be classified either as Slavophiles or West-ernizers. For all of them, the Messiah was Jesus Christ, the Truth and the Horizon of the human person, in whom history merges with Eternity. The Russian Idea of Chaadayev, Soloviev, and Berdyaev refused the nationalist temptation—the temptation that seduced both the Slavophiles and many Westerners—as well as the socialist-Marxist and the liberal traps that se-duced many Slavophiles and Westerners as well.

Berdyaev saw the real danger of Marxist-Leninist communism in the ease with which it had managed to create a "new person," something with which it had much greater success than with building a "new economy." No less important was Berdyaev's firm conviction that the discourse of liberal-ism is not as radically opposed to the communist ideology as it sounds. "The implacably hostile attitude of communism to all religion," Berdyaev observes, "belongs to the very essence of the communist general outlook on life," and this is the case because communism "wants to be a religion itself, to take the place of Christianity."[12] For this reason, Berdyaev contin-ues, "A free-thinking, atheist and materialist bourgeoisie is to be preferred to Christians who sympathize with communism; it can be used for the socialist work of construction; it is usually indifferent to the question of a 'general outlook,' whereas the Christian communists make a breach in the integral wholeness of the communist 'world outlook.'"[13] As Berdyaev writes elsewhere, "The greedy bourgeois person is more acceptable, more tolerable than the Christian communist. The former can be a travel companion."[14]

⮌

That assessment is no longer so surprising in light of final changes in the former Soviet bloc or those we see in China today. Marx and Lenin were wrong when they said that the last stage of the revolution was communism, as history has shown that communism can become capitalism—and not even as something new but precisely as a return to the origins, which are nothing more than secularized modernity.

Dostoyevsky prophetically perceived this in in his novel *The Devils*, which represents, as Henri de Lubac reminds us, a harrowing analysis of the reality hidden within liberal ideas, not socialist ones, as some have mis-takenly tried to suggest: "The revolutionary socialists are the heirs of the liberals who, in the Western school, embraced atheism. 'To annihilate God'

12. Berdyaev, *Origin of Russian Communism*, 158.
13. Ibid., 167.
14. Berdyaev, *El cristianismo y el problema del comunismo*, 142.

is the first point in their program and the first watchword spread abroad by their tracts. They draw the inferences of that atheism. No longer contenting themselves with a vague belief in progress, they undertake to build up humanity without God."[15]

## THE FUTURE OF THE PROMISE

The ease with which the communist countries adopted liberal slogans only confirmed Berdyaev's sense that the new person created by communism—*homo sovieticus*, in the words of Alexander Zinoviev[16]—was nonplussed by the free-thinking, atheist, and materialist bourgeoisie. In the words of Berdyaev, they were natural travel companions. This new person, this *homo sovieticus,* was willing, as Józef Tischner puts it, to set fire to a cathedral without even a second thought in order to use the heat to fry some eggs.[17] Zinoviev, a philosopher who served as a professor in the Department of Logic at the University of Moscow, was expelled from the Soviet Union in 1977. After the fall of the Soviet Union, however, he radically changed his position and supported Gennady Zyuganov, the communist candidate who lost to Boris Yeltsin in 1996. In his book *The Radiant Future,*[18] Zinoviev illustrates the closeness of the two creations of modern European civilization. He describes the astonishing ease with which Professor Kanareikin, one of the central characters of the novel and head of the Institute of Philosophy of the Academy of Sciences of the USSR at the time of Khrushchev's thaw, becomes not only an exemplary apologist for Stalin but a liberal devoted to the observation from the window of his office all the attractive women passing down the Marxism-Leninism Avenue. "In Moscow," we are told, "you can find absolutely anything you want. Any wines, any food, any kind of girl."[19]

The novel's title is taken from the following slogan, which was very popular in Zinoviev's time: "Long live communism: the radiant future of all humankind." The Institute of Philosophy of the Academy of Sciences, with Kanareikin at the helm, is in charge of caring for and arranging a huge banner attached to a concrete building, the location of which is the exit to Cosmonaut Square on Marxism-Leninism Avenue. It is a building, however,

15. de Lubac, *Drama of Atheist Humanism,* 322–23.

16. Zinoviev, *Homo Sovieticus.*

17. Tischner, *Etyka solidarności oraz Homo sovieticus* [Ethic of Solidarity and Homo Sovieticus], 25.

18. Zinoviev, *Radiant Future.*

19. Ibid., 282.

marked by a fatal technical error that forces those in charge of it to make constant repairs, especially on the eve of the 25th Congress of the CPSU.

Neither this image about the truth of communism—a system built on corrupt foundations—nor the figures of those responsible for taking care of this structure, however, are the protagonists of the story of *The Radiant Future*. The only thing we know about the narrator—the author himself?—is that he also works at the Institute and is the head of the department of Theoretical Issues of the Methodology of Scientific Communism.

One day, on his way to work, he encounters an old woman dressed in rags. Drunk and pushing a cart full of trash, she is looking for money to buy more alcohol. The protagonist has never seen her before, even when he looked out the window. On those rare occasions, he would only see elegant and smiling passersby. When he nearly collides with this woman, he thinks, not with anger but rather with sadness, "We have a developed form of socialism. We are moving towards communism at an ever-increasing rate. But she doesn't give a damn for all that."[20] Despite the unpleasantness of this experience, he cannot get the image of the woman—a kind of shadow of human dignity who slides frightened through the beautiful streets of the city—out of his mind. It becomes an obsession for him. Her presence even haunts his dreams. In his dreams, he sees himself carrying in the cart of the old women books written with great effort. When he wants to begin to walk, he cannot. The indifferent crowd that surrounds him, everyone pursuing his or her own affairs, prevents him from moving his cart.

This scene permits the protagonist to see that he is located in a different dimension of existence from the unknown people that surround him. As an intellectual, he works to realize the theoretical Marxist dream of a better world, while the faceless mass of humanity images this dream as it is worked out in reality. Within the uniform sea of individuals, he can only clearly distinguish the face of the old women. And this woman—homeless, living on the margins of the society created by him—becomes the symbol of freedom, of the human capacity to decide one's own destiny. Although the narrator is not fully conscious of it, she nevertheless becomes an important image of contradiction, of resistance to the absurd and totalitarian imposition of the propaganda of the state.[21]

Years after the publication of *The Radiant Future*, in the era of Mikhail Gorbachev's *Perestroika*, Alexander Solzhenitsyn experienced something

20. Ibid., 106.

21. Along these lines, it is important to mention the figure of Venedict Yerofeyev, who, in large measure and for much time, was the real life and tragic incarnation—though he in all likelihood would not have used these phrases—of the figure of the old woman of *The Radiant Future*.

similar to the protagonist of *The Radiant Future*. The famous Russian Nobel Prize winner not only had to assume that his countrymen did not understand him as he had hoped, but that they were perhaps even living in different realities altogether.

In June 1987, in the newspaper published by Russian immigrants in New York, *New Russian Word*, there appeared an article by Ivan Suslov under the title "Why Are You Silent, Master?"[22] This article was directed to Solzhenitsyn, asking him to comment on Gorbachev's reforms. Three years passed before Solzhenitsyn gave his answer, in September 1990, which was published first in the Moscow daily *Komsomol Truth*, and then, three days later, in the supplement of the monthly *Russian Thought*. In an article titled "How Are We to Rebuild Russia?"[23] Solzhenitsyn began with the famous pronouncement, "The clock of communism has stopped striking," and he proceeded to focus primarily on what he considered the two fundamental issues: the situation of the Soviet Union and the possibilities offered by *perestroika* for an attempt to construct a Russia based on the ideas once presented by Leo Tolstoy. These ideas consisted, *a grosso modo*, in regarding Imperial Russia, together with Ukraine and Belarus, as the backbone—both geopolitically, as well as in the moral-religious sense—of the attempt to resurrect the Slavic nations of the east.

The project found, in principle, a positive reception, especially among Russian immigrants, which was reflected in Zoya Krajmalnikova's "Is It Possible to Rebuild Russia Without God?" also published in *Russian Thought*.[24] When Solzhenitsyn returned to Russia, however, euphoria turned into great disappointment. The until-now charismatic Master of Vermont became known as the "Carthusian of Troitse-Lykovo." The main cause of the intellectual and spiritual disagreement in these different proposals for the renewal of Russia's former glory and future aspirations resided in the fact that Solzhenitsyn failed to take into account that, in his country's new reality, religion did not occupy the position he expected. After years of supremacy in *theoria*, *praxis* was now taking its revenge. The Russia of Solzhenitsyn's time had little in common with the idealized image of the Holy Russia of the nineteenth century. It had much more in common with secularized Europe at the beginning of the twenty-first century.

22. Suslov, "Pochiemu moltchitie, Mastier?" 3.

23. Solzhenitsyn, "Kak nam obustroit' Rossiyu?"

24. Krakhmalnikova, "Mozhna li obustroit' Rossiyu biez Boga?" 9.

∽

Toward the end of his time in office, President Boris Yeltsin promoted a contest for the contemporary definition of the Russian Idea. All proposals reflected a distinctly secular character, devoted to describing different variants of a modern state. None of them even tried to recover the thought of Soloviev or Berdyaev.

In Viktor Pelevin's novel *Generation "P"*,[25] a marketing professional receives a unique assignment: to prepare the material to promote the Russian Idea. He fails. He fails because it is no longer possible to identify the Russian Idea.

The disintegration of the Soviet Union came as an unexpected blow to its inhabitants. Much of the society and many of its writers in particular expressed their experience apocalyptically, which often reflected what happened with more success than many academic treatises. "The principal problem posed by this year [1989]," writes the famous Russian dissident Mikhail Epstein, "is no longer a (derivative) social or a political one, but rather an eschatological one: how to live after one's own future, or, if you like, after one's own death."[26] The solution to this problem was the center of the various attempts to re-define the identity of the ordinary citizens of the now defunct communist empire and of the Russian state itself. Some sought support in the Orthodox Church; others in pan-Slavic discourse or in the pragmatism of a new liberal state; and others still, in the manner of Solzhenitsyn, in dreams of the restoration of the ideals of Old Russia.

In *Generation "P"*, Viktor Pelevin succeeds in offering an image as revealing as it is accurate of the situation of the new generation of Russians and their attempt to re-define themselves after having discovered that their "future is over." The abbreviation "P" of the title stands for everything that is related to "P" in the modern world and ultimately comes to symbolize the modern world as such: the "P" is for Pepsi, as well as for the prefix "post-," as in post-communist, post-colonial, post-modern, post-humanistic, post-historical, and so on. The emergence of capitalism meant that the destiny of the generation that appeared after the fall of the Berlin Wall was bound to capitalism. But it also meant that this generation found itself marginalized, expelled from the space created by the new reality—a reality dominated by new Russians: businessmen, Mafiosos, politicians, and new (and not so

25. Pelevin, *Generation "P"*. This book was published in Great Britain under the title *Babylon*, and in the United States under the title *Homo Zapiens*. Because the body of the author's text continually references the original Russian title, I have translated accordingly. —Trans.

26. Epstein, *After the Future*, 71.

new) oligarchs. The response of this generation to the new situation was that of assimilation; they not only accepted the new rules of the game, but they did their best to become one with the new culture.

Pelevin's book explores the importance of advertising for capitalism and the way advertising attempts to create a new language of propaganda. The new iconography fabricated by capitalist advertising, it turns out, is not a radical departure from Russia's religious, national, and cultural past. Rather, it has roots in Russia's tsarist and communist history. Marketers insert new commercial content in designs borrowed from old communist posters. They also apply the same basic rule as their forbearers: the message must be as simple as possible and must be as effective with as wide a social audience as possible. Consequently, they create a language that obeys the most primitive instincts and aesthetic preferences.

The head of the Institute of Philosophy of the Academy of Sciences, Professor Kanareikin of Alexander Zinoviev's novel *The Radiant Future*, would no doubt feel very comfortable in the new reality of Generation "P". He could continue to care for the banner that proclaimed a new "radiant future." This time, however, instead of working to instantiate Marxist ideas, he could work to instantiate something closer to his dreams: any wine, any food, any kind of girl. What is more, this transformation need not cost him much, perhaps nothing at all, because, at bottom, there is no need for transformation. In order to facilitate the transition from communism to liberalism, one can even use the same music that accompanied the construction of the former "future." It is no coincidence, for instance, that the current occupant of the Kremlin, President Putin, known both for his formation in the KGB as well as for his fine taste in music (Tchaikovsky, Liszt, and so on), chose as the official anthem of modern Russian the famous composition of Aleksandr Aleksandrov. This composition has, since the days of Stalin, fulfilled the same function. It was composed by the same author, Sergey Mikhalkov, who, throughout his more than ninety years of life, adapted it three times. Throughout all these years, the same music has accompanied the parades, the official acts of state, the executions, and, of course, the funerals. The communists shot their enemies to the sound of this march. With the same musical background, Comrade Kovalenko, who served for thirty-five years as the Kremlin's official undertaker, buried the leaders of the revolution. With great skill, he would always finish his work at the last sounds of the hymn, such that the hymn marked the exact time of the operation: four and a half minutes. The same four and a half minutes marked—or terminated—the lives of several generations of Russian people. And it continued to mark the rhythm to which the free-thinking, atheist, and materialist bourgeoisie of Generation "P"—the natural travel companion of *homo sovieticus*—marched toward its own radiant future.

☞

With a few brushstrokes, I have tried to reproduce an image—a simplified image, of course, but one that I hope is suggestive—of the changes experienced by contemporary Russian society. It is an image offered by many Russian authors, several of whom I have considered here. It is an image of a landscape that increasingly bears striking resemblances to our own. In short, just as Russia never left the European framework behind but only offered a variation on the same theme, now Russia returns once again to its primary design: the post-modern liberal society. It is a society in which even those who are recognized as the "opposition" are tied with the same chains as the rest of society. They are alone: Solzhenitsyn in his internal exile, the old woman of Zinoviev's novel, Yerofeyev in the alcoholism that plagued his life. Each in their own way faced an extreme and desperate internal exile, like so many others in modern societies.

But more than "being alone," they do not know that they are not alone. And this is the living center of the reflection that culminates in the Russian Idea, which is nothing more than an attempt to find an alternative to the tendency—so characteristic of contemporary civilization—to build humankind on the basis of the temporal and the finite, leaving behind the religious dimension, as Soloviev underscores in the first of his lectures on Divine Humanity (*bogochelovechestvo*).[27] The Russian Idea is nothing more than the discovery that we are not alone, that our future is not a slave of death, that we are a unique and irreplaceable part of a Community.

## THE RUSSIAN IDEA OF VLADIMIR SOLOVIEV

As we already saw in chapter 1, in Russia, as in the rest of Europe, the question of the nature of the human person and of history had profound social implications. As we saw above, Berdyaev observes that in Russia these social implications were notably religious, even for atheists, whether socialist or anarchist. We see this especially in the writings of Dostoevsky, but as we also saw above, the figure that most popularized the Russian Idea was certainly Vladimir Soloviev. Soloviev focused the concept and masterfully demonstrated the universality of the idea itself, as well as the thought that created

---

27. Soloviev, *Lectures on Divine Humanity*, 1–3.

it. He located the Russian Idea soteriologically and historiosophically in such a way that it carried no nationalistic overtones but represents a new aspect of the Christian idea as such, a sketch of the realization of the fullness of life.[28] In this way, it surpassed the Slavophile conception of Russian messianism, which was based on the idea that Russia embodied among the peoples of the world the role of redeemer nation. Soloviev's studies of the sources of Christianity led him to conclude that this mission is not Russia's but already embodied in the Church—the undivided Church, the Universal Church. The basis of Soloviev's *Russian Idea* was the lecture he delivered in Paris in order to launch his book *Russia and the Universal Church*. Later, *The Russian Idea* would also appear in the form of a separate brochure. During his stay in Paris until the fall of 1888, amid the controversy that prompted the lecture and the publication of *The Russian Idea*, Soloviev finished making corrections and wrote the final chapter of *Russia and the Universal Church*, perhaps his best-known book. At this time, *The Russian Idea* was making quite a stir throughout Europe. Soloviev's judgments and proposals were written about in newspapers and magazines, and were discussed in salons, universities, sacristies, and government offices. As one might expect, neither the Russian imperial government nor the authorities of the Russian Orthodox Church liked the content of the lecture or the book very much. In December of 1889, in a letter to Canon Rački, Soloviev described the reaction to his ideas: "They do not approve of my book on both sides: the liberals for its clericalism, the clerics for its liberalism."[29] When Cardinal Strossmayer presented Pope Leo XIII with *L'Idée Russe*, the pope apparently said, "Bella idea ma fuori d'un miracolo e cosa impossibile" (Beautiful idea, but impossible without a miracle).[30]

*Russia and the Universal Church* consists of three parts. In the first, "The Religious State of Russia and the Christian East," Soloviev indicates that in the official Russian Orthodox Church, the place of highest spiritual authority is the tsar, whose representative is the Chief Procurator (Ober Prokurator), which is contrary to the canons of the Seventh Ecumenical Council. Therefore, in the Christian East, it is impossible to find a point of union for the whole Church, since she lacks one. The Church, in her earthly reality, needs a center of power and authority. In the case of the East, Soloviev suggests, there are three options: either the visible Church does not exist; or, as the so-called Old Believers think, she ceased to exist in 1666

28. Soloviev, "Historia i budushchnost' teokratiy" [History and Future of Theocracy], 243.

29. Solovyov, *Vladimir Solovyov*, 357.

30. Ibid., 349.

and the antichrist rules in her place; or the real power established by Christ is found in the West. Soloviev leans toward the latter option. In the second part, "The Ecclesiastical Monarchy Founded by Jesus Christ," Soloviev argues that, from the beginning, the Church acquired its structural model from the Roman Empire, which was nothing but a foreshadowing of the Church. Also in this part he openly defends the dogma of papal infallibility for the first time in his writings. The third part of the book, "The Trinitarian Principle and Its Social Application," has a dogmatic-theosophical character, and it concludes the line of thought Soloviev began in his youth with *Philosophical Principles of Integral Knowledge* and *Lectures on Divine Humanity*. As Sergey Soloviev indicates in the biography of his uncle, the earliest forms of Soloviev's theory of the Holy Trinity and of Sophia begin to acquire depth and clarity in *Russia and the Universal Church*. In it, there is also a visible change, especially in terms of the influence of Christian dogma on the narration of Sophia. In the last chapters, the philosopher offers a sketch of the ideal human society, the Universal Church. He conceives this society as an embodiment of the divine Sophia and a reflection of the Holy Trinity. The high priest of the Universal Church, the Pope of Rome, corresponds to God the Father; the Christian monarch corresponds to the Son; and the prophet corresponds to the Holy Spirit. The prophetic role is the principal one, unifying the first two.[31]

The great debate from which the Russian Idea arises and to which it tries to give shape is therefore also a debate about the relationship between the Church and the state, and between faith and reason. It becomes the front line of the fight between good and evil, life and death.

⤳

With regard to the path down which he travels, Soloviev's point of departure remained unabashedly the same: the conviction of the intimate unity between faith and reason, God and world, Christ and the human person. This conviction led Soloviev to seek forms of social organization capable of responding to the challenge of this unity. Towards the end of his life, he saw that the discussion needed to return to its natural dimension: to eschatology. His profound analysis of the development of the modern world led him to these conclusions.

*Russia and the Universal Church* may seem to be a text written by a Roman Catholic theologian to defend papal primacy. It may also seem somewhat naïve in its proposals for a theocratic state, the fruit of the union

31. Ibid., 351–54.

between Moscow and Rome. But what also stands out in Soloviev's text, as in all his work—and Hans Urs von Balthasar stresses this against the opinion of Berdyaev—is that the Russian thinker appears as "universal heir" of the history of Europe and its thought. He knows and understands in a profound way the roots and fruits of "the French Revolution, German idealism, the Hegelianism of the Left, together with Feuerbach and Marx, Comte's positivism, Darwin's evolutionism, Nietzsche's doctrine of the superman, and the fashionable pessimism of Schopenhauer in the form finally given it by E. von Hartmann."[32] In the introduction to *Russia and the Universal Church*, we read:

> I do not presume to pass judgment on the special circumstances of France, nor to decide whether, as distinguished writers more competent than myself declare, the Revolution did this country more harm than good. But let us not forget that if each nation in history works more or less for the whole world, France has the distinction of having taken a step of universal significance in the political and social sphere.
>
> Though the revolutionary movement destroyed many things that needed to be destroyed, though it swept away many an injustice and swept it away forever, it nevertheless failed lamentably in the attempt to create a social order founded upon justice. Justice is simply the practical expression and application of truth; and the starting-point of the revolutionary movement was false. The declaration of the Rights of Man could only provide a positive principle for social reconstruction if it was based upon a true conception of Man himself. That of the revolutionaries is well-known: they perceived in Man nothing but abstract individuality, a rational being destitute of all positive content.
>
> I do not propose to unmask the internal contradictions of this revolutionary individualism nor to show how this abstract "Man" was suddenly transformed into the no less abstract "Citizen," how the free sovereign individual found himself doomed to be the defenseless slave and victim of the absolute State or "Nation," that is to say, of a group of obscure persons borne to the surface of public life by the eddies of revolution and rendered the more ferocious by the consciousness of their own intrinsic nonentity. No doubt it would be highly interesting and instructive to follow the thread of logic which connects the doctrines of 1789 with the events of 1793. But I believe it to be still more important to recognize that the πρῶτον ψεῦδος, the basic falsehood, of the Revolution—the conception of the individual man

---

32. Balthasar, *Glory of the Lord*, 3:279–81.

as a being complete in and for himself—that this false notion of individualism was not the invention of the revolutionaries or of their spiritual forbears, the Encyclopedists, but was the logical, though unforeseen, issue of an earlier pseudo-Christian or semi-Christian doctrine which has been the root cause of all the anomalies in the past history and present state of Christendom.

Men have imagined that the acknowledgment of the divinity of Christ relieves them of the obligation of taking His words seriously. They have twisted certain texts of the Gospel so as to get out of them the meaning they want, while they have conspired to pass over in silence other texts which do not lend themselves to such treatment. The precept "Render to Caesar the things that are Caesar's, and to God the things that are God's" is constantly quoted to sanction an order of things which gives Caesar all and God nothing. The saying "My Kingdom is not of this world" is always being used to justify and confirm the paganism of our social and political life, as though Christian society were destined to belong to this world and not to the Kingdom of Christ. On the other hand, the saying "All power is given Me in Heaven and Earth" is never quoted. Men are ready to accept Christ as sacrificing Priest and atoning Victim; but they do not want Christ the King. His royal dignity has been ousted by every kind of pagan despotism, and Christian peoples have taken up the cry of the Jewish rabble: "We have no king but Caesar!" Thus history has witnessed, and we are still witnessing, the curious phenomenon of a society which professes Christianity as its religion but remains pagan not merely in its life but in the very basis of that life. This dichotomy is not so much a logical *non sequitur* as a moral failure. . . .

That all human relationships should be governed by charity and brotherly love is undoubtedly the express will of God and the end of His creation; but in historic reality, as in the Lord's Prayer, the fulfillment of the divine will on Earth is only realized after the hallowing of God's Name and the coming of His Kingdom. The Name of God is Truth; His Kingdom is Justice. It follows that the knowledge of the truth and the practice of justice are necessary conditions for the triumph of evangelical charity in human society.

In truth, all are one; and God, the absolute Unity, is all in all. But this divine Unity is hidden from our view by the world of evil and illusion, the result of universal human sin. The basic condition of this world is the division and isolation of the parts of the Great Whole; and even Man, who should have been the unifying rationale of the material universe, finds himself split up and scattered over the Earth, and has been unable by his own efforts to achieve more than a partial and unstable unity, the universal monarchy of paganism. . . . Since mankind is objectively separated from the divine unity, this unity must in the first place be given to us as an objective reality independent of ourselves—the Kingdom of God coming amongst us, the external, objective Church. But once reunited to this external unity, men must translate it into action, they must assimilate it by their own efforts—the Kingdom of God is to be taken by force, and the men of violence possess it. At first manifested *for* us and then *by* us, the Kingdom of God must finally be revealed *in* us in all its intrinsic, absolute perfection as love, peace and joy in the Holy Spirit.

Thus the Church Universal (in the broad sense of the word) develops as a threefold union of the divine and the human: there is the priestly union, in which the divine element, absolute and unchangeable, predominates and forms the Church properly so called (the Temple of God); there is the kingly union, in which the human element predominates and which forms the Christian State (the Church as the living Body of God); and there is lastly the prophetic union, in which the divine and the human must penetrate one another in free mutual interaction and so form the perfect Christian society (the Church as the Spouse of God).

The moral basis of the priestly union, or of the Church in the strict sense of the word, is faith and religious devotion; the kingly union of the Christian State is based on law and justice; while the element proper to the prophetic union or the perfect society is freedom and love.[33]

This passage reveals something of the character of Soloviev's thought, which was born from a profound Christian experience—an experience lived within a world that formed a part of that experience, but ultimately rejected it. This is also the tragic experience of the search for answers to offer a lost humankind, answers that implicated public life. If Soloviev's theocratic solutions belonged, in Berdyaev's words, to his "rosy vision" of the world around him, their basis was the unifying action of Christ, who breaks into human history, along with Soloviev's perception of the Church as a perpetual seal of Christ's unifying presence in this same history. Moreover, they already suggested the direction Soloviev's later thinking would take. In his final work, the idea of a Christian state disappeared to give way to the final design of the United Church as the antithesis of the state.

33. Soloviev, *Russia and the Universal Church*, 7–10.

The fact that Soloviev was also the privileged trustee of patristic and classical thought, along with Russian Orthodox spirituality, was also crucial. The challenge of dialogue between Orthodoxy and Catholicism began with a deep knowledge of both traditions and opened out onto a broader perspective that became a dialogue between East and West.[34] It was a dialogue in which all his work, "the most universal intellectual construction of modern times,"[35] participated. Balthasar thought the work of Soloviev was "'beyond question the most profound vindication and the most comprehensive philosophical statement of the Christian totality in modern times,'" "'a work of art on a massive scale,' a drama and epic, a hymn of the universe," that his "skill in the technique of integrating all partial truths in one vision makes him perhaps second only to Thomas Aquinas as the greatest artist of order and organization in the history of thought."[36] But the main rationale for Balthasar's appreciation of Soloviev was that Soloviev's system "aims at bringing a whole ethical and theoretical scheme to perfection in a universal theological aesthetic—a vision of God's coming to be in the world."[37] Soloviev's opposition to "Kantian-Hegelian formalism" characterized all of his thought, and Balthasar's conclusion, although expressed in the context of theological aesthetics, helps us better define that opposition:

> Here, then, is the same universal trend of thought as in Hegel; but in place of the Protestant "dialectic," which relentlessly transcends all things to find its term in the absolute Spirit, the basic conceptual model in Soloviev's thought is the Catholic "integration" of all partial points of view and forms of actualization into an organic totality that annuls and uplifts (*aufhebt*) all things in a manner that pervades that which is transcended far more successfully than in Hegel. It establishes God's becoming man as the abiding pivot and organizing focus of worldly reality and its relation to God. What is preserved is the eternal, ideal kernel of every person in so far as it has been integrated into the entirety of the cosmic body of God; which means that its real bodily form is preserved in the same way. There is no ultimate absorption of all things into an absolute spiritual subject; instead there is the resurrection of the dead. So for Soloviev aesthetics and eschatology coincide, in practical terms; and in connection with this we must note simply that if God has become man in Christ, the Kingdom of God does not break in "unilaterally" from

34. Balthasar, *Glory of the Lord*, 3:281.
35. Ibid.
36. Ibid., 281, 284.
37. Ibid., 281.

> above and from outside; it must necessarily grow to maturity
> just as much from within.[38]

*The Russian Idea* already suggested Soloviev's later shift from theocracy to eschatology. Upon affirming that the Russian Idea consists in "building on earth the faithful image of the Divine Trinity," he continues along a path whose ultimate expression will be found only at the end of his life. In the same year, in a 21 July 1888 letter addressed to the Jesuit E. Tavernier, Soloviev writes that he was "more or less looking at all things *sub specie aeternitatis* or at least *sub specie antichristi venturi*."[39] On this road we find that the biggest obstacle to the emergence of Divine Humanity—humanity "transubstantiated" by and in Christ—is those who assert themselves as gods. "Once mankind has renounced God," writes Dostoevsky in *The Brothers Karamazov*, "Man will be exalted with the spirit of divine, Titanic pride, and the man-god will appear."[40]

The idea of Divine Humanity, which is the heart of Soloviev's thought, was also the basis of his understanding of theocracy. According to Soloviev, theocracy was the "materialization" in history of the idea of Divine Humanity, its social and political instantiation, the fulfillment of the idea of a "Christian politics."[41] Divine Humanity was Soloviev's response to the question of evil in the world. The Russian philosopher's theandrism, which embraced society, politics, and ecclesiology, encountered the problem of evil visible in reality, present in the structures of the surrounding world. The problem was evidenced in the triumph of the "abstract principles," in the "abstract dualism," that led to the division between the world, on the one hand, and Christ and the Church, on the other; between the divine and the human. This division is also reflected in the separation between the Eastern and Western Church.

This, then, was the challenge Soloviev faced, and it is this which allows us to understand the background of the Russian Idea: the problem of evil, not just in its social or political dimensions, but above all as a fundamentally ontic or existential problem, "the last, the extremist manifestation of evil in history, the picture of its short-lived triumph and its final destruction."[42] The search for the answer to the question of where to find help in the fight against evil became the heart of the Russian Idea. It is a question that belongs to the

38. Ibid., 283–84.

39. Mochulsky, *Wladimir Solowiow*, 184.

40. Dostoevsky, *Brothers Karamazov*, 648–49.

41. Soloviev, "Vielkiy spor i christianska política" [Great Controversy and Christian Politics], 3–103.

42. Soloviev, *War, Progress, and the End of History*, 21.

culture and religious consciousness of Russia, full of existential tension and of ongoing moral debate.

### MYSTERIUM INIQUITATIS—THE DAMN PROBLEM

This *damn problem*, as Dostoyevsky called the problem of evil, which is so present in the Orthodox East, was inescapable for Western philosophy as well. Western philosophy mortgaged its future in the attempt to eliminate the concept of evil, to reduce the problem of evil to the level of a relic or myth. In so doing, western philosophy lost the capacity to perceive the presence of personal evil, the devil. "Before the problem of evil," writes Etienne Borne, "philosophy faces total risk, recognizing that until it passes through the fire of this issue, it is unsure of what it is, or even if it is."[43] This failure of Western thought to face evil became clear to philosophy itself, but this failure is not reflected in secularized Western consciousness. As Leszek Kolakowski writes, "There came a point, however, when philosophers had to confront a simple, painfully undeniable fact: that of the questions which have sustained European philosophy for two and a half millennia, not a single one has been answered to general satisfaction. All of them, if not declared invalid by the decree of philosophers, remain controversial."[44] In Russia, however, as Jan Krasicki quite rightly points out, the problem of evil always belonged intrinsically to the universal and eschatological vision of human history, and within this horizon, the interpretation of the ontic experience of each person as integral and central to God's plan of salvation for the whole universe.[45]

In the spring of 1898, during his last trip to Egypt, Soloviev experienced the reality of evil, and this real-mystical encounter with real evil, the devil, marks the beginning of the last stage of his work. In 1900, the year of his death, he wrote his brilliant, and, as Berdyaev considered it, prophetic work, *War, Progress, and the End of History: Three Conversations, Including a Short Story of the Anti-Christ*. This work presented only an apparent rupture with his previous thought. As Berdyaev indicates, it is better understood as the key to the interpretation the entirety of Soloviev's life and work. This "Apocalypse According to Soloviev" is essential to the interpretation of the corpus of Russian philosopher, including his articulation of the Russian Idea.

---

43. Borne, *Le problème du mal*, 4.

44. Kołakowski, *Metaphysical Horror*, 1.

45. Krasicki, "Bogoczlowiecznstwo i zlo" [Divine Humanity and Evil], 27.

The purpose of this apocalypse, as Alain Besançon indicates, is the interpretation of the present moment when viewed in light of the entirety of the historical process—an apocalypse that clarifies *hic et nunc* by illumining it with the light of last things.[46] This method is already applied in the third century by Hippolytus of Rome in the text known as *On the Antichrist*.[47] Soloviev might have known this text, since it was very popular at the time. To this day, there are translations of the original Greek into ancient Slavic, Georgian, and Ethiopian manuscripts, as well as fragments in Syriac and Aramaic.[48]

There are interesting similarities between Soloviev's text and Hippolytus's, but for our purposes, the most important is that the empire—the sacred state—is clearly identified with the antichrist. This fact enables us to situate Soloviev's vision within the most genuine Christian tradition, overcoming some interpretations which, following that of Dante in *Monarchy*, seem to situate Soloviev's thought outside the tradition. Ultimately, the issue of whether or not Soloviev knew Hippolytus's text is irrelevant, for a prophetic character clearly and intimately links both texts. Soloviev, in his final work, uniquely overcame his previous theocratic monism, as well as the no less dangerous dualism between the divine and the human that he identified as pagan "moral bankruptcy." He avoided formulating yet another of what Étienne Gilson calls "parodies of the City of God," of which the history of our own time abounds.[49] Theocratic monism and pagan dualism tend to generate precisely such parodies—parodies that, over the course of the Church's history, have enticed and continue to entice many. Soloviev realized that there was a common denominator to all these "parodies of the City of God": their seed and fruit were the double process of the secularization of the Church and the sacralization of the state. The common denominator was nothing other than the desperate attempt to evade the "damn problem" of evil, of death. This evasion inevitably led such parodies to become bearers and victims of their own "culture of death."[50] Not without reason did Pope John Paul II, while still a cardinal, say during the spiritual exercises that he preached in 1976 to Pope Paul VI and the Roman Curia: "Laicist anthropocentrism is even more opposed to admitting man's relationship with Satan than it is to acknowledging man's relationship with God or with any *'sacrum.'* Man is alone, and his greatness requires that this be so: that he be

46. Besançon, *La falsification du Bien.*
47. Hippolytus of Rome, "O antychryscie" [On the Antichrist].
48. Ibid., 112.
49. Gilson, *Les métamorphoses de la Cité de Dieu,* 11.
50. John Paul II, *Evangelium Vitae,* §12.

alone, independent of good and evil, independent of God and of Satan. All the same, might not the perfection *sui generis* of temptation of man lie in precisely this, that man should believe himself to be alone?"[51] In last years of his life, Soloviev became aware of this increasingly visible feature of modern civilization, which Catherine Pickstock describes this way: "In spite of its claims, the staging of reason does not result in an excess of life after all, nor in a successful management of the terrain of death. Although death's narrative is discreetly elided and removed to a space outside the *polis*, and although there are truly no places for death, that is because death has been universalized."[52] The culture that Pickstock describes is a culture that condemns life to suffer what she calls the "necrophilia of modernity": "For this life as separated from death, which claims to take death hostage, is at once given over to death, according to a sacrificial logic which does not immolate just one host, but instead, everyone."[53]

Soloviev's concepts of All-Oneness (*vseedinstvo*) and of Divine Humanity are deeply rooted in patristic anthropology. As Henri de Lubac writes, "For the divine image does not differ from one individual to another: in all it is the same image." To which he then adds: "The same mysterious participation in God which causes the soul to exist effects at one and the same time the unity of spirits amongst themselves."[54] The rootedness of Soloviev's thought in patristic anthropology leads him to consider social and political questions from a strong ontological perspective. In Soloviev's thought, the question of good and evil in the world erupts with the same existential force as in his reflection on the modern state. In this final description of the modern state that Soloviev bequeaths to us, we see once again the state as *privatio communitatis*.

Shortly before his death, Soloviev wrote an article that was published in the journal *Rossiya* under the title "On the True Good." It then appeared as the preface to the first edition of *War, Progress, and the End of History*. In it, Soloviev asks the question, "Is *evil* only a natural *defect*, an imperfection disappearing by itself with the growth of good, or is it a real *power*, *ruling* our world by means of temptations, so that to fight it successfully assistance must be found in another sphere of being?"[55] Although, as Soloviev himself indicates, he has addressed this "vital question" before, this final work was the product of an evolution in the way of treating "the problem of evil":

51. Wojytla, *Sign of Contradiction*, 35.
52. Pickstock, *After Writing*, 106.
53. Ibid., 105.
54. de Lubac, *Catholicism*, 29.
55. Soloviev, *War, Progress, and the End of History*, 15.

"Some two years ago a change in the tenor of my spiritual life (which there is no need to dwell upon now) created in me a strong and full desire to illumine in some clear and generally accessible way the main aspects of the problem of evil which, as I say, is of concern to all."[56]

Indeed, in the first stage of his life, according to his biographer, Konstantin Mochulsky, Soloviev did not have "a clear notion of sin":

> He did not perceive the tragedy of evil in the world. Although he quoted the words of the Apostle saying that the world was fallen, this seemed to him only a subjective state of consciousness, a wrong direction of the will. It was enough to change this direction, straighten the crooked will, and evil would disappear. For this reason, Redemption remained for him completely covered by the Incarnation, as if it were its appendix. He seemed to forget entirely the high-priestly mission of Christ, the only one who was without sin and bore the sins of the world. This mission was not at the center of Soloviev's religious experience. He reduced redemption to Christ's victory over the three temptations, over the self-confidence of human nature. He barely mentioned the struggle in Gethsemane and at Golgotha, where in a real and living way the Savior embraced the sins of the whole world, died, and conquered death. He barely mentioned the resurrection either. Only in the 1890s, after the hard experience of a spiritual crisis, was Soloviev liberated from his theosophical optimism and reached a tragic perception of the world's history. His evolutionism became apocalypticism.[57]

Jan Krasicki, too, contends that the problem of evil was not basic to Soloviev's philosophical system. Otherwise, Soloviev's philosophy would possess a quasi-Manichean or quasi-Gnostic tendency, and as such, it would be foreign to Christianity. But, at the same time, we cannot underestimate the importance of evil for the formation and crystallization of Soloviev's thought. These two aspects of Soloviev's thought comprise two inseparable parts of a diptych; they condition and need each other; we can study the one only in the light of the other. Together, they represent a paradigmatic response to the problem of evil. They reflect the process, *in statu nascendi*, of Soloviev's relationship with the *mysterium iniquitatis*—a relationship that forms an integral part of the other key concepts of the author of the Russian Idea: Divine Humanity, Sofia, Theocracy, and so on. The question of evil in the world and in history nourishes the definitive meaning and significance

56. Ibid.

57. Mochulsky, *Wladimir Solowiow*, 102–3.

of the work and philosophical vocation of Soloviev. Moreover, the vantage from which a philosopher approaches the problem of evil determines the overall construction of the philosophical system.[58]

Mochulsky continues, "*War, Progress, and the End of History* bears witness to a definitive transformation. Before Soloviev inclined towards the view of St. Augustine: evil is not substantial, it is only *privatio boni*. But now evil was present before him in all its terrifying realism. Before he did not believe in the devil, but now he believed. . . . But this encounter with demonic forces not only did not darken Soloviev's soul, but, on the contrary, it strengthened the light within it."[59] Although, as Krasicki suggests, Leon Shestov and to a certain extent Berdyaev are probably right when they affirm that, in his later works, Soloviev "hid" the ultimate truth about himself and "took this secret with him to another world," these later works nevertheless show us a great deal not only about the "history of Soloviev's soul," but they also shed light on one of the greatest mysteries, which for centuries has faced the human spirit: the *mysterium iniquitatis*. This light is especially precious, because it arises out of the profound experience of this philosopher-mystic.[60]

## The World of Yesterday?

The Russian Idea, when viewed from the height of Soloviev's thought and experience, gives us valuable insights in our own search for answers at the beginning of the twenty-first century, for our world is not that different from the world that we have been examining in these pages—the world in response to which the Russian Idea was first formulated. That time sought more than to proclaim a radiant future. It wanted to be the beginning of that future, to be, as Hannah Arendt reminds us, the "Golden Age of Security." Arendt takes this phrase from Stefan Zweig as the title of one of the chapters of her *Origins of Totalitarianism*. In the decades before the outbreak of the First and then the Second World War, precious few were aware of the "inherent weakness of an obviously outmoded political structure" still standing in that world.[61] "The world of yesterday," as Stefan Zweig calls it in the title of his book, can seem to be a surprisingly current world:

58. Krasicki, *Bog, człowiek, zło*, 9.
59. Mochulsky, *Wladimir Solowiow*, 250–52.
60. Krasicki, *Bog, człowiek, zło*, 26.
61. Arendt, *Origins of Totalitarianism*, 50.

Everything in our almost thousand-year-old Austrian monarchy seemed based on permanency, and the State itself was the chief guarantor of this stability. The rights which it granted to its citizens were duly confirmed by parliament, the freely elected representative of the people, and every duty was exactly prescribed. Our currency, the Austrian crown, circulated in bright gold pieces, an assurance of its immutability. Everyone knew how much he possessed or what he was entitled to, what was permitted and what was forbidden. Everything had its norm, its definite measure and weight. He who had a fortune could accurately compute his annual interest. An official or an officer, for example, could confidently look up in the calendar the year when we would be advanced in grade, or when he would be pensioned. Each family had its fixed budget, and knew how much could be spent for rent and food. . . . No one thought of wars, of revolutions, or revolts. All that was radical, all violence, seemed impossible in an age of reason.

This feeling of security was the most eagerly sought-after possession of millions, the common ideal of life. . . . The century of security became the golden age of insurance. One's house was insured against fire and theft, one's field against hail and storm, one's person against accident and sickness. Annuities were purchased for one's old age, and a policy was laid in a girl's cradle for her future dowry. . . .

In its liberal idealism, the nineteenth century was honestly convinced that it was on the straight and unfailing path toward being the best of all worlds. Earlier eras, with their wars, famines, and revolts, were deprecated as times when mankind was still immature and unenlightened. But now it was merely a matter of decades until the last vestige of evil and violence would finally be conquered, and this faith in an uninterrupted and irresistible "progress" truly had the force of a religion for that generation. One began to believe more in this "progress" than in the Bible, and its gospel appeared ultimate because of the daily new wonders of science and technology. . . . People became handsomer, stronger, healthier, as sport steeled their bodies. Fewer cripples and maimed persons with goiters were seen on the streets, and all of these miracles were accomplished by science, the archangel of progress. Progress was also made in social matters; year after year new rights were accorded to the individual, justice was administered more benignly and humanely, and even the problem of problems, the poverty of the great masses, no longer seemed insurmountable. . . . There was as little belief in the possibility of such barbaric declines as wars between the peoples of Europe as there was in witches and ghosts. Our fathers were comfortably saturated with confidence in the unfailing and binding power of tolerance and conciliation.[62]

This description speaks even more strongly if we remember the story of its author, Stefan Zweig. One of the great writers of the twentieth century, his work was translated into dozens of languages around the world. He was friends with Maxim Gorky, Rainer Maria Rilke, Auguste Rodin, and Arturo Toscanini. A humanist and pacifist of Jewish origin, he settled in Brazil in 1941, after several years of life in exile. There, in the city of Petrópolis, upon hearing news of the bombardment and fall of Singapore, he and his wife committed suicide. In *The World of Yesterday*, his final book, which was edited after his death in 1944, he wrote these words: "Even in the abyss of despair in which today, half-blinded, we grope about with distorted and broken souls, I look up again and again to those old star-patterns that shone over my childhood, and comfort myself with the inherited confidence that this collapse will appear, in days to come, as a mere interval in the eternal rhythm of the onward and onward."[63] Zweig's confidence in the "eternal rhythm of the onward and onward," however, was not enough to save him, to extricate him from the trap that lay at the center of the world whose destruction so disturbed him, which was nothing but devastating emergence of evil, the encounter with which Zweig could not bear. On all the pages of *The World of Yesterday*, there appears an overwhelming sense of loneliness—a sense that seems to accompany the writer throughout the entirety of his life, but that is cruelly multiplied by the events he describes in the final pages. Driven from his homeland because of his Jewish origins, and after the declaration of war between England and Germany, he was no longer an alien but a "foreign enemy." He then received a final, devastating blow: "And one who had the heart and soul all his life for human and spiritual unity found himself, in this hour which like no other demanded inviolable unity, thanks to this precipitate singling out, superfluous and alone as never before in his life."[64] To reiterate Arendt's observation, it is loneliness—the hallmark of our world today—that tills the ground for totalitarian rule:

> What prepares for totalitarian domination in the non-totalitarian world is the fact that loneliness, once a borderline experience usually suffered in certain marginal social conditions like old age, has become an everyday experience of the evergrowing masses of our century. The merciless process into which

62. Zweig, *World of Yesterday*, 1–4.

63. Ibid., 5.

64. Ibid., 222.

totalitarianism drives and organizes the masses looks like a suicidal escape from this reality. The "ice-cold" reasoning and the
"mighty tentacle" of dialectics which "seizes you as in a vice" appears like a last support in a world where nobody is reliable and
nothing can be relied upon. It is the inner coercion whose only
content is the strict avoidance of contradictions that seems to
conform a man's identity outside all relationships with others.[65]

Vladimir Soloviev perceived the inherent danger of this way of understanding and of building human society. He saw that the true *telos* of this
process was a pseudo-Christian society based on Christian principles but
that ultimately rejected the Person of Christ as its living center. For this reason, in his 1898 essay "The Idea of Humanity in Auguste Comte," Soloviev
contrasts the concept of humanity in Comte, "The Great-Being" (*"Le Grand-
Etre"*), with the idea of Divine Humanity.[66] He was well aware of the danger
of this mystification. In "A Short Story of the Anti-Christ," the protagonist
writes his "famous" work, *The Open Way to Universal Peace and Prosperity*,
which convinces "even some of his former critics and adversaries." "Nobody
raised his voice against the book. On every side it was accepted by all as
the revelation of the complete truth."[67] Soloviev was also well-aware of the
internal complexity of reality that he was trying to unmask. In the article
"The Idea of the Superman," originally published in 1899 in the magazine
*The World of Art*, Soloviev indicates three main ideas that, in his view, char-
acterize the modern world: in addition to the "economic materialism" of
Marx, he signals the "abstract moralism" of Tolstoy and the "demonology of
the *Übermensch*" of Nietzsche. Soloviev writes, "Of these three ideas . . . the
first appeals to the urgency of the 'now,' the second captures in part tomorrow as well, and the third is tied to what will happen the day after tomorrow
and beyond."[68]

At least since the appearance of *The Spiritual Foundations of Life*
(1882–1884), we can see in Soloviev's work a clear debate with his com-
patriot Tolstoy, the famous writer who held great influence in the Russia
of his time. But we must recognize that this debate never reached the level
of a personal confrontation. Tolstoy's name was scarcely mentioned in Soloviev's writings. Only in his final work was Soloviev more explicit. For
instance, he describes the Prince with some biographical details of Tolstoy.

65. Arendt, *Origins of Totalitarianism*, 478.

66. Soloviev, "Ideya cheloviechestva u Avgusta Komta" [Idea of Humanity in Auguste Comte].

67. Soloviev, *War, Progress, and the End of History*, 169–70.

68. Soloviev, *Politics, Law, and Morality*, 256–57.

The relationship of these two giants of world culture did have its ups and downs over the years. But, overall, it was marked by a great respect, especially by the younger Soloviev toward Tolstoy.

We should remember that it was the young philosopher whose influence led to a transformation in Tolstoy's thought. In May 1875, Soloviev, who was then twenty-two, was invited to visit the writer in his legendary estate of Yasnaya Polyana. A few months earlier, Tolstoy had encountered Soloviev's philosophical debut in the treatise *The Crisis of Western Philosophy: Against the Positivists* (1874). In one of his letters, which began by complaining about his work on the "boring and banal *Anna Karenina*," Tolstoy wrote: "My acquaintance with the philosopher Soloviev gave me a great deal of new material, stirred up the philosophical ferment in me very much and did a lot to conform and clarify for me those thoughts of mine which are so necessary for the rest of my life and death, and which are so comforting to me that if I had the time and was able, I would try to pass them on to others."[69] In an unexpected way, Soloviev became the "godfather" of Tolstoy's ideological shift. The next time they saw one another was 1881. The meeting took place in the new home of the Count, in Moscow. Tolstoy had by then published various works—*The Confession*; his translation of the Four Gospels, which came to be known as *The Gospels of Tolstoy*; the *Critique of Dogmatic Theology*—and he was working on the treatise *What I Believe*.

This time the conversation was not so cordial. The two men had become clear adversaries. The change in the relationship between the philosopher and the writer was apparent when Tolstoy, after having participated in the seventh lecture on Divine Humanity on 10 March 1878—an event at which, incidentally, Dostoevsky was also present, putting the two great Russian writers in the same room for the first and only time, and probably without even realizing it—told his companion Nikolay Strakhov that what they had just heard was "nonsense." What increasingly separated Soloviev and Tolstoy was Tolstoy's effort to construct a Christianity without Christ, the Son of God, without Christ incarnate and risen, opting instead for a Christianity consisting of a vast compendium of insights based on an abstract morality. Soloviev understood the danger of materialism, as well as of Tolstoy's abstract idealism. Years later, Soloviev wrote in a letter to Tolstoy the phrase that accurately reflected the substance of the matter: "Christ's

69. Tolstoy, *Tolstoy's Letters*, 1:281.

resurrection."[70] As Soloviev puts it in his *Easter Letters*: "The risen Christ is *more than spirit*—a spirit does not have flesh and bones, a spirit does not eat food. As spirit, the *eternally incarnated* Christ, with all the fullness of His inward mental essence, all the positive possibilities of physical existence without its external limitations, *all that lives* in Him is preserved, all that is mortal is overcome absolutely and finally."[71]

The works of Tolstoy have provoked harsh criticism from the Russian Orthodox Church, and his social criticism has received similar criticism from government circles. Since Tolstoy, like Soloviev, appealed to Tsar Alexander III not to execute the perpetrators of 1881 attacks that ended the life of Alexander II, he became the object of special attention from the censors. The difference between the appeals of Soloviev and Tolstoy, however, lay in the reasons that compelled such audacity. Soloviev did so because of his belief that a sovereign cannot be Christian without being governed by love, by the compassion that God reveals to human beings in Christ. Tolstoy, on the other hand, did so in the name of a morality identified with social justice. Consequently, the highly significant history of Tolstoy's treatise *What I Believe* should not surprise us.

Banned by the censors, publishers rapidly appreciated its value, and they risked their lives to publish it illegally. In addition, it was very profitable: the clandestine edition sold extraordinarily well at the price of four rubles. The editors were none other than the organization *Narodnaya Volya*, already well-known for perpetrating Tsar Alexander II's assassination. This is an important fact, which confirms Soloviev's critique of Tolstoy: not only did Tolstoy's social criticism attract revolutionaries, but it attracted terrorists like the *Narodnaya Volya* as well.[72] We can likewise see the malleability of Tolstoy's abstract morality in the ease with which, a few decades later, the communist regime promoted him as the "prophet of the revolution." So before us there appears a revealing scene: both the revolutionaries of *Narodnaya Volya* and "the Demons" of Dostoevsky's vision found common ground in this treatise of Russian literature's patriarch.

70. Soloviev, "Vladimir Soloviev's Letter to L. Tolstoy," 8.

71. Soloviev, *Politics, Law, and Morality*, 94.

72. It is perhaps an irony of history that in the last days of his life, Dostoyevsky lived in an apartment in the same building as a small group of *Narodnaya Volya*, sharing, without knowing it, a common wall with his own "Devils."

## Tolstoy and Nietzsche

We have already commented on the way Soloviev influenced Tolstoy's religious-ideological change. But the influence cuts both ways: Tolstoy's ideas motivated part of Soloviev's work as well. Tolstoy helped Soloviev to identify what he called "false Christianity" (*Izhekhristiyanstvo*).

With time, and after years of more or less direct dialogue with Tolstoy, Soloviev grew aware of the danger contained in his idea to establish the Kingdom of God on earth. *War, Progress, and the End of History,* was Soloviev's final attempt to overcome the theocratic idea, the fight against evil by way of socio-political means. With regard to the stance of the human creature in the face of evil, Soloviev's response was in full union with the hypostatic kerygma, the same answer given by the Church for two thousand years. Tolstoy's response, in effect, reduced Jesus Christ to the message of the Sermon on the Mount, a teacher on the same level as Confucius, Lao-Tse, Buddha, Socrates, and so on. In the passive attitude toward evil in the moral teaching of Tolstoy—criticized in *War, Progress, and the End of History* and represented in the figure of the Prince—we find falsehood justified by human reason. Soloviev, in contrast, thought the "glorification" of God always involved the "glorification" of the human person. The conciliar formula of the hypostatic union, Soloviev emphasized, had been fruitful since the time of the first doctrinal statements until the present. The "Event" of the Incarnation—the fact that, according to Cardinal Joseph Ratzinger, "the interlocking of God and man appear[ed] as the truly decisive, redemptive factor"[73]—meant that humankind also reached a new level of deification in its history—a theosis, whose "summit" is Christ himself. If, as Evdokimov puts it, in the Incarnation, "God is not only God but God and man at the same time," then, in the confrontation with evil, this "Event" has profound repercussions.[74] After the Incarnation, we are not the same as before, and in the fight against evil, each one of us is not simply a subjective moral consciousness, as for Tolstoy. We face evil as theandric beings, Divine Humanity. In the fight against the greatest evil—against death itself—a humanistic ethic, and compliance with the commands of abstract conscience and reason, are radically insufficient. We need the power of the Word Incarnate, the power of the Love who is stronger than death.

When Soloviev writes that the ideas of Tolstoy marked a "tomorrow" and the work of Nietzsche is "tied to what will happen the day after

---

73. Ratzinger, *Introduction to Christianity*, 229.
74. Evdokimov, *Sacrament of Love*, 58.

tomorrow and beyond,"[75] he highlights the internal logic common to both thinkers. Although for Nietzsche, Tolstoy represents the decadent modernism against which he rebelled,[76] Soloviev warns that Nietzsche shares the same premises of the "Christian pity" he critiques, which Soloviev denounces as "false Christianity."

What Marxism, Tolstoyism, and Nietzscheism have in common, despite all the obvious differences between them, is the denial of what belonged to the innermost center of Soloviev's philosophical consciousness: the Truth about Divine Humanity and the Resurrection of Jesus Christ. This denial becomes the foundation of society "today, tomorrow, and beyond." The promises of Zinoviev's *Radiant Future* pass through Zweig's *Golden Age of Security* and Pelevin's *Generation "P"*, only to end irrevocably in the violence, self-destruction, and death that reign in a society saturated with necrophilia. Soloviev was aware that "the whole of contemporary civilization is characterized by this striving to organize humanity outside of the absolute religious sphere, to establish itself and make itself comfortable in the realm of temporal, finite interests." But he also understood that, though neither socialism nor positivism "stands in any direct relation, negative or positive, to religion," each in its own way attempts "to occupy the empty place that religion has left in the life and knowledge of contemporary civilized humanity."[77] Both were therefore incapable of facing the *mysterium iniquitatis*—the question of evil, the question of death.

In 1894, in "A Preliminary Conception of the Moral Meaning of Life," the preface to the first edition of his *Justification of the Good*, Soloviev writes:

> In its rejection of different institutions moral amorphism[78] forgets one institution which is rather important—namely, death, and it is this oversight which alone renders the doctrine plausible. For if the preachers of moral amorphism were to think of death they would have to affirm one of two things: either that

75. Soloviev, *Politics, Law, and Morality*, 257.

76. "The instinct of life should prompt us to seek some means of puncturing any such pathological and dangerous accumulation of pity as that appearing in Schopenhauer's case (and also, alack, in that of our whole literary decadence, from St. Petersburg to Paris, from Tolstoy to Wagner), that it may burst and be discharged. . . . Nothing is more unhealthy, amid all our unhealthy modernism, than Christian pity." Nietzsche, *Anti-Christ*, 21.

77. Soloviev, *Lectures on Divine Humanity*, 2–3.

78. Soloviev defines moral amorphism in the following way: "When . . . [the] necessary subjective condition of the good and rational life is taken to be its essence and purpose, the result is a new moral error, namely, the rejection of all historical and collective manifestations and forms of the good, of everything except the inner moral activities and states of the individual" (lxv). —Trans.

with the abolition of the law courts, armies, etc. men will cease to die, or that the good meaning of life, incompatible with political kingdoms, is quite compatible with the kingdom of death. The dilemma is inevitable, and both alternatives to it are equally absurd. It is clear that this doctrine, which says nothing about death, contains it in itself.[79]

In 1899 Soloviev directly confronted Nietzsche in the previously mentioned article, "The Idea of Superman."[80] In light of the question about "the greatest evil" that confronts humankind, which is death, Soloviev critically analyzes the idea of the Superman. In accordance with the principle he so often applied, *audiatur et altera pars*, he tried to find an element of truth in Nietzsche's thought, on the basis of which to demonstrate the way Nietzsche's thought departs from it. Soloviev observes,"The bad side of Nietzscheism is striking. Contempt for weak and ill humanity, a pagan view of Strength and Beauty, the appropriation to oneself in advance of some exclusive superhuman significance—first to oneself personally and then to oneself collectively, as a selected minority of 'the best'—that is, the stronger, more talented, powerful, or 'lordly' natures, to which all is permitted insofar as their will is the supreme law for others. Here is the obvious error of Nietzscheism. Where is that truth which makes Nietzscheism strong and attractive to a living soul?"[81] Indeed, where is the truth in Nietzsche? Soloviev responds that, in order to differentiate the lie from the truth, we do not have two separate words, but only one. "One and the same word combines in itself both the lie and the truth of this amazing doctrine. The entire matter is in how we understand and how we pronounce the word 'superman.' Within it resounds either the voice of narrow and hollow claims or the voice of a profound self-consciousness—open to the best possibilities and anticipating the future."[82]

Soloviev thought that our nature itself pushes us to seek to overcome our limited condition. Both the discovery of this calling and the capability to respond to it determines our being. Despite all this, however, we face an insurmountable limit. This limit is death. We cannot, by ourselves, cross the boundary of death and at the same time remain *only human*. Already in Homer, observes Soloviev, "man" and "mortal" are synonymous. To say "man" is to say "mortal," because only human persons, in the proper sense

79. Soloviev, *Justification of the Good*, lxv.
80. Soloviev, *Politics, Law, and Morality*, 255–63.
81. Ibid., 257.
82. Ibid., 258.

of the word, are mortal, beings "subject to death" (*theoi te Brioi te*).[83] We do not say that animals others than humans are "mortal." We experience "death" in our consciousness of it. Becoming conscious of death, we identify it as an "existential peculiarity" of our "actual condition," and we almost never want to accept it. Other animals do not "struggle (consciously) with death and consequently cannot be conquered by it; and thus, its mortality has no pangs or description for it." Human persons, in contrast, are "first and foremost 'mortal'—in the sense of conquered, overcome by death. And if so, then this means a 'superman' must be first of all, and particularly, a *conqueror of death*."[84]

According to Soloviev, Nietzsche's "superman" is nothing but a caricature of the "true Superman": Jesus Christ, the God-Man who conquered death, and who did not limit the fruits of his victory to a select few, but graciously offered them to all people. We continue to be offered the Resurrection of Jesus Christ as the victory over death, over "absolute evil," and also as "testimony" of his Godhood. Contrary to Nietzsche's proclamation, after the "death of God and man," God still lives and we are "not yet born."[85]

## Epilogue

Since his first work, *The Crisis of Western Philosophy: Against the Positivists*, until his final work, *War, Progress, and the End of History*, Soloviev's intellectual path was an attempt to unify faith and reason, theology and philosophy. Soloviev's work was characterized by the conviction that the Incarnation of God, Jesus Christ, was the central event in the history of humankind, in the whole cosmic process, and that it comprised the center of all human *theoria* and *praxis*. It was an Event that overcame the dualism, the separation between God and world, God and humankind. As he traveled along this intellectual path, Soloviev's perception of evil, as well as his idea of theocracy, underwent an evolution. He eventually abandoned an immediate social and political application of the theocratic principle.

In the last decade of his life, Soloviev overcame the Hegelian vision of historical progress, and he definitively immersed himself in the dynamism of the Event of the Incarnation and Resurrection of Jesus Christ, the Christ Event. As Soloviev put it in his *Lectures on Divine Humanity*: "If we examine the entire theoretical and moral content of Christ's teaching, as set forth in the Gospels, we shall find that the only new teaching specifically different

83. Ibid., 261.
84. Ibid.
85. Tischner, "For the Existence of Man," 74.

from all other religions is Christ's teaching about Himself, His reference to Himself as living, incarnate truth: 'I am the way, the Truth and the Life' [John 14:6]. 'He that believeth on the Son hath everlasting life' [John 3:36]."[86]

In the United Universal Church, Soloviev found the full realization of his theocratic idea, as well as ecumenism and Divine Humanity. The unitotality of the Trinity reflected the unity of creation. Soloviev constructed with his work a narrative based on an "essential deduction and inexhaustible projection: that the absolute unity is necessarily triune. In other words, that, even though God is infinitely one, God is Trinity."[87]

This narrative finds clear expression in Soloviev's Russian Idea. But for its proper interpretation we must attend to the entirety of Soloviev's corpus, especially its final stage. The theocratic idea contained in the Russian Idea was only an attempt to contrast Christianity with the "kingdom of death." Soloviev's ongoing effort to understand the world around him, along with his deep love for others, led him to overcome the limitations of these theocratic ideas, bringing his Russian Idea to its ultimate consequences. The Russian Idea became for Soloviev the attempt to put into practice the response to death. The transposition of this response into the fields of politics, economics, and so on, deprived it of its power. Soloviev eventually realized this. He also eventually realized that death has been overcome *hic et nunc*, and that the victory over death likewise takes place *hic et nunc*. The Church reveals this victory and offers it to all humankind.

The kingdom built by the antichrist in *War, Progress, and the End of History* was the kingdom of Marx, Tolstoy, and Nietzsche. It was not the kingdom that Soloviev sought in the Russian Idea. While it is true that in Soloviev's thought there is a union of priest and king, the kingdom proclaimed by Soloviev also included the prophet. The modern secular world strives to create its own anthropology, its own historiosophy, even its own ecclesiology of the state—ongoing "parodies of the City of God." We are witnesses of the way that "the kingdom of death" can falsify the king and even the priest but it cannot falsify the Spirit.

On 27 February 2007, during the catechesis of Lent, Cardinal Giacomo Biffi, the archbishop emeritus of Milan, presented a talk to Pope Benedict XVI and the Roman Curia entitled, *Vladimir Soloviev: The Unheeded Prophet*. The Pope listened while Cardinal Biffi identified the Antichrist as "the reflection, almost the incarnation, of the confused and ambiguous religiosity of our time." Biffi went on to say: "One sees here described—and condemned—a Christianity of 'values,' of 'openings,' of 'dialogue,' a Christianity

---

86. Soloviev, *Lectures on Divine Humanity*, 105.

87. Lira, "Prologo," xxxiii.

where it seems there is little room left for the person of the Son of God crucified for us and risen, little room for the actual event of salvation. . . . The teaching that the Great Russian philosopher left us is that Christianity cannot be reduced to a set of values. At the center of being a Christian is, in fact, the personal encounter with Jesus Christ." At the conclusion, Cardinal Biffi affirmed that "if Christianity—on opening itself to the world and dialoguing with all—dilutes the salvific event, it closes itself to a personal relationship with Jesus and places itself on the side of the Antichrist."[88]

It was reported that when in May 1900 Soloviev finished his last public lecture, in which he presented "A Short Story of the Anti-Christ," he picked the manuscript off the table and said, "I wrote this to teach definitively my point of view on the question of the Church."[89] This is the heart of the great message of the Russian Idea—a message that reminds us that we are not condemned to the slavery of the Antichrist's "kingdom of death," of the modern state. We are continually given the possibility of living in freedom. And this freedom can only be given to us by Jesus Christ, and the space of this freedom is the Church.

88. "Retreatants Hear of Guises of the Antichrist."
89. Soloviev, "Tri razgavora, Kratkaya poviest' ob anticristie," 784.

# CHAPTER III

# Between the Icon and the Idol

*The human person has been thought [into being]*
*by God as an icon, a marvelous icon.*

—Irina Yazykova

## INTRODUCTION

There are still places in Europe where the air tastes different. The difference is evident with your first breath. The air inundates you. It sinuously invades your lungs and penetrates your body with the damp weight of memory that is still *memory*. It has not yet become *the past*. The air is bound to change you. It first changes the way you breathe, but it soon transforms the way you feel and think as well. Those who have had the occasion to stay even a few days in one of the provincial cities of Bessarabia,[1] for instance, could recognize this air that still shudders with memory, still vibrates with the light of the Menorah.

---

1. This is the region of southeastern Central Europe that we know today as western Ukraine and Moldova.

❧

The design of these cities was the result of ethnic politics that developed in the Russian Empire from the late seventeenth to the nineteenth century. As a result of a series of decrees, those of Jewish origin were forbidden to live in villages, and they were forced to move to the cities west of the Dnieper River. The history of nineteenth-century Russian Jews, largely unknown in the West, was the prologue to their destiny in the rest of Europe in the twentieth century. They suffered a systematic limitation of their freedom, institutionalized discrimination, and numerous *pogroms* that were, in large measure, promoted in accordance with the interests of power.

The massive influx of Jewish people to the cities, along with the reforms of Tsar Alexander II that opened access to education for children of all classes, conditioned a social and cultural evolution that profoundly transformed the character of the Jewish community in Russia. From the 1860s onward, the Russian intelligentsia of Jewish origin began to grow in number and in importance. Distancing themselves from their cultural and religious backgrounds, many began to secularize and Russianize themselves. They viewed Western post-Enlightenment thought with great interest. They stood firm in their perception of social injustice and the need for profound change. The remarkable economic progress that accompanied and brought about these changes permitted the Jewish community in Russia to establish a dynamic relationship with European cultural and academic life. These developments together marked a profound change in the largest Jewish population of Europe, and therefore in the culture and way of life for people in the western regions of the Russian Empire.

❧

In the heart of western Ukraine, in the region of Zhytomyr, on the eastern bank of the Gnilopyat River, is the city of Berdichev. Founded in the fifteenth century as a regional trading center, it had more than fifty thousand inhabitants by the end of the nineteenth century. The vast majority of these inhabitants—approximately 80 percent—were of Jewish origin. The city center lay at the foot of a fortified Carmelite monastery dating from the seventeenth century. Over time, an Orthodox cathedral and several *cerkiev*, along with Catholic churches and Jewish synagogues, were built there. The city was a center of Hasidism, with the figure of Rabbi Levi Yitzchak at the forefront. At the city's Catholic church, Santa Barbara, Honoré de Balzac married Evelina Hanska in 1850. The Polish writer Józef Teodor Konrad

Korzeniowski, otherwise known as Joseph Conrad, was born in Berdichev in 1857. At the beginning of the twentieth century, in 1903, one of the greatest piano virtuosos, Vladimir Horowitz, was born there. Two years later, in 1905, so was Vasily Grossman.

By the time of Grossman's birth, Berdichev had already reached a good level of economic and social development. A lively hustle and bustle marked the atmosphere of this small town surrounded by fertile fields of oily black earth, as well as numerous forests, lakes, and rivers. The city center had a Western, bourgeois character. There were wide streets with public buildings, synagogues, churches, schools, hospitals, shops, banks, hotels, and restaurants. Soberly decorated façades of two- and three-floor buildings surrounded the central streets, where in the midst of all the activity, one could find ladies dressed in Parisian clothes, men preoccupied with business deals in Odessa and Berlin, and artisans and farmers en route to market.

In the old quarter of Berdichev, it is still possible to see the house where Vasily Grossman, the only son of Ekaterina Grossman and Semyon Grossman, was born. It is a two-story brick building with a solid wood door, large windows, and a prominent balcony at the center of the second floor. An arch above the attic window projects from the roof. It is a house that suggests the thriving stability of the family that inhabited it. Vasily was enrolled in the birth record under the name of Iosif, although he was called Vasily from the beginning. His parents belonged to very wealthy Russified Jewish families. It was the custom then that, although Jews were officially enrolled in the records with Jewish names, they used Russian names in everyday life. The family of Vasily's mother, Ekaterina, was comprised of rich and enlightened merchants who years earlier had moved from Lithuania to Odessa. Ekaterina was educated in France and married an Italian of Jewish origin. Once in Italy, however, she met Semyon Grossman, who had studied chemistry in Switzerland at the University of Bern. As Ekaterina Korotkova-Grossman, Vasily's daughter, later recalled, Semyon won Ekaterina's hand: she left her husband and the two moved to Berdichev.[2]

Semyon Grossman, an activist of the Social Democratic Workers' Party, left his wife and young son in Berdichev in order to join the Revolution of 1905, and he was one of the organizers of the uprising of Sevastopol. Once the revolution was over, he abandoned militancy in the party, but he remained in close contact with his Bolshevik friend Shcheglov. He returned, for a short time, to Berdichev before leaving for Donbass, where for many years he worked in the mining industry, and then for Kiev, where he worked for the Chemical-Bacteriological Institute. According to Ekaterina

2. Rapoport, "Iz protivostoyania s sistemoy otciets vyshol pobeditelem."

Korotkova-Grossman, although Vasily's parents would never again live together, they maintained a close relationship. They did not consider their geographical separation a formal break. Semyon's living conditions and the climate of the mining region were undesirable given Ekaterina Grossman's fragile health. Ekaterina would often travel to Odessa for rest and relaxation.

When Vasily was five, his mother took him to France and then to Switzerland. In Switzerland, he studied at a high school for two years. They then returned to Russia at the very beginning of World War I, first to Kiev and then to Berdichev, and in the city of his birth Vasily completed high school. During the hard times of the Russian Civil War, when his mother taught French classes, Vasily helped the ailing household economy by sawing wood. In 1921, he enrolled in a college preparatory course at the Kiev Institute of Popular Education. At that time he met his first wife, a young woman from a Cossack family, Anna Petrovna Matsuk, who was a classmate of his. In 1923, Vasily went to Moscow to begin his studies in mathematics and chemistry at Moscow State University. He and Anna married before he finished his studies, and, in 1929, Anna gave birth to their only child, to whom they gave the name of Vasily's maternal grandmother, Ekaterina. The marriage of Vasily and Anna did not last long: they separated in 1929, divorced in 1933, and Anna, along with Ekaterina, returned to Kiev. Nevertheless, they maintained a good relationship, and Ekaterina frequently visited her father and paternal grandmother. During one of our conversations, I asked Ekaterina why her parents' marriage failed. She said that it was the passion of a love between two young people who were used to getting attention but not to giving it—Anna was the youngest daughter, with a large age gap between her and her siblings; Vasily was an only child and could not stand the pressures of adult life,[3] especially in the harsh conditions of Soviet reality in the late 1920s and early 1930s.

Vasily, who came of age in the years of revolutions, civil war, and the birth of the Soviet Union, could not separate himself from the events that surrounded his life and transformed the world in which he lived. Although Vasily's father was extremely interested in social and political issues, Vasily did not actively participate in them—perhaps precisely because his father did so. When, years later, in his novel *Everything Flows*, Vasily describes the protagonist's memories of his time at the university, Vasily shows that he was in fact extremely attentive to everything that was going on around him. It is likely that he heard about the lectures of Berdyaev,[4] who greatly

3. Ekaterina Korotkova-Grossman currently lives in Moscow. After the war she studied English philology. In her retirement she dedicated herself to the translation of English literature into Russian, and she is the author of various historical novels.

4. Olbrych, *Wasilij Grossman*, 36.

influenced the cultural and intellectual atmosphere of Russia in the 1920s. Berdyaev presented these lectures before his expulsion in 1922 from the Soviet Union, and they were so popular that crowds filled the largest halls in Moscow. In those years, Berdyaev focused on two topics: history and the human person. This opened two lines of investigation: historiosophy and anthropology. Both lines were united by the same spirit of freedom, and their confluence produced the lectures that would later become *The Meaning of History* and *Dostoevsky: An Interpretation.*[5]

During his studies in Moscow, Grossman lived in the house of his cousin, Nadiezhda Almaz, an activist in the Comintern. Grossman worked as a tutor at a center for orphaned children. After finishing his studies in 1929, he worked as a chemical engineer in the deepest and most polluted mine in the Donetsk mining basin, Smolanka II. He later described this stage of life in his story "Phosphorus."[6] During this time his health suffered severely due to the harsh working conditions. He contracted tuberculosis and, in 1932, returned to Moscow. There he resumed contact with his cousin and began working as a chemist in a Moscow factory. At that time, he already had a clear desire to write.

His friendship with Nadiezhda was very important to him. In 1933, she fell victim to the system she served with such passion. She was arrested, expelled from the party, and exiled to Astrakhan. In letters to his father, Vasily described what had happened to his cousin. He had no doubt of the injustice that, in the name of the state, was inflicted on a good woman. Two years later, his cousin returned to Moscow. Her return was possible because the Great Purge had not yet begun. The Great Purge started after the death of Sergei Kostrikov-Kirov, the First Secretary of the Communist Party in Leningrad, who was assassinated on 1 December 1934, probably not without the consent of Stalin.[7] After the return of his cousin, and despite the danger that it entailed, Vasily maintained a close friendship with her.

As Ekaterina Korotkova-Grossman told me, throughout her father's life, certain women represented for him fundamental existential reference points. It is unsurprising, therefore, that this period in Vasily's life was an important turning point. What happened to Nadiezhda led him to look differently at the life that surrounded him and the great history that with increasing force was beginning to sweep him up.

---

5. Berdyaev, *Meaning of History*; Berdyaev, *Dostoevsky.*

6. Grossman, "Fosfor."

7. Guber, Osuschestvliayuschiy zhizn' tak, kak hotelos . . . "Iz knigi o Vasilii Grossmanie" Pamiat' y pisma," 265–66, 272–73.

## THE ONTOLOGICAL STATE

When I refer to the state, I think of the modern state. This explanation is probably a pleonasm, because "the state" is, after all, a modern concept, first proposed, as is well known, by Machiavelli. Such clarification seems necessary in light of the trend to label all similar social organizations, both before and after the beginning of the sixteenth century, as well as those that are completely foreign to Western civilization, "the state." It is a ubiquitous trend, which is reflected in numerous translations of classical texts, in which, for instance, *res publica*, with surprising ease, becomes *the state*. It is not the coordinates of space and time in a definitive mode that allows us to use the term "the state." For instance, Eric Voegelin, in his 1938 work *Political Religions*, distinguishes between what is "the state" and what is not, introducing concepts of "immanent religion" and "transcendental religion" in order to do so. The role of "immanent religion" in this case is "to sacralize" earthly power, endowing it—whether it be the nation, a race, or other social group—with a sovereign power that is sustained by the development of an "immanent religion," whose ultimate legitimacy comes, for instance, from science. In this way, Voegelin finds the first example of a state built upon an immanent religion in 1376 BC, when Egypt's pharaoh Amenhotep IV changed his name to Akhenaton and introduced a new sun religion. Then, moving to the modern era, Voegelin ends his book with Hitler as a new Akhenaton.[8]

Three years earlier, in his *Religion and the Modern State* (1935), Christopher Dawson had analyzed the process in which "the modern state" occupied spaces "in which the statesmen of the past would no more have dared to meddle with than the course of the seasons or the movements of the stars," motivated by the determination to build, here and now, an earthly Jerusalem. This determination intended to encompass, according to Dawson, the totality of life. Once accepted, it required total submission of its members and the establishment of a new political order that was intolerant and violent.[9] Raymond Aron defined this "secular religion" in the following way: "I propose to call 'secular religions' doctrines which, in the souls of our contemporaries, take the place of vanished faith, and situate here below, in the distance of the future, in the form of a social order to be constructed, the salvation of humanity."[10]

---

8. Voegelin, *Political Religions*.

9. Dawson, *Religion and the Modern State*, 45.

10. Cited in Anderson, *Raymond Aron*, 66.

I hope that, over the course of this reflection, we will better understand what we mean by the "totalitarian state." It might be the case that this concept, like the concept of the "modern state," is also a pleonasm.

⤚

I understand the modern state as William Cavanaugh describes it in his book *Theopolitical Imagination*: "By 'state' I mean to denote that peculiar institution which has arisen in the last four centuries in which a centralized and abstract power holds a monopoly over physical coercion within a geographically defined territory. I am aware of the danger in ignoring the differences between actual states, or between states in theory and states in practice. Nevertheless, I think it is a useful exercise to consider in general terms the pathologies which modern states seem to share—especially that of atomization of the citizenry—and the common stories which serve to enact these pathologies."[11] For an approach to the analysis of the birth of the modern state, the work of Benedict Anderson, *Imagined Communities*,[12] and the classic studies, Ernst Kantorowicz's *The King's Two Bodies*[13] and Étienne Gilson's *The Metamorphoses of the City of God*,[14] are also helpful.

The context of these reflections does not permit us to enter into a detailed analysis of the modern state. At this juncture, I must offer some comments that will help us understand the historical and cultural constraints of the Soviet state.

When thinking of totalitarian states in modern European history, the memories of the national-socialist system in Western Europe and communist-Marxist system in Eastern Europe automatically present themselves to us. Despite the similarities and common features of these two systems, which share the same roots, there are important differences between them. One of these differences is the literature that appeared under their respective domains. It is evident that the wealth of literature that, in one form or another, opposed the totalitarian state has been much more significant in the eastern than in the western part of Europe. The reasons for this originated in the social and cultural background in which both of these totalitarianisms took place. Voegelin sought to demonstrate that national-socialism, communism, and fascism were not simply "the stupidities of a couple of intellectuals of the nineteenth and twentieth centuries . . . [but] the

11. Cavanaugh, *Theopolitical Imagination*, 10.
12. Anderson, *Imagined Communities*.
13. Kantorowicz, *The King's Two Bodies*.
14. Gilson, *Les métamorphoses de la Cité de Dieu*.

cumulative effect of unsolved problems and shallow attempts at a solution over a millennium of Western history."[15]

⌒

It is easy to verify that the state as such does not exist, as Cavanaugh has emphasized,[16] following Philip Abrams and others.[17] The state is not a *being*; it is, we might say, a *state* of relationships—or the lack thereof—between people. The modern state is not only a social construction[18] but also a social deconstruction—a deconstruction of the Community—as Robert A. Nisbet demonstrated magisterially in his classic work, *The Quest for Community*.[19]

In order to advance in our understanding of the state, we must see that the reality of the state is ontological in terms of the persons the state brings into *being*. In the summer of 1918, in one of his first works, Berdyaev, immersed in the revolutionary storm, wrote: "This power [of the state] has an ontological foundation, which it takes from the original source of ontological reality."[20] He later adds: "That's why all social ideas, in a hopeless and insurmountable way, are formal ideas, so you can never find in them real content and purpose; you can never find in them an ontological core."[21] Perhaps it was Heidegger, as Julio Quesada demonstrates, who perceived the first processes and the ultimate consequences of the ontological relationship between person-people-state.[22] "The being of the state rests anchored in the political being of the men who, as a people, bear that state, and have decisively committed themselves to it," Heidegger said in a seminar titled "On the Essence and Concepts of Nature, History, and State."[23] When we ask about the state, therefore, we must ask about the society that bears it; and when we ask about society, we must ask about the kind of people who comprise it.

15. Voegelin, "Gnostic Politics," 240.

16. Cavanaugh, *Theopolitical Imagination*.

17. Abrams, "Notes on the Difficulty of Studying the State," 77; Miliband, *State in Capitalist Society*.

18. Bierdiajew, *Filozofia nierówności*, 50.

19. Nisbet, *Quest for Community*.

20. Bierdiajew, *Filozofia nierówności*, 51. Years later, and in a more developed way, Berdyaev would return to these reflections on the nature of the state in *The Realm of Spirit and the Realm of Caesar*.

21. Ibid., 109.

22. Quesada, *Heidegger de camino al holocausto*.

23. Heidegger, "Über Wesen und Begriff von Natur, Geschichte und Staat," 78.

◡

I remember the way that, during several conversations I had with him, Arseny Roginskiy, chairman of the organization Memorial in Moscow, spoke of "sovetskoye obschestvo" rather than "sovetskoye gosudarstvo." In other words, he spoke of Soviet "society" rather than the Soviet "state." It is worth recalling also that, as Hannah Arendt suggests, the social sphere "is a relatively new phenomenon whose origin coincided with the emergence of the modern age and which found its political form in the nation-state."[24] Following Arendt, Igor Kondakov, in his analysis of the history of Russian culture in the communist era, speaks of society as a carrier of the virus of totalitarianism.[25] He then goes on to argue that that the totalitarianization of society cannot take place if cultural, historical, geopolitical, and psychological conditions do not permit it.[26] This clarification is important because it helps us to see that we must first confront the problem of totalitarianism ontologically, particularly with regard to the way ontology shapes anthropology. "Here the devil is struggling with God, and the battlefield is the human heart," as Dostoyevsky put it.[27] As Berdyaev saw, the real danger of Marxist-Leninist communism was the ease with which it managed to create a "new man"—Zinoviev's *homo sovieticus*[28]—something it achieved with far greater success than a "new economy."[29]

Berdyaev's statement is clear: there are ideas whose force transforms people in the innermost depths of their being—transforms the human condition itself. In this way, such ideas can create a *homo sovieticus,* or a *homo germanicus* for that matter.[30] Ideologies can transform people, and people in turn form—or better, transform—societies.


THE IDOL

Where does the power of ideologies to transform people—to transform their very being—come from? This power is the power of the "idol," which

---

24. Arendt, *Human Condition,* 28.

25. Kondakov, *Vvedenie v istoriiu russkoi kul'tury,* 579.

26. Ibid., 584–85.

27. Dostoevsky, *Brothers Karamazov,* 108.

28. Zinoviev, *Homo sovieticus.*

29. See, for instance, Berdyaev, *Origin of Russian Communism*; Berdyaev, *El cristianismo y el problema del comunismo,* 143.

30. Lepenies, *La seducción de la cultura en la historia alemana,* 48.

takes the place of the "icon." It is a process in which our being loses its mode of being as icon and becomes an image of itself—an idol.

What determines the difference between the icon and the idol? The difference lies with the function of distance—does distance entail difference or division? John D. Zizioulas, one of the best-known contemporary Orthodox theologians, writes that when fear of the other pathologically pushes us to identify difference with division, it is upon these divisions that we construct ways of relating to the world. Upon these divisions we organize clubs, associations, and even "churches." A communion built upon division becomes a fragile pact of mere coexistence, which lasts only as long as mutual interest lasts. "Different beings," writes Zizioulas, drawing on the theology of St. Gregory of Nyssa and St. Maximus the Confessor, "become distant beings: because difference becomes division, distinction becomes distance."[31]

But distance is also the space that makes donation possible. Jean-Luc Marion offers a contemporary restatement of the Solovievian opposition between Divine Humanity and those who assert themselves as gods when he indicates that the absolute measure of distance is the Father's abandonment of the Son on Good Friday: "From the bottom of the infernal abyss that opened at the very heart of our history, once and for all, there issues the unsurpassable filiation that eternally confesses the paternity of the Father. Revealing himself as Father, God advances in his very withdrawal."[32] The icon is the manifestation of donation directed beyond its own distance, becoming an ever-new event of paternal-filial love in which visible and invisible, divine and human, unite without confusion. St. Maximus the Confessor teaches that God, as totally Other—as alterity par excellence—transcends created being. But created being appears as a being-in-movement-toward-unity. "God is Creator in that God gives being to what was not. And if created being is always being in movement, then God—along with being—gives to beings the movement for their realization."[33] The cause of this movement is the goodness and the will of God, in which God is revealed ultimately as desire. According to Maximus, as Pablo Argárate argues, God, in a certain sense, is moved in that God moves and attracts all beings to Godself.[34] "He moves and is moved as one who thirsts to be the object of thirst," Maximus

---

31. Zizioulas, *Communion and Otherness*, 3.

32. Marion, *Idol and Distance*, xxxv. At this juncture, it is important to signal that John Milbank's critique of Marion, which charges that Marion arbitrarily privileges the recipient subject (*l'adonné*), does not seem to take sufficiently into account the paternal-filial relation that for Marion establishes the basis of all donation.

33. Argárate, "La noción de Dios en Máximo el Confesor," 297, 305.

34. Ibid., 307.

writes, "and who desires to be desired and loves to be loved."[35] This dona-tion, this "movement" of God, finds its fullness in the Incarnation, in Jesus Christ who gives himself to us, according to St. Maximus, as a "living icon of love and goodwill toward God and neighbor, an icon that has the power to elicit in us the dutiful response."[36]

⤙

The idol, in contrast, does not abide distance but devours it. It refuses dona-tion, directs the human gaze toward itself, and offers access to the "divine" without the necessity of donation, without distance. The idol is the deified self, in which we reflect our selves back to ourselves—selves we think we can dominate. But above all, the idol helps us justify our selves to ourselves. The idol, therefore, is our reflection dressed in the image we have of the divine. It is the divine made in our own image and likeness. As Marion writes:

> The idol reflects back to us, in the face of a god, our own ex-perience of the divine. The idol does not resemble us, but it resembles the divinity that we experience, and it gathers it in a god in order that we might see it. The idol does not deceive; it apprehends the divinity. It apprehends the divinity, and, even when it terrorizes, it reassures by identifying the divinity in the face of a god. Hence its prodigious political effectiveness: it renders close, protective, and faithfully sworn the god who, identifying himself with the city, maintains an identity for it. This is indeed why politics always gives rise to idols, even after paganism; "Big Brother," the "Great Helmsman," the Führer, or the "Man we love best" must be divinized: made into gods, they conjure the divine or, more vulgarly, destiny. Idolatry gives the cult of personality its true dignity—that of a familiar, tamed (and therefore undangerously terroristic) figure of the divine. Idolatrous temptation for ancient Israel always depended upon political necessities. Conversely, it is to politics first that our time owes the fact that we are not lacking for new idols.[37]

Marion's definition of idol is already reflected in Soloviev's analysis of selfishness. In *The Meaning of Love*, Soloviev writes: "The basic falsehood and evil of egoism lie not in this absolute self-consciousness and self-eval-uation of the subject, but in the fact that, ascribing to himself in all justice

35. Ibid.

36. Schönborn, *God's Human Face*, 129.

37. Marion, *Idol and Distance*, 6.

an absolute significance, he unjustly refuses to others this same significance. Recognizing himself as a center of life (which as a matter of fact he is), he relegates others to the circumference of his own being and leaves them only an external and relative value."[38] And then later on he writes:

> A human being (in general and every human being in particular), being in fact only *this* and not *another*, may *become* [*stanovitsia*] all, only by doing away, in his consciousness and life, with that internal boundary which separates him from another. "This" may become the "all" only together with others; only together with others can an individual realize his absolute significance. . . . There is only one power which can from within undermine egoism at the root, and really does undermine it, namely love, and chiefly sexual love. . . . Every kind of love is the manifestation of this capacity, but not every kind realizes it to the same degree, nor does every kind as radically undermine egoism. Egoism is a power not only real but basic, rooted in the deepest center of our being, and from thence permeating and embracing the whole of our reality—a power, acting uninterruptedly in all aspects and particulars of our existence. In order genuinely to undermine egoism, it is necessary to oppose to it a love equally concretely specific, permeating the whole of our being and taking possession of everything in it.[39]

This Solovievian becoming (*stanovitsia*) resonates with Maximus's anthropology in which the human person simply is the "mutual movement of inter-penetration" of body and soul, in which such interconnectedness and comingling bears the trace of the perichoresis of the Divine Persons,[40] and with the anthropology of St. Ignatius of Antioch, who conceives of the human person as "God's runner" (*theodromos*), "a being strained between its present and its *telos*; a being in a dramatic process of *becoming*, with all the deficiency that this process implies."[41]

This simple ontological approach helps us begin to understand the fundamental difference between the natures of the anthropological and sociohistorical foundations of totalitarianism in Western and Eastern Europe respectively.

Most simply put, we might say that the difference resides in the relationship between the idol and the icon. In the West, the evolution of

38. Soloviev, *Meaning of Love*, 43.

39. Ibid., 44–46.

40. Argárate, "El dinamismo de la constitución antropológica en Máximo el Confesor," 64.

41. Argárate, "El concepto de discípulo en Ignacio de Antioquía," 295.

modernity brought about the idol's domination. But in the Slavic part of Europe, the relationship to modernity has been sufficiently different such that the response to totalitarianism has also been different. Consider two basic facts: National Socialism was the product of the dominant culture and could count on the support—implicit or otherwise—of the overwhelming majority of German society; the Soviet regime, in contrast, was established as a result of a Bolshevik *coup d'état* and a subsequent civil war. In addition, and no less important, while the German idol of modernity was a product of the irrationality of "secular reason," in Russia, it was the result of a peculiar transformation of the icon. Yet both are different stages of the same process. In Germany, the culmination of the transformation of the icon was the Reformation. Centuries later, it was German philosophy, heir of the Reformation, which in Russia came into conflict with the icon once again.

## Two Ideologies, One Idol

The first decades of the twentieth century witnessed the final formation of two new faces of the idol. In both cases, a Christian theology, already wounded for centuries by dualism, was the irrational background. In the pre-national-socialist Germany of the early twentieth century, however, the new impulse on the part of secularized society for the study of religious phenomena was the "kiss of death."[42] In Russia, where the Russian Idea—the experiment in the return to the union between faith and reason, between theology and philosophy—was at its maturity, there was an important response to these developments, which was eventually buried in the avalanche of Russian history itself.

∾

No less important was the fact that, in Germany, the idolatry of the state shaped, in large measure, German society and its history.[43] As Erich Fromm explains, this identification with the state stifled opposition to National Socialism once it had attained power. Although many people were not National Socialists, the majority supported the regime and perceived any attack on it as an attack on German state.[44] And later, remembering the importance

42. Junginger, *Study of Religion under the Impact of Fascism*, 14.

43. Lepenies, *La seducción de la cultura en la historia alemana*, 21.

44. Fromm, *Fear of Freedom*, 179.

of economic conditions, Fromm adds, "In addition to these factors, the last stronghold of middle-class security had been shattered too: the family."[45]

When asked for the reason of the profound influence of National Socialist ideology, Fromm replied that it was possible thanks to the union of this ideology with the state. Fromm's reflection provides a fundamental insight: it is not the ideology that marks the state; it is the idol of the state that offers ultimate power to the ideology. For this reason, ideologies need the state as much as the state needs ideologies. Although Hitler in *Mein Kampf* makes clear his interest in controlling the structure of the state, and although Lenin proclaims, following Marx and Engels, the intention of bringing the state to its own withering,[46] both Hitler and Lenin, with their respective ideologies, were equally bearers of the idol of the state.

As Wolf Lepenies indicates, it is hard to deny that the idolatry of the state has shaped the character of German society and its history.[47] One of the most paradigmatic expressions of this phenomenon was the 4 October 1914 manifesto *An die Kulturwelt* (*To the World of Culture*), which was written by the Jewish poet Ludwig Fulda and signed by ninety-three top representatives of German science and culture. In this manifesto, the signatories declared that Germany—a nation that loved peace and that was victim of the atrocities of its enemies, both Western and Eastern—had been forced into war, preempting the troops of the allies who sought to destroy German *Kultur*.[48] Perhaps the most tragic epilogue of this manifesto was written by the author, Ludwig Fulda, when he committed suicide in 1939.

In Russia, despite the programmatic authoritarian character of imperial power, the idolatry of the state did not appear, especially in the educated classes of society. It is enough to mention Odoevsky, Chaadayev, and Soloviev in order to sketch a line of thought that, despite its declared patriotism, was very far from the cult of the state. Over the course of the nineteenth century, it prepared the soil for the emergence of a considerable number of intellectuals capable of critiquing the totalitarian processes of modern society. In 1914, the same year as the manifesto *An die Kulturwelt*, Vladimir Ern delivered a famous lecture at the Vladimir Soloviev Religious-Philosophical Society titled "From Kant to Krupp." Ern spoke of the profound union between German tradition and culture, as well as the totalitarian trends within Germany, whose clearest expression was German militarism, symbolized by the arms industry. "In the first place," said Ern, "I believe that violent

---

45. Ibid., 185.
46. Lenin, "Państwo a rewolucja."
47. Lepenies, *La seducción de la cultura en la historia alemana*, 21.
48. Ibid., 26.

outbursts of Germanism were previously prepared by the Kantian analytic. In second place, I believe that Krupp's guns have profound philosophical significance. And in the third place, I believe that the interior transcription of the German spirit in Kant's philosophy rightly and inevitably coincides with the external transcription of the same spirit in the weapons of Krupp."[49] Ern's words were soon confirmed in a way that, even for him, was surprisingly explicit. The University of Bonn gave the son of Frederic Alfred Krupp and the then-owner of Krupp-Werke, Gustav Krupp von Bohlen, and the company's general director, Alfred Hugenberg, honorary doctoral degrees, which were awarded by the department of philosophy.[50]

Sixty-five years later, Ern's words were echoed in those of Leszek Kolakowski, who described the "recurrent German philosophical desire as one which consists in the attempt to discover God without God, to find a secular and transcendental foundation for moral and epistemological security apart from God."[51] According to Ern, when human persons are stripped of the objective and absolute character of the sources of their identity—tradition, history, grace, and so on—they are turned over to the hands of "the legislative character of reason." Kant is above all a legislator, who, "with the heavy hand of phenomenological principles," wants to dictate what is good and what is bad, what is true and what is a lie.[52]

⌁

The Russian idol of communism originates both in Western thought—especially German Western thought—as well as in Russia's own culture. As indicated in the previous chapter, Marxism was for the Bolsheviks a philosophy and a religion, not just a struggle to transform socio-political life. Neither Marx nor Western Marxists foresaw this profound and intimate union of two messiahs: Russian national messianism and the messianism of the proletarian class.[53]

We can say that the presence of the icon—a word that, in the case of Russia, has connotations that are not accidental—constituted a sufficiently different space in the Slavic world such that the response to totalitarianism was distinct. This is not the moment to delve into the historical reasons for this phenomenon. I would only point out an important fact: one of the

49. Ern, "Od Kanta do Kruppa," 241–49.

50. Bohun, *Oczyszczeni przez burze*, 93.

51. Kolakowski, "Reprodukcja kulturalna i zapominanie," 80.

52. Ern, "Od Kanta do Kruppa," 241–49.

53. Berdyaev, *Russian Revolution*, 71.

primary reasons is the difference in the interpretation of the inheritance of Pseudo-Dionysius the Aeropogite. This difference is evident, for instance, when we compare Étienne Gilson's *Being and Some Philosophers*[54] with Vladimir Lossky's *The Mystical Theology of the Eastern Church*[55]—the title of which is significant. What influenced these two different lines of interpretation was, without a doubt, the difference in the exposition of two great interpreters of Pseudo-Dionysius's corpus: John Scotus Eriugena[56] in the West and Maximus the Confessor[57] in the East. The Western interpretation, fortunately, now seems to be undergoing a major change, due to the work of Hans Urs von Balthasar, who took the decisive step to recover the Dionysian "garden" that was devastated by the "tank formations" of modern German scholarship, to revive the "corpse beneath the triumphal car of modern philology."[58]

⤺

As we have been examining, the renewal of Russian cultural and intellectual life in the nineteenth and twentieth centuries crystallized the Russian Idea, in which the most fundamental question about Russia's vocation was the question of evil, *unde malum*? "The fundamental problems of universal philosophy," writes Boris Vysheslavtsev, "are obviously shared by Russian philosophy, and, in this sense, a specifically Russian philosophy does not exist. There is, however, a distinctively Russian manner of approaching universal philosophical problems, a Russian style of living them and reflecting upon them."[59] Russian thought refused to eliminate the problem of evil from cultural and philosophical consciousness, or to relegate it to the realm of the abstract, as did much modern mythology. Russian thought did not assimilate philosophical currents that programmatically rejected metaphysis, such as positivism and analytic philosophy; or that programmatically dehumanized, such as structuralism, neo-structuralism, and psychoanalysis, in which the problem of good and evil is treated as the result of ridiculous errors or superficial language games.[60] There is no doubt that Russian thought felt the full force of the question of evil. And this question cannot be separated

54. Gilson, *Being and Some Philosophers*.

55. Lossky, *Mystical Theology of the Eastern Church*.

56. Eriugena, *Periphyseon*.

57. Pseudo-Dionysius, *Complete Works*.

58. von Balthasar, *Glory of the Lord*, 2:144.

59. Vysheslavtsev, "Viechnoye w russkoy filosofii," 154.

60. Kolakowski, *Metaphysical Horror*, 2–3.

from *praxis*, as has been the case in the West. In the Philosophical Society of Amsterdam, in a conversation between Shestov and Husserl entitled "What is philosophy?" Lev Shestov said this is "the great and ultimate struggle," to which Husserl replied, "No, philosophy is reflection."[61]

## THE HUMAN PERSON AND THE ICON

The Russian language itself reflects this difference, this vital existential attitude of Russian thought. To express the truth, the Russian language has two words: *pravda* and *istina*. Pravda concerns truth in an abstract sense, as in mathematical truth. Frank indicates the way istina, in contrast, connotes the sense of vital relationship,[62] and Florensky signals its relation with being (iest),[63] such that recognizing the truth involves becoming truthful ourselves. And becoming truthful ourselves, according to the etymology given by Florensky that derives from the Sanskrit root for breathing, means, in the words of Cardinal Tomáš Špidlik, becoming alive.[64] Our vital need to search for truth constitutes a space in which the boundaries between theology, philosophy, and literature are much more provisional, or even tend to disappear altogether, and in which the concept of the contemporary tends to overcome the limits of mere chronological systematization.[65]

"A Russian thinker," Frank writes, "whether a simple, religious person or a Dostoevsky, Tolstoy, or Soloviev, always looks for the truth. A Russian thinker wants to understand not only the world and life but tries to capture the religious-moral principle of the universe in order to transfigure and to save the world. He desires the absolute victory of truth as the only true way of rising above lies, falsehood, and injustice."[66] Perhaps this is the secret of Russian culture that made it possible for a former KGB colonel, Anatoliy Golisyn, in one of the most valuable books for interpreting the transformation of the Soviet Union into capitalist Russia—a book that, at bottom, is nothing more (or less) than a painful catharsis—to write in the book's dedication: "In memory of Anna Akhmatova, conscience and soul of Russian literature." In the final words of the prologue, he adds: "And I thank Russian

---

61. Shestov, "Egzystencjalizm jako krytyka fenomenologii," 218.

62. Frank, "Sushchnost' y viedushchyie motivy russkoy filosofrii," 151–52.

63. Florensky, *Stolp i utvuerzhdieniye istiny*, 41.

64. Tomáš Špidlik, "Presentación," in López Sáez, *La belleza, memoria de la resurrección*, 12.

65. Leyderman and Lipoveckiy, *Sovremennaya russkaya literatura*.

66. Frank, "Sushchnost' y viedushchyie motivy russkoy filosofrii," 152.

history and literature for the inspiration they gave when guiding me toward my decision of conscience to serve the people rather than the party."[67]

This power to enter and to transform readers' lives arises only out of experience that reaches the depths—or the heights—of the human being.

In the mid-1980s, I received a very tattered *samizdat* edition of a text written by a writer, poet, and dissident Lithuanian, Tomas Venclova. It was an essay titled "Poetry as Penance," and it was about the difference between the poetry of Eastern and Western Europe. Venclova summarizes his conclusion in one sentence: "The poetry of Eastern Europe is the poetry of life and death; the poetry of the Western Europe is that of the college campus. While the latter is written on campuses, the former is written in concentration camps."

Over twenty years have passed since I read that sentence. Tomas Venclova is now a professor of literature at Yale University, and the Berlin Wall has long since become a block of cement that I keep as a souvenir in my desk drawer. But Venclova's phrase has not lost any of its force. What is more, it becomes increasingly clear not only that the poetry of Eastern and Western Europe, but also their respective politics, belong to two different orders of life. Both the poetry and the politics of the cultures of Eastern Europe arise out of and develop as expressions of vital experience, while in the West they belong to an abstract academic world and the no less abstract world of politics. Czeslaw Miłosz, in *The Captive Mind*, was right when he wrote:

> A man is lying under machine-gun fire on a street in an embattled city. He looks at the pavement and sees a very amusing sight: the cobblestones are standing upright like the quills of a porcupine. The bullets hitting against their edges displace and tilt them. Such moments in the consciousness of a man *judge* all poets and philosophers. Let us suppose, too, that a certain poet was the hero of the literary cafés, and wherever he went he was regarded with curiosity and awe. Yet his poems, recalled in such a moment, suddenly seem diseased and highbrow. The vision of the cobblestones is unquestionably real, and poetry based on an equally naked experience could survive triumphantly that judgment day of man's illusions. In the intellectuals who lived through the atrocities of war in Eastern Europe there took place what one might call the elimination of emotional luxuries. Psychoanalytic novels incite them to laughter. They consider the literature of erotic complications, still popular in the West,

67. Golitsyn, *New Lies for Old*.

as trash. Imitation abstract painting bores them. They are hungry—but they want bread, not hors d'oeuvres.[68]

Donation (the gift) cannot appear in "abstract space" but only in the reality that is the space of donation. Flannery O'Connor's definition of literature as incarnational does not sound strange to Russian poets; indeed, it almost perfectly reflects Russian Acmeist poetry's self-understanding.[69] This understanding of literature's task makes it possible for us to perceive the power a novel or a poem can have.

While philosophical treatises do not possess this power, literature, novels, and poetry do. It is a power that the best philosophers know how to recognize and that the best poets and writers know how to live. The evolution of Soloviev's thought, life, and work offers a paradigmatic example of the intimate union between life, thought, and art. Kondakov regards Soloviev as a symbolic figure of all of Russian culture—one who was uniquely able to bring harmonic balance to the contradictions and the dualisms of the Russian tradition.[70] The tripartite structure of the Russian Idea—anthropology, historiosophy, and ecclesiology, conformed in each case to a fundamental ontology—finds fullest expression in the work of Soloviev. The roots of his exposition of the opposition between the icon and the idol, upon which I have drawn to examine the relationship between human persons, literature, and state, can be found in his metaphysics. In the first paragraph of his first academic paper, "The Mythological Process in Ancient Paganism," we see Soloviev's lifelong interest in the relationship between human persons, society, and the state.[71] His analysis of the evolution of contemporary thought and of modern societies, as well as of the human challenges that still beset us, illumines not only the reality of late nineteenth century, but ours as well.

Here I want to emphasize a detail that I think is particularly revealing: Soloviev's last work, the text with which he ends and crowns his life's work, in which he transcends the question of the human person and the state, is not a philosophical treatise. It is a dialogue and a narration; it is literature. (We see something similar in the case of Hannah Arendt's *Eichmann in Jerusalem*[72]

---

68. Miłosz, *Captive Mind*, 39.

69. Acmeist poetry is a school of poetry that arose in Russia around 1910, associated with Anna Akhmatova and Osip Mandelstam, among others. Its valorization of the concrete and of direct expression through image is commonly regarded as a reaction to Symbolism. See, for instance, Wachtel, *Cambridge Introduction to Russian Poetry*, 8. —Trans.

70. Kondakov, *Vvedzienie v istoriu russkoy kultury*, 501–2.

71. Soloviev, "Mitologicheskiy proces v' drevniem' yazychestvie," 1.

72. Arendt, *Eichmann in Jerusalem*.

and in the work of Michel Henry[73]). This formal evolution of Soloviev's work seems to suggest that literature possesses a power to explain us to ourselves that philosophical essays do not. Literature that follows O'Connor's definition of incarnational art seeks to instantiate the truth about the human being. Years earlier, Soloviev wrote these words: "the understanding of truth (*istina*) we have achieved has shown us again that truth (*istina*) is not only eternally in God but it *comes to be* (*stanovitsia*) in the human person."[74] This process in which truth comes to be, in which it grows in us, was given special expression in Russian thought and especially in Russian literature, thereby evidencing Isaiah Berlin's thesis that the artistic-literary-political sense of great writers tends to reach much deeper in the search for truth (*istina*) than others.[75] These great artists, painters, poets, and writers succeed in overcoming with their work the suffocating concept of verisimilitude and its artificial sense of self-sufficiency. According to Berlin, literature has the ability to offer us not only a picture of our past but to make our past speak to our fundamental existential problems. According to Berlin, Tolstoy did this especially well[76]—a fact that perhaps suggests some of the possible reasons for the fascination Grossman also felt for Tolstoy.

In December 1941, Grossman was working on the front as a war reporter, experiencing in a direct way everything he would later write about. At the same time, in German-occupied France, in the town of Clamart, near Paris, Berdyaev wrote about first philosophy, the metaphysics that informed the tradition in which both he and Grossman participated, incarnated, and continued to return to as an always-new gift. Berdyaev writes:

> My thought is not by any means abstract, it is concerned above all with a revolution in the mind, in other words, with the liberation of the mind from the power of objectification. Nothing but a radical change in the set up of the mind can lead to vital changes; a wrong attitude of the conscious mind is the source of the slavery of man. At the root of the metaphysical considerations of this book there lies an acute sense of the evil which reigns in this world, and of the bitter lot of man as he lives in it. My thought reflects a revolt of human personality against an illusory and crushing objective "world harmony," and the

73. Henry, *L'Amour les yeux fermés*; Henry, *Le fils du roi*.
74. Soloviev, "Kritika otvliechennyh nachal," 745.
75. Zdybel, "Intelektualna droga Isaiaha Berlina," 54.
76. Berlin, *Russian Thinkers*, 22–81.

objective social order, against any form of investing the objective world order with a sacrosanct character.[77]

According to Berdyaev, German and Russian thought are characterized by
the way they grapple with "ultimate problems and eschatology."[78] Following
Berlin, however, Berdyaev argues that we see the eschatological character of
Russian thought especially in the work of Russian literary figures.[79] What
unites thought and literature are their existential foundation. According to
Berdyaev, the act of knowing is not a purely intellectual act, the dispassion-
ate duplication of reality. The power of philosophy arises out of the existential tension of the philosopher as a human person present in the act of
knowing. "It is decided by the intensity of the will to truth and meaning."
The act of knowing, therefore, is an act of the whole person; thought is a
function of life. "The whole man, not reason, constructs metaphysics."[80] But
just as thought cannot be separated from the thinker, the thinker cannot be
separated from "the corporate experience of his brothers in spirit."[81] Knowing therefore depends largely on the shape of these communities and the
relationships between people who live inside and outside them. The act of
knowing can have as an effect the frigid form of objective expression, but
this is a derivative process, because the primary one is the intuition of the
existing person in the fullness of existence. Berdyaev therefore opposes the
view that emotional knowledge is subjective in a pejorative sense, and that
intellectual knowledge is objective in a positive sense. Philosophical knowledge has an indispensable personal character, such that the more personal
it is, the more significant. But this personal act of knowledge does not entail
the alienation of the person. We know within communities. Through our
relationships with the world and with other people, we learn to unite experience and common thought. Truth has two meanings, writes Berdyaev: truth
as knowledge about reality and truth as reality itself. Truth is not simply an
idea; it is being and existence itself.[82]

Berdyaev's reflections by no means exhaust the richness of the thought
and artistic expression of the Russian tradition. But he certainly expresses
much of its essence. Living in exile, his works display a clear desire to
explain his inheritance to the West. Something similar is the case of Paul
Evdokimov—a friend of Berdyaev—who, in his book *Orthodoxy* argues that

77. Berdyaev, *Beginning and the End*, vii.
78. Ibid., 35.
79. Ibid.
80. Ibid., 37.
81. Ibid.
82. Ibid., 42.

the metaphysical freedom of Byzantine theology profoundly expresses its human and social character. In Byzantine theology, writes Evdokimov, fascination with the most intimate theological distinctions "is not the preserve of the learned few, but is enjoyed by the whole people."[83] He then continues: "The theology of the Fathers has always been open to human wisdom in all its branches, especially the magnificent humanism of the Greeks, but it does not stop there; it is a practical and realistic *paidagogos* that gradually raises human thought to the experience of direct relationship with God."[84] The West has often treated this Byzantine inheritance with the same attitude with which it treats Orthodox iconography, perceiving its beauty but not its rationality. For this reason, the West often adopts a condescending attitude toward it. But, as Florensky notes in *Reverse Perspective*, the Western linear perspective that informs such condescension already bespeaks a process of fragmentation and isolation:

> When the religious stability of a Weltanschauung disintegrates and the sacred metaphysics of the general popular consciousness is eroded by the individual judgment of a single person with his single point of view, and moreover with a single point of view precisely at this specific moment—then there also appears a perspective which is characteristic of a fragmented consciousness. . . . [T]his initially happens not in pure art, which is essentially always more or less metaphysical, but in *applied art*, as an element of decoration, which has as its task *not the true essence of being, but verisimilitude to appearance.*[85]

According to Evdokimov, it is the relationship to and the experience of the true essence of being that makes us partakers of the living "symbiosis" of truth and goodness, sealing the integrity of existence and giving birth to beauty.[86]

One of the greatest gifts to the West of the tradition out of which Berdyaev, Evdokimov, and Florensky speak is the art and aesthetic theory of Wassily Kandinsky. His art and his theory are equally important. As Michel Henry indicates, despite the enormous influence of the aesthetics of Plato, Aristotle, Kant, and Hegel, among others, "the common trait of all these thinkers was that they really expect nothing from painting. This renders their analyses of little use for those who would like beauty to increase their

---

83. Evdokimov, *Orthodoxy*, 21–22.
84. Ibid., 22.
85. Florensky, *Beyond Vision*, 208–9. Florensky's italics.
86. Evdokimov, *Art of the Icon*, 1.

ability to feel and to enrich their personal experience."[87] Kandinsky begins his work *Point and Line to Plane* with this claim: "Every phenomenon can be experienced in two ways. These two ways are not arbitrary, but are bound up with the phenomenon—developing out of its nature and characteristics: Externally—or—Internally."[88] The Internal does not belong to the world; it is not the world's replication. "In what way, then," Henry asks, following Kandinsky, "can the Internal be revealed, if it is not in or as a world? It is revealed in a way of life. Life feels and experiences itself immediately such that it coincides with itself at each point of its being. Wholly immersed in itself and drawn from this feeling of itself, it is carried out as a pathos."[89] This process not only takes place within cultural space but in-forms that space. It is an *ethos* informed by a living metaphysics—not a speculative, abstract one—and it arises from the sense that knowing the truth is not most fundamentally a process of objectification. Knowing the truth has its own dynamism, which coincides with life itself, and which constantly invites the transformation of our lives.[90] This dynamism makes possible the Russian tradition's distinctive *logos*.

As we have seen, this existential dynamism has its origin in the specific history and culture of Russia, which bequeathed to us as its inheritance figures from the pre-Communist era such as Odoevsky, Chaadayev, Khomyakov, Gogol, Chekov, and Dostoevsky. Moreover, this existential dynamism did not disappear when the Bolsheviks came to power. It continued in the work of Pavel Florensky, Nikolay Berdyaev, Sergei Bulgakov, Mikhail Bulgakov, Boris Pasternak, Osip Mandelstam, as well as so many others whose names we may possibly never know. Writers, thinkers, and poets who, like Anna Akhmatova in 1938, in the prison lines of Leningrad, was asked the question, "Can you describe this?" and answered, "Yes, I can."[91] Before the altar of the idol that devours its own children, these figures were capable of donation, of offering their lives, and, in this way, preserving the truth of their being. Not without reason have Kondakov and Shneyberg compared Akhmatova to the image of a mother who, in her poetry, addresses the Russian people. With compassion, prayers, and words of solace and hope in spite of everything, she tends to her children.[92]

87. Henry, *Seeing the Invisible*, 2.

88. Kandinsky, *Point and Line to Plane*, 17.

89. Henry, *Seeing the Invisible*, 7.

90. Berdyaev, *Truth and Revelation*, 22–23.

91. Akhmatova, *Complete Poems*, 384.

92. Kondakov and Shneyberg, *Ot gorkovo do Solzhenicyna*, 396.

☞

This process in which truth becomes increasingly present in the life of the writer is at the heart of the evolution of Vasily Grossman's work. Like Akhmatova when asked the question, "Can you describe this?," he too answers, "Yes I can." At the outset of his literary journey, living amidst the state machinery that put into practice Lenin's idea that culture is "the servant of politics" and Stalin's idea that writers are the "engineers of human souls,"[93] Grossman offered all of us an exceptional study of human persons, their products, modern society, and the totalitarian state—the same state whose final withering away Lenin himself proclaimed.[94] Grossman took up the poet Zbigniew Herbert's challenge: "you were saved not in order to live / you have little time you must give testimony."[95]

Grossman's testimony is of special value because it assumes all the consequences of the human condition; it accepts on behalf of us all the responsibility for being as we are. At the end of chapter seven of his novel, *Everything Flows*—the chapter on the trial of the Judases, the collaborators of the totalitarian state—Grossman writes: "All the living are guilty . . . You, the defendant, are guilty—and you, the prosecutor, and I myself, as I think about the defendant, the prosecutor, and the judge"[96] But this realization, so tragically sincere, is not all that Grossman has to say about human nature. There is something else, something that leads him to end the chapter with the question: "Why is all this so painful? Why does our human obscenity make us feel such shame?"[97] At this juncture, I would simply point out that there are some interesting parallels between *Everything Flows* and Dostoyevsky's *The Idiot*—parallels that appear from the first scene in which Ivan, like Prince Myshkin, arrives in Moscow on the train, which find their ultimate justification in the natural goodness of both characters.

By way of an experiment, we can point to a constant in the work and life of Grossman: a profound and painful dialectic between the idol and the icon, each of which battle for the human heart. It is a battle whose first stage is the life of the author himself, which, as Yuriy Druzhnikov argues in his article "The Lessons of Vasily Grossman," is more captivating than his work.[98] Grossman gives expression to this experience in a masterful and

93. Kondakov, *Vvedzienie v istoriu russkoy kultury*, 565.
94. Lenin, "Państwo a rewolucja."
95. Herbert, *Selected Poems*, 79.
96. Grossman, *Everything Flows*, 71.
97. Ibid.
98. Druzhnikov, "Uroki Vasiliya Grossmana."

direct way through the characters in his stories. The dichotomy between good and evil, the encounter between the idol and the icon, is deeply rooted in Russian culture. It is guided by the Solovievian truth (*istina*) that is "coming to be" in the vital experience of the writer and that is being worked out over the course of Grossman's work. His own work as "icon"—literature as incarnational, as the space of donation—participates in the opposition to the idol, to the totalitarian state created by modern society and incarnated by Lenin and Stalin. And this property of Grossman's narrative as icon is present in a unique and, to my mind, particularly characteristic way, in the figure of the mother and of motherhood.

## Idol against the Woman

In Grossman's work, we see the masterful depiction and evolution of the figure of woman as icon, as a being uniquely endowed with the capacity of donation, of opposition to egoism *par excellence*. The woman bears the living power of truth that liberates from the bondage to the idol. This truth, which "takes possession of the internal being of a human and actually rescues him from false self-assertion," Soloviev simply calls "Love."[99]

Grossman characteristically situates the woman as icon, who ultimately holds the gift of donation, before the idol of the state. This evolution is fully consistent with the thought of Soloviev, who begins with the figure of the mother and culminates in the primary figure of the woman, who gives herself in the spousal union—a union that shelters total reciprocal donation and permits the equal participation of both lovers. Only in this union, explains Soloviev—physical union, sexual union—does there appear the fullness of the proper recognition of the unconditional importance of the beloved, the fullness of reciprocity, and the total communication of life.[100]

In the story "In the Town of Berdichev"[101] we find these reference points. In this story, which was made into a film in the 1960s by Aleksandr Yakovlevich Askoldov that was quickly censored, Vavilova, the pregnant commissar of a Red Army unit, remembers when she attended a speech by Lenin directed to soldiers being dispatched to the front—a speech that caused tears of emotion among those who attended it. It was probably this description of the idol that caught the attention of Maxim Gorky. Despite his harsh criticism of Grossman's previous work, after reading "In the Town of Berdichev," Gorky invited the young writer to his home. Over the course

99. Soloviev, *Meaning of Love*, 41.
100. Ibid., 42, 47–48.
101. Grossman, "In the Town of Berdichev."

of the story, Vavilova undergoes a profound change, one that leads to the discovery of her humanity. She becomes pregnant. And until the birth of the child, she stays with the family of a poor Jewish blacksmith, Yefim, and his wife, Beila—a family whose life together, despite the terrible experiences of the civil war, helps Vavilova learn her true vocation. The birth of Vavilova's son, along with the short experience of living with Yefim and Beila, occasions a new and unexpected relationship with the revolution.

Already we see in Grossman's work the dichotomy of totalitarianism—the state-idol personified in the figures of Lenin and Stalin, which condemns, demands sacrifice, and so on—and woman—the icon, the image of the mother, of the wife, who donates herself completely.

The idol appears in all its power—the power to control desire—in *Life and Fate*. Shtrum's internal struggle is a struggle between the desire to be simply human and honest, and a desire for recognition and success. In the grip of the idol, the desire for God becomes egotistical desire, which is encouraged, controlled, and directed by the self alone. The idol makes us turn in upon ourselves and especially devalue others—a process described by Soloviev in *The Meaning of Love*.[102] The more we are turned inward upon ourselves, the more we lose our capacity for donation and the more our alienation deepens. It is much easier to try to control others than to learn to love them. Once again, Leszek Kolakowski's observation is apt that the difference between despotism and totalitarianism is that the latter is characterized by an inherent tendency to destroy the ties that bind people and to drown the natural human propensity to create community life.[103] And, once again, we see the fundamental characteristic of modern society, and therefore of the modern state, as *privatio communitatis*. The extent to which the dominant culture is immersed in this process of alienation can be glimpsed in a significant detail: Tzvetan Todorov, in the preface to the French edition of the works of Grossman,[104] repeatedly uses the concept of "the individual"—rather than, as Grossman does, "the human being" or "the human person"—to describe totalitarianism. The conception of the human being as an "individual" is among the first in the process of the totalitarianization, which is also the dehumanization, of societies.

Arendt concludes *The Origins of Totalitarianism* with an insight that helps us see that all is not lost. Drawing on St. Augustine's words from *City of God*, *Initium ut esset homo creatus est* (that a beginning be made, man

---

102. Soloviev, "Smysl lubvi," 3–60.

103. Kolakowski, "Euro- i azjatokomunizm," 375.

104. Todorov, "Les combats de Vassili Grossman," xix.

was created),[105] she indicates the permanent possibility of a new beginning within history: "This new beginning is guaranteed by each new birth; it is indeed every man."[106]

This truth about the birth of each new person is present in the work of Grossman in the image of the mother and wife. This is the icon of life that opposes the idol of death. Though we encounter a premonition of it in the figure of commissar Vavilova in "In the Town of Berdichev," we find its fullness in Grossman's short text "The Sistine Madonna." We also find it tragically expressed in the character of Sofya Osipovna in *Life and Fate*, who experiences and offers motherhood by embracing little David in his last moments in the gas chamber. We find it in the drama of Masha. In *Everything Flows*, we find it in Anna's patient goodness.

To the chilling vision of the idol-state—cold like the steel and concrete of the gas chamber—Sofya opposes her heartbreakingly beautiful embrace of her new son, David. "Now I am a mother" or "I've become a mother" (*ya stala materiu*),[107] she says, embracing the child's still body. The icon of motherhood, which reemerges even in gas chambers, is always attacked by the idol. It is the idol's principal enemy, because, apart from the spousal embrace, it is the supreme donation. The massacre of the innocents will always distinguish totalitarian societies and states. It is their unmistakable feature. Where women, wives, and mothers are attacked, the idol is present. And where this attack has acquired a condition of normalcy, the idol is already master of persons, societies, and the states incarnated by them. In *Everything Flows*, the only thing that can extinguish Masha's hope of finally finding herself with her husband and her daughter is her sense of the normalcy of her tragedy. Upon leaving to work outside the fences of the Gulag, she finds a *normal* world.[108] Imre Kertész describes this kind of normalcy in *Fatelessness*[109] and Hannah Arendt gives expression to it in *Eichmann in Jerusalem* in her famous definition of the banality of evil.[110] Grossman's description of Lenin and Stalin in *Everything Flows* differs from that of *In the Town of Berdichev*. In *Everything Flows*, the cruelty and banality of Soviet totalitarianism find their reflection in the deified figure of

105. Augustine, *City of God against the Pagans*, XII.20.

106. Arendt, *Origins of Totalitarianism*, 479.

107. Grossman, *Life and Fate*, 554. I refer to the original text because the Spanish translation of Galaxia-Gutenberg fails to reflect the richness of the phrase. And for the purposes of this work, the presence of the verb *stat,' stanovitsa*, as we have already noted, is significant.

108. Grossman, *Everything Flows*, 101–14.

109. Kertész, *Fatelessness*.

110. Arendt, *Eichmann in Jerusalem*.

Lenin.[111] As Berdyaev observes, "The apotheosis of Caesar is the source of totalitarianism in its extreme forms."[112] The phenomenon commonly called "cult of personality" entails a process of deification. This was the process Lenin began in the first moments of creation of the communist empire. As early as 1918, Demian Biedny wrote, "Lenin, though far away, was always with the Russians."[113] In the same year Gregory Zinoviev published the first biography of Lenin, a work that followed the strict rules of hagiography. The protagonist was an atheist saint, ascetic, and martyr who lived only for his faith in the idea of the Bolshevik Revolution. Zinoviev writes this about Lenin: "Truly he is the chosen one among millions, our leader by the grace of God." Zinoviev continues: "Lenin is the true leader who is only born once every five hundred years." It should be said that Zinoviev neither explains why exactly five hundred years nor what it means for a communist to experience this curious grace of god—lowercase *g*, of course—that legitimized the power of Lenin.[114] Zinoviev, one of Lenin's closest collaborators in their times of exile, returned with Lenin to Russia. Because of a disagreement, Zinoviev fell from favor at the beginning of the revolution. Although Zinoviev still belonged to the party leadership, Leon Trotsky took his place as second in command. Zinoviev's biography of Lenin was an attempt to redeem himself and to demonstrate his commitment to the idea as well as to the idol, but he never recovered his old position. It was Stalin who in time received the Lenin Legacy and control over the party. Years later, Zinoviev became a victim of Stalin's purges. He was condemned in 1936, in the case of the Trotskyite-Zinovievite Terrorist Center, for the attempted murder of Kirov and Stalin himself. This so-called Trial of the Sixteen was the first of the show trials mounted in Moscow—the first in which the accused were old Bolsheviks. Increasingly elaborate and based on absurd charges of monstrous crimes—espionage, poisoning, and so on—these cynical demonstrations of the power of the idol-state were acts of faith requiring allegiance from all. "If you are genuinely capable of sincere repentance, if you still feel any love at all for the Party, then help the Party with your Confession," says the judge Nikolay Krymov in Grossman's *Life and Fate*.[115] These trials demonstrate the power of the state, the idol: "Viktor felt a shiver of fear, the fear that was always lurking in his heart—fear of the State's anger, fear of being a

---

111. Grossman, *Everything Flows*, 173.

112. Berdyaev, *Realm of Spirit and the Realm of Caesar*, 76.

113. Stobiecki, *Bolszewizm a historia*, 134.

114. Ibid., 130. Cf. Zinovev and Lenin, *Lenin Vladimir Ilich*.

115. Grossman, *Life and Fate*, 777.

victim of this anger that could crush a man and grind him to dust."[116] This is a power that is total, divine, and omnipresent. It is estimated that more than forty cities in the Soviet Union were named after Lenin, and more than 51,000 museums dedicated to him have been constructed.[117] The perpetual presence of the creator of the state in his work guarantees the state's survival: "Lenin lives in the soul of every member of our party," read the statement by the Communist Party Central Committee that was issued after his death in 1924.[118] The idol inserts itself in relationships at all levels; it cannot permit relationships that "have nothing to do with the State."[119]

The role of the justice system is of fundamental importance for the modern state, and it is the cornerstone of totalitarian society. In the twentieth century, the most elemental and ordinary repressions, to the most well-known atrocities, have enjoyed legal justification. Isaac Steinberg, Commissioner for Justice in Lenin's government, wrote: "Terror is a *system* . . . a legalized plan of the regime for the purpose of mass intimidation, mass compulsion, mass extermination. Terror is a calculated register of punishments, reprisals, and threats by means of which the government intimidates, entices, and compels the fulfillment of its imperative will. Terror is a heavy, suffocating cloak thrown from above over the entire population of the country, a cloak woven of mistrust, lurking vigilance, and lust for revenge."[120] Whoever is not part of the system is a natural enemy of the system. Thus, in *Everything Flows*, Masha is charged for failing to denounce her husband, who had been arrested for failing to denounce his friends.[121] Another protagonist of the same novel, Nikolay, despite living with doubts similar to those of Shtrum of *Life and Fate*, signed the letter condemning the Killer Doctors of the famous 1937 trials, and, at a meeting, voted in favor of the death sentence for Rykov and Bukharin. The power the judicial system exerts in everyday life in Grossman's work is no accident. He himself, as his stepson Fedor Guber remembers, after a terrible inner struggle signed along with others a letter in which Russian intellectuals of Jewish origin distanced themselves from the behavior of the Killer Doctors. "He never forgot this letter for the rest of his life."[122]

---

116. Ibid., 569.

117. Stobiecki, *Bolszewizm a historia*, 130.

118. Zaremba, "Nieboszczyk w służbie partii," 31.

119. Grossman, *Life and Fate*, 569.

120. Pipes, *Russian Revolution*, 792.

121. Grossman, *Everything Flows*, 101.

122. Guber, "Osuschestvliayuschiy zhizn' tak, kak khotelos . . . "Iz knigi o Vasilii Grossmanie" Pamiat' y pisma," 283.

## THE THEOLOGIAN AS LAWYER

It is no coincidence that, from its inception, the process of the creation of the modern state—which is the same process as the sacralization of the state—bears the signature of the theologian as lawyer. *Corpus mysticum*, from the twelfth century onward, became *corpus iuridicum*, and this process extended to include the state, eventually leading to the state's sacralization and the development of new foundational ideologies.[123] Once again, we are reminded of Gogol's words about the legal and juridical occupying the empty spaces left by the culture of the Christian community.[124]

It was likewise no accident that the original purpose of the first secular university, the University of Naples, which was founded by Emperor Frederick II in 1224, was the formation of lawyers dedicated to the service of the empire's interests. The same effort to construct the legal foundation and fabric of the state—although founded on assumptions that invoked theological sources—drove Louis IX. Both espoused a conception of the law that, while incompatible with the thought of St. Thomas Aquinas,[125] was more than sufficient to serve as the pistol shot that started the race to the modern state. It was more than sufficient to support Dante Alighieri's claim in *The Monarchy* that "the whole of mankind is ordered to one goal. . . . There must therefore be one person who directs and rules mankind, and he is properly called 'Monarch' or 'Emperor.' And thus it is apparent that the well-being of the world requires that there be a monarchy or empire."[126]

St. Augustine perfectly understood the essence of the problem, and he rejected the concept of the city dominated by the notion of justice defended by Cicero and proposed instead an entirely different definition:[127] "A people is an assembled multitude of rational creatures bound together by a common agreement as to the object of their love. In this case, if we are to discover the character of any people, we have only to examine what it loves."[128] Berdyaev locates the difference between a state and a people in the fundamental fact that the state was created by an act of violence in a world that refuses love.[129] We must keep in mind, Berdyaev points out, that Cel-

---

123. Kantorowicz, *King's Two Bodies*, 206–7.

124. Zenkovsky, "N. V. Gogol," 58.

125. MacIntyre, "Natural Law as Subversive," 63–65.

126. Dante, *Monarchy*, 11.

127. Gilson, *Les métamorphoses de la Cité de Dieu*, 48–52.

128. Augustine, *City of God against the Pagans*, XIX.24. It is important to clarify that St. Augustine does not reject justice per se. True justice includes sacrifice to God (cf. II.21, XIX.21). According to Augustine, justice is a form of love.

129. Berdyaev, *Realm of Spirit and the Realm of Caesar*, 77.

sus defended the empire and imperial power using arguments very similar to those used to defend the totalitarian state in our own time. Moreover, Berdyaev observes, "the so-called liberal democracies, which claimed to be neutral in regard to the realm of the Spirit, no longer exist: they have increasingly become dictatorships. . . . [W]here once the emperors said that they were called not only to rule the state, but to look out for the salvation of the souls of their subjects, the caesars of today are also concerned with saving souls, if only from religious superstitions. Caesar always and irresistibly tends toward demanding for himself not only that which is Caesar's, but that which is God's."[130]

There is a clear correspondence between ontology and the will to legislate—a correlation that found one of its most famous expressions in the relationship between Heidegger's fundamental ontology and the will to legislate of the Third Reich. As Julio Quesada argues, there is a close relationship between metaphysics and law.[131] Carl Schmitt's *Constitution of Freedom* intimately relates to Heidegger's reflections in *Introduction to Metaphysics,* and these, in turn, to the Nuremberg Laws. As we saw above, the Nuremberg Laws were characterized by the same offer of salvation as the Soviet Criminal Code of 1922 or the legal system of the People's Republic of Poland.[132] This offer, however, was not only limited to the conception of law as a repressive instrument. It also established the *legal* possibility—and justification—for the expulsion, isolation, and elimination of others, whether Jews, the bourgeois, kulaks, enemies of the proletariat, enemies of progress, neighbors, brothers, sisters, the elderly, or fetuses. This offer of salvation characterizes all modern states. It includes the control of all aspects and levels of life, and it encourages the response to evil with counter-evil, that is, with the accusation. As Marion writes in *Prolegomena to Charity*: "If I (passively) undergo evil, it is actively that I kindle a counter-evil. And if evil is universal, in me and around me—as, in fact, it clearly is—then the counter-evil of the accusation will have to become universal also. And, in fact, the accusation does become universal. For accusation, obviously, offers itself as the final weapon of those who do not have, or no longer have, any other. But truly, must one own a weapon?"[133] This first victory of evil is decisive, because it leads those who suffer to affirm their innocence through accusation, to perpetuate suffering by demanding the suffering of others. It entices them, in other words, to oppose evil with counter-evil. Marion continues:

130. Ibid., 78.

131. Quesada, *Heidegger de camino al Holocausto*, 254.

132. Kładocznyn, *Prawo jako narzędzie represji w Polsce Ludowej (1944–1956)*.

133. Marion, *Prolegomena to Charity*, 5.

"The triumph of the logic of evil within the very effort to be rid of it stands out markedly in the universal accusation. This phenomenon can take the following formulation: just because the cause of evil remains to me unknown, uncertain, and vague doesn't mean that I must give up trying to suppress it. . . . In order to speak of such a cause, our time has invented expressions: 'round up the usual suspects,' but above all, 'determine accountability.'"[134] In order to fulfill this undertaking, the state offers us the guarantees of the *rule of law*, sustained by the structure of the *ministry of justice*. The ministry of justice stealthily usurps the place of the ministry of forgiveness, conquering us with the logic of the accusation and erecting its power upon the structure of institutionalized vengeance. The rule of law offers us a space in which the other is the one upon whom I unload my sufferings and my responsibilities. It perpetually returns us to the position of Cain and makes us participants in his question: Am I my brother's keeper? (Gen 4:9). As Marion indicates, our response turns out to be this: "Of course not! If someone is my brother's keeper, it would be anyone other than me! If, of the two of us, one has to be responsible, it is my brother, who is responsible for my unhappiness by the simple fact that he remains happy when I no longer am."[135] This is the response accepted by all, in the sense that the normalcy in which we live is the normalcy of Cain, where the solitude of alienation devours the space of donation.

But despite all this, in the work of Grossman, the normalcy of evil—its terrible banality—cannot extinguish the normalcy we carry within ourselves, which is simply the freedom to love, which is donation. The logic of donation, which is the inverse of the logic of accusation, and which defeats alienation, permits a new question to appear, which Grossman dares to formulate with a terrible honesty, "Abel, where is your brother Cain?"[136] To my mind, it is significant that the same question appears in Berdyaev's *Destiny of Man*, published in Paris in 1931.[137] This fact not only suggests that Grossman knew the book, but it also allows us to affirm that Grossman himself belonged to the best tradition of Russian thought—a tradition that refused to capitulate before the dominant culture and that made possible the exposure of the true reality of the modern state.

134. Ibid.

135. Ibid., 8.

136. Grossman, "Abel," 113–36.

137. In *The Destiny of Man*, Berdyaev writes, "Moral consciousness began with God's question: 'Cain, where is your brother Abel?' It will end with another question on the part of God: 'Abel, where is your brother Cain?'" (276–77).

## The Weddings of the Icon

Throughout his life and work, Grossman identified the totalitarian features of the modern state, whether socialist, national-socialist, communist, or liberal. He exposed the anthropological truth of totalitarian society, masterfully describing the ontological tragedy of human persons enslaved by the idol of the modern state. He intuited that the icon of the woman, mother, and wife opposed the idol of the state. Their freedom to love—their participation in and extension of the space of donation—continues to serve us as icons of the freedom of donation we see in Christ—the one in whom the mystery of the human person takes on light.

Shortly before his death, Grossman encountered a place where the *polis* for which those from the ancient Greeks to MacIntyre[138] searched was a reality in the simple life of a people, the Armenian people—a people who welcomed a broken Grossman and graciously gave him back to himself, a community that loved the same thing: life. This offering and this love helped him discover his own humanity.

Grossman's consciousness of his own impending death influenced the last novel he wrote, *Everything Flows*. It influenced the last trip he took, as well. These sketches from his time in Armenia comprise an internal dialogue that aims to respond definitively to the questions that had marked his entire life—questions upon which the greatness of Russian literature has been constructed.

One of these questions is: If not the state, then what? The answer is not so much the classical *polis*, but *sobornost'*—a community in which the virtues are not so much the object of study but gifts given in the vital experience handed down from one generation to another; in which tradition is not just a narrative but a lived gift, and as lived, donated; donated, and therefore, lived. As Marion suggests, "a gift is not repeated, nor is it received as gift unless the recipient donor becomes integrally and in person—hypostatically—a gift."[139]

For economic reasons, Grossman took a job editing and retranslating a war novel by Rachiya Kochar. But it is also likely that he did so because of the trip to Armenia included in the task. Grossman's first long trip since the war ended helped him find some distance, not only from the ostracism prevalent in official circles, but also from a difficult familial situation.[140] The result of this trip was the essay *Dobro vam*, or *Good Wishes*, the Rus-

---

138. See, for instance, MacIntyre, *Ethics and Politics*, 3–40.

139. Marion, *Idol and Distance*, 168.

140. Druzhnikov, "Uroki Vasiliya Grossmana."

sian translation of the Armenian traditional greeting, *Barev dzez* (literally, "Good to you").

This journey through an extraordinarily beautiful land, inhabited by a people heir to a unique history, generates a series of strikingly intimate reflections by Grossman. Perhaps it was the difficult blow of the seizure and confiscation of his life's work, *Life and Fate*; perhaps it was the awareness of his immanent death; perhaps it was both; in any case his journey through Armenia and his encounters with its inhabitants led to a profoundly introspective work. *Good Wishes* is written in first person. Throughout his trip, Grossman reflects upon himself, because in many ways, this land speaks to him of his own life. He meets numerous families who receive him with simplicity and generosity in their humble homes. He has long conversations with them about what he and they care most about: "love for other people, right and wrong, good and evil, faith and lack of faith."[141] In one of these conversations, Grossman is struck by the way his interlocutor speaks about human evil without judging anyone.

In Grossman's sketches of his travels we encounter a gallery of ordinary people whose faces are illumined by truth, goodness, and beauty. Grossman describes Vazgen I, the Supreme Patriarch Catholicos of the Armenian Apostolic Church, who introduces him to Rachiya Kochar, the author of the novel that Grossman edits and translates—a man Grossman calls Martirosyan. When the Catholicos asks Grossman about his impressions of Armenia, Grossman speaks about the beauty of the ancient Armenian churches: "I said I wanted books to be like these churches, simply made and expressive; and that I would like God to be living in each book, as in a church."[142]

The title of Grossman's text is significant. As I pointed out above, it is a translation of the Armenian traditional greeting, *Barev dzez*. As the trip progresses, the ordinary kindness that this traditional greeting evokes becomes the centerpiece of Grossman's reflections. In this work, Grossman's style does not so much evoke Tolstoy or Dostoevsky as Chekhov. Far from pondering "great ideas," Grossman's concern is Chekhovian humanism, the ordinary goodness that Ikonnikov proclaims in *Life and Fate*,[143] and which Grossman finds among his Armenian hosts.

141. All citations from Grossman's *Good Wishes* come from Robert and Elizabeth Chandler's translation of *Dobro vam*, titled *An Armenian Sketchbook*. Many thanks to the Chandlers for their willingness to share drafts of their translation while the work was in progress. —Trans.

142. In the original, the word *God*, for reasons of censure, begins with a lowercase *g*.

143. Grossman, *Life and Fate*, 27–29.

His journey ends at a wedding celebration for a nephew of Martirosyan. The young man works as a driver, and his betrothed works in a village shop. It is a celebration in which Grossman discovers the celebration of life—a celebration in which he also participates. "I seemed to be taking part for the first time in a splendid and solemn, perfectly structured one-act drama," he writes, "the drama of *life*."[144] The sincerity and the goodness with which he is welcomed lead him to this recognition: "I was at home; I was among my own kind." And this "translator from Armenian who knows no Armenian,"[145] as Grossman describes himself, depicts, without translation, the life of a people—a people he encounters at the end of his own life.

At the wedding, during the time of toasts and speeches, in which the guests speak "little about the newlyweds and their future happy life" but instead "about good and evil, about honorable labor, about the bitter fate of the Armenian nation, about the nation's past and its hopes for the future, about the fertile Armenian lands to the west where so much innocent blood was spilt, about how the Armenian nation has been scattered throughout the world, about how labor and true kindness will always be stronger than any lie,"[146] Grossman is unexpectedly welcomed with the speech of a carpenter about the history of Grossman's own people, the Jews.

> The carpenter was talking about the Jews, saying that when he had been taken prisoner during the war he had seen all the Jewish prisoners being taken away somewhere separate. All his Jewish comrades had been killed. He spoke of the compassion and love he felt for the Jewish women and children who had perished in the gas chambers of Auschwitz. He said how he had read articles of mine about the war, with portrayals of Armenians, and had thought how this man writing about Armenians was from a nation that had also suffered a great deal. He hoped that it would not be long before a son of the much-suffering Armenian nation would write one day about the Jews. To this he now raised his glass.[147]

After the carpenter's speech, many others, "both old and young," address Grossman: "All spoke about the Jews and the Armenians, about how blood and suffering had brought them together."[148] Overcome, Grossman writes, "Never in my life have I bowed to the ground; never have I prostrated myself

---

144. Grossman, *Armenian Sketchbook*, 101.

145. Ibid., 114.

146. Ibid., 111–12.

147. Ibid., 112.

148. Ibid.

before anyone. Now, however, I bow to the ground before the Armenian peasants who, during the merriment of a village wedding, spoke publicly about the agony of the Jewish nation under Hitler, about the death camps where Nazis murdered Jewish women and children. I bow to everyone who, silently, sadly, and solemnly, listened to these speeches."[149]

In Grossman's description of the wedding, the celebration of life closes with a scene of dancing, with the simplicity and the humility of the truth, goodness, and beauty incarnated in the perichoresis that he encounters in this village, among this people:

> Each of the guests was given a thin wax candle, and holding hands, we began to dance a slow and solemn round dance. Two hundred people—old men and old women, young boys and girls—all holding lighted candles, moved slowly and solemnly the length of the rough stone walls; the little lights swayed in their hands. I saw interlaced fingers; I saw a chain that would never rust or break—a chain of dark-brown laboring hands; I saw many little lights. It was a joy to look at people's faces: The soft sweet flames seemed to be coming not from the candles but from people's eyes. What kindness, purity, merriment, and sadness there was in these eyes. There were old men saying goodbye to a life now slipping away from them. There were old women in whose crafty eyes I saw a defiant joy. The faces of the young women were full of shy charm. There was a quiet seriousness in the eyes of the young boys and girls.
>
> This chain, the life of the nation, was unbreakable. It brought together youth and maturity, and the sadness of those who would soon be leaving life. This chain seemed eternal; neither sorrow, nor death, nor invasions, nor slavery could break it.[150]

Grossman ends this final scene of *Good Wishes* with a fundamental insight: "I understood that all the wise speeches—speeches that had seemed to have so little to do with this wedding—did in fact have everything to do with this wedding and this young couple."[151] The center of the wedding, the center of the celebration in which they all participated, was the union of the bride and groom. The union of a couple—a young man who worked as a driver and a young woman who worked in a village shop—offered all those present a new chance at life, a new possibility of donation.

149. Ibid., 113.
150. Ibid., 113–14.
151. Ibid., 114.

When, in 1963, Grossman returned to work on *Everything Flows*—a text that he left unfinished in 1955—he picked up in a remarkably compassionate way the motif of the wedding night, the first night. This time, the couple is not young, and there is no banquet. But there are people to celebrate it: the people that appear in Anna's narrative. There also remains, despite everything, the liberating power of donation—the power of the woman who, through donation, opens the way to life. In a dream, Ivan, the protagonist of *Everything Flows*, calls to his mother, and Anna comes to him:

> He had called out to his mother in a dream, and this woman had come to him.
>
> She was there beside him. He felt at once, with all his being, that she was beautiful. She had heard him cry out in his sleep and she had come to him, feeling tenderness and pity toward him. . . .
>
> She was beautiful because she was kind. He took her hand. She lay down beside him and he sensed her warmth, her tender breasts, he shoulders, her hair. . . .
>
> She was kindness, all kindness, and he understood with the whole of his corporeal being that her tenderness, her warmth, her whispers were beautiful because her heart was full of kindness toward him, because love is kindness.[152]

This first night of love makes it possible that, shortly before Anna's death, when she is already in the hospital, Ivan, in the solitude of another night, faces his most difficult memory: his conversation with Aleksey, his cell companion during the interrogations, "the most intelligent man I've ever met."[153]

Aleksey has endured the sufferings of prison and of torture with Ivan, which makes him gain credibility. And Aleksey's intelligence enables him to exposit with brilliance the logic of evil. In this way, Aleksey becomes the only man who makes Ivan doubt about the goodness of the human heart and the possibility of the freedom to love. In this conversation, which will mark Ivan unlike any other, Aleksey declares, "The history of life is the history of violence triumphant. Violence is eternal and indestructible. It can change shape, but it does not disappear or diminish."[154] Despite the relief

152. Grossman, *Everything Flows*, 115.

153. Ibid., 201.

154. Ibid., 204.

that comes to Ivan after the following interrogation, he never forgets Aleksey's words.

As the years passed, the love—the donation—of Anna, breaks the chains that have bound Ivan's heart since the night of his conversation with Aleksey. Anna is the icon of motherhood, of a donation that is gratuitous and total, of freedom. Anna makes it possible for Ivan to find the final answer to the question of evil put to him by Aleksey—a man who seems to accept freely his being the bearer of the idol. As the victim of evil, Aleksey proclaims the triumph of evil. But more than just proclaiming its triumph, he becomes its apologist. What Ivan sees in the figures of Lenin and Stalin, he finds reaffirmed in the most intelligent person he had ever known: his cellmate. This makes Ivan doubt what is most important to him, what he has been looking for all his life. It makes Ivan doubt in his own capacity to be free, to forgive, which is the only path toward the reaffirmation of his belief in the goodness of the human heart.

What makes Grossman's work unique is that it does not accuse; it does not condemn. Accusation and condemnation are what the idol-state does. Rather, Grossman illumines the way of donation, the way of suffering with those who suffer. Before others, Grossman asks forgiveness, as he also forgives—something that mothers and wives do. It is also something the Father did in sending the Son—an event in relation to which these mothers and wives stand as icons.

The last three chapters of *Everything Flows*, in many ways, summarize Grossman's literary corpus. In them, we find Grossman's final answer to the dialectic of the icon and the idol. In the face of the idol, the novel ends with a definitive affirmation of the human person as an immutable bearer of the gift of freedom—the freedom that is found in donation, in forgiveness. This is the act of reconciliation of Christians that Soloviev describes in his final work, "A Short Story about the Anti-Christ," the prophetic response before the question of evil in the world. Grossman transfers the tension locked in the Russian Idea to the existential plane. He masterfully translates Solovievian ontology and eschatology to the language of personal experience. In the end, Grossman shows us that only the ordinariness of goodness defeats the banality of evil. Among Grossman's final words, we find the following:

> Never before had he seen his life as a whole—but now here it was, lying there before him.
> And, seeing his life, he felt no resentment toward anyone.
> All of them—those who had prodded him with their rifle butts as they escorted him toward the investigator's office, those who has subjected him to long interrogations without letting

him sleep, those who had said vile things about him at public meetings, those who has officially renounced him, those who had stolen his camp ration of bread, those who had beaten him—all of them, in their weakness, coarseness, and spite, had done evil without wanting to. They had not wanted to do evil to him.

They had betrayed, slandered, and renounced because there had been no other way for them to survive. And yet they were people; they were human beings. . . .

People did not want to do evil to anyone, but they did evil all through their lives.

All the same, people were people. They were human beings. And the wonderful, marvelous thing is that, willingly or unwillingly, they did not allow freedom to die. In their terrible, distorted, yet still-human souls, even the most terrible of them looked after freedom and kept it alive.[155]

Again, what makes Grossman's work unique is that it neither accuses nor condemns, as the idol-state does. His work seeks to lay plain the truth that resides in the human person as icon—an icon that we all are and that constitutes a perpetual invitation to the nuptial dance. His work neither abandons those who suffer nor seeks escape from the horrors of reality. It lays plain the way of donation, the way of suffering with those who suffer. It asks for forgiveness, as it also forgives. It invites us to go and do likewise.

Grossman's final message to us, therefore, is one of hope. Before the power of the idol—and even the idol's identification with the state—the human person always bears the icon of a nature created to love, to donate (*don*), and to forgive (*per-don*). The person who forgives is free.

155. Ibid., 208.

# Bibliography

Abrams, Philip. "Notes on the Difficulty of Studying the State." *Jounal of Historical Sociology* 1 (1977) 58–89.

Akhmatova, Anna. *The Complete Poems of Anna Akhmatova*. Boston: Zephyr, 1997.

Anderson, Benedict. *Imagined Communities: Reflections on the Origin and Spread of Nationalism*. New York: Verso, 2006.

Anderson, Brian C. *Raymond Aron: The Recovery of the Political*. Lanham, MD: Rowman & Littlefield, 1998.

Anniekov, P. *Literaturnyie wspominaniya* [Literary Memories]. Moscow: Gosudarstviennoye Izadtielstvo Jydozhestvennoy Literatury, 1960.

Antonov, Konstantin. *Filosofia religii v russkoy metafizike XIX- nachalo XX veka* [Philosophy of religion in Russian metaphysics in the nineteenth century and early twentieth century]. Moskow: Izdatelstvo PSTGU, 2009.

Aquinas, Thomas. *On Kingship*. Toronto: Pontifical Institute of Mediaeval Studies, 1949.

Arendt, Hannah. *Eichmann in Jerusalem: A Report on the Banality of Evil*. New York: Penguin Classics, 2006.

———. *The Human Condition*. Chicago: University of Chicago Press, 1998.

———. *The Origins of Totalitarianism*. New York: Harcourt, Brace, 1968.

Argárate, Pablo. "El concepto de discípulo en Ignacio de Antioquía." *Studia Monastica* 43 (2001) 269–96.

———. "El dinamismo de la constitución antropológica en Máximo el Confesor." *Studia Monastica* 43 (2001) 47–65.

———. "La noción de Dios en Máximo el Confesor." *Studia monastica* 42 (2000) 295–317.

Augustine, Saint. *The City of God against the Pagans*. Edited by R. W. Dyson. Cambridge Texts in the History of Political Thought. Cambridge: Cambridge University Press, 1998.

———. "True Religion." In *The Works of Saint Augustine: A Translation for the Twenty-First Century*, vol. 8, *On Christian Belief*. Edited by John Rotelle. Translated by Edmund Hill. New York: New City, 2005.

Baader, Franz Xaver von. "Über Das Durch Die Französische Revolution Herbeigeführte Bedürfniss Einer Neuen Innigeren Verbindung Der Religion Mit Der Politik." In *Romantics, Reformers, Reactionaries: Russian Conservative Thought and Politics in the Reign of Alexander I*, edited by Alexander Martin. DeKalb: Northern Illinois University Press, 1997.

Balthasar, Hans Urs von. *The Glory of the Lord: A Theological Aesthetics.* Vol. 2, *Studies in Theological Style: Clerical Styles.* Translated by Andrew Louth et al. Edited by John Riches. Edinburgh: T. & T. Clark, 1986.

———. *The Glory of the Lord: A Theological Aesthetics.* Vol. 3, *Studies in Theological Style: Lay Styles.* Translated by Andrew Louth et al. Edited by John Riches. Edinburgh: T. & T. Clark, 1986.

Bazylow, Ludwik. *Historia Rosji* [History of Russia]. Warsaw: Ossolineum, 2005.

———. *Społeczeństwo rosyjskie w pierwszej połowie XIX wieku* [Russian Society in the First Half of the Nineteenth Century]. Wrocław: Ossolineum, 1973.

Bentham, Jeremy. "Defense of Usury." In *Jeremy Bentham's Economic Writings,* edited by W. Stark, 1:121–207. London: Blackfriars, 1952.

———. *A Fragment on Government.* Oxford: Clarendon, 1891.

Berdyaev, Nicholas. *The Beginning and the End.* New York: Harper & Row, 1952.

———. *El cristianismo y el problema del comunismo.* Madrid: Espasa-Calpe, 1968.

———. *The Destiny of Man.* London: G. Bles, Centenary, 1937.

———. *Dostoevsky: An Interpretation.* San Rafael, CA: Semantron, 2009.

———. *The End of Our Time.* New York: Sheed & Ward, 1924.

———. *The Meaning of History.* San Rafael, CA: Semantron, 2009.

———. *The Origin of Russian Communism.* Translated by R. M. French. London: G. Bles, 1937.

———. *The Realm of Spirit and the Realm of Caesar.* Translated by Donald A. Lowrie. New York: Harper, 1952.

———. *The Russian Idea.* Hudson, NY: Lindisfarne, 1992.

———. *The Russian Revolution.* Ann Arbor: University of Michigan Press, 1961.

———. *Truth and Revelation.* New York: Collier, 1962.

Berlin, Isaiah. *Four Essays on Liberty.* Oxford: Oxford University Press, 1969.

———. *Russian Thinkers.* New York: Penguin, 1994.

Besançon, Alain. *La falsification du Bien: Soloviev et Orwell.* Paris: Julliard , 1985.

Bierdiajew, Mikolaj. *Filozofia nierówności: listy do nieprzyjaciół, rzecz o filozofii społecznej.* Kety: Antyk, 2006.

Blachowska, K. *Narodziny Imperium* [The Birth of the Empire]. Warsaw: Neriton, 2001.

Bohun, Michal. *Oczyszczeni przez burze. Wlodimierz Ern i moskiewscy neoslowianofile wobec pierwszej wojny swiatowej.* Krakow: WUJ, 2008.

Borne, Etienne. *Le problème du mal.* Paris: Presses Universitaires de France, 1958.

Boudou, Adrien. *Le Saint-Siège et la Russie, 1814–1847.* Paris: Plon, 1922.

Bulgakov, Sergei. "Evharisticheskiy Dogmat" [The Dogma of the Eucharist]. *Put'* 20 (1930) 3–46.

———. "Evharisticheskiy Dogmat" [The Dogma of the Eucharist]. *Put'* 21 (1930) 3–33.

———. "Tragedia filosofii." In vol. 1 of *Sochinieniya.* Moscow: Nauka, 1993.

———. *The Unfading Light.* Grand Rapids: Eerdmans, 2012.

Cavanaugh, William T. *The Myth of Religious Violence: Secular Ideology and the Roots of Modern Conflict.* Oxford: Oxford University Press, 2009.

———. *The Theopolitical Imagination: Christian Practices of Space and Time.* New York: T. & T. Clark, 2003.

Chaadayev, Peter Yakovlevich. "Apologie d'un fou." In vol. 1 of *Polnoye sobraniye sochinieniy i izbranyie pisma.* Mowcow: Nauka, 1991.

———. "Nieopublikovannaya satiya" [Unedited Article]. In *Zvieniya.* Moscow-Leningrad, 1934.

———. *Philosophical Letters and Apology of a Madman.* Knoxville: University of Tennessee Press, 1969.

———. *Philosophical Works of Peter Chaadaev.* Edited by Raymond T. McNally and Richard Tempest. Sovietica 56. Dordrecht: Kluwer Academic, 1991.

———. *Polnoye sobranyie sochinieniy i izbranyie pisma* [Complete Works]. Vol. 1. Moscow: Nauka, 1991.

———. "Zamiecheniya na broshuru A. S. Khomiakova (1854)" [Notes in S. Khomiakov's Notebook (1854)]. In *Polnoye sobranyie sochinieniy i izbranyie pisma.* Moscow: Nauka, 1991.

Cobban, Alfred. *Edmund Burke and the Revolt against the Eighteenth Century: A Study of the Political and Social Thinking of Burke, Wordsworth, Coleridge, and Southey.* London: G. Allen & Unwin, 1929.

Congar, Yves. *After Nine Hundred Years.* Westport, CT: Greenwood, 1959.

Dante Alighieri. *Monarchy.* Translated and edited by Prue Shaw. Cambridge: Cambridge University Press, 1996.

Dawson, Christopher. *Religion and the Modern State.* New York: Sheed & Ward, 1935.

Dostoevsky, Fyodor. *The Brothers Karamazov.* New York: Farrar, Straus & Giroux, 2002.

Druzhnikov, Yuriy. "Uroki Vasiliya Grossmana." *Literaturnye vesti* 39 (1999).

Egorov, Boris. *Oblicza Rosji. Szkice z historii kultury rosyjskiej XIX wieku* [The Faces of Russia: Essays on the History and the Culture of Russia of the Nineteenth Century]. Gdansk: Slowo/Obraz Terytoria, 2002.

Epstein, Mikhail. *After the Future: The Paradoxes of Postmodernism and Contemporary Russian Culture.* Translated by Anesa Miller-Pogacar. Amherst: University of Massachusetts Press, 1999.

Eriugena, Johannes Scotus. *Periphyseon: On the Division of Nature.* Indianapolis: Bobbs-Merrill, 1976.

Ermichev, Aleksandr, and Alla Zlatopolskaya, editors. *P. J. Chaadayev: Pro et contra.* St. Petersburg: Izdatelstvo Russkogo khristianskogo gumanitarnogo instituta, 1998.

Ern, Vladimir. "Od Kanta do Kruppa." In *Niemarksistowska filozofia rosyjska.* Lodz: Editorial Ibidem, 2002.

Evdokimov, Paul. *The Art of the Icon: A Theology of Beauty.* Translated by Steven Bigham. Redondo Beach, CA: Oakwood, 1990.

———. *El conocimiento de Dios en la tradición oriental.* Madrid: Paulinas, 1969.

———. *Orthodoxy.* New York: New City, 2011.

———. *The Sacrament of Love.* Crestwood, NY: St. Vladimir's Seminary Press, 1985.

Eydelman, N. *Pushkin. Istoriya y sovremennost' i hudozhestvennom soznaniy poeata* [Pushkin: History and Contemporaneity in the Artistic Knowledge of the Poet]. Moscow: Sovietskiy Pisatiel, 1984.

Faye, Emmanuel. *Heidegger: The Introduction of Nazism into Philosophy in Light of the Unpublished Seminars of 1933–1935.* New Haven: Yale University Press, 2009.

Felmy, Karl Christian. *Teología Ortodoxa Actual.* Salamanca: Sígueme, 2002.

Florensky, Pavel. *Beyond Vision: Essays on the Perception of Art.* London: Reaktion, 2002.

———. *The Pillar and Ground of the Truth: An Essay in Orthodox Theodicy in Twelve Letters.* Princeton: Princeton University Press, 1997.

———. *Stolp i utvuerzhdieniye istiny: Opyt pravoslavnoy tieodyccei.* Moscow, 2003.

Florovsky, Georges. "Offenbarung, Philosophie und Theologie." *Zwischen den Zeiten* 9 (1931) 463–80.

——. "The Orthodox Church and the Ecumenical Movement Prior to 1910." In *Collected Works of Georges Florovsky*, 2:161–232. Belmont, MA: Nordland, 1974.

——. *Ways of Russian Theology*. 2 vols. Belmont, MA: Nordland, 1979.

——. "Western Influences in Russian Theology." In *Collected Works of Georges Florovsky*. Belmont, MA: Nordland, 1975.

Frank, Siemion. "Sushchnost' y viedushchyie motivy russkoy filosofrii." In *Russkoye mirovozrieniye*. St. Petersburg, 1996.

Fromm, Erich. *The Fear of Freedom*. New York: Routledge, 2001.

Gagarin, Ivan. *Le archives russes et la conversion d'Alexandre I, Empereur de Russie*. Lyon, 1877.

Gershenzon, Mikhail. *Sochineniya i pisma P. Ia. Chaadaeva*. Vol. 1. Moscow, 1913–1914.

Gilson, Étienne. *Being and Some Philosophers*. 2nd. ed. Toronto: Pontifical Institute of Mediaeval Studies, 1952.

——. *Les métamorphoses de la Cité de Dieu*. Paris: Vrin, 1952.

Golitsyn, Anatoliy. *New Lies for Old: The Communist Strategy of Deception and Disinformation*. Rancho Palos Verdes, CA: GSG, 1990.

Gouhier, Henri. *La jeunesse d'Auguste Comte et la formation du positivisme*. Paris: Vrin, 1970.

Grigorian, M. *Czaadayev i yego filosofitskaya sistema* [Chaadayev and His Philosophical System]. Moscow: Nauka, 1958.

Grossman, Vasily. "Abel." In *V gorode Berdicheve*, 7–24. Ekaterinburg: U-Faktoria, 2005.

——. *An Armenian Sketchbook*. Translated by Robert Chandler and Elizabeth Chandler. New York: New York Review of Books, 2013.

——. *Everything Flows*. Translated by Robert and Elizabeth Chandler with Anna Aslanyan. New York: New York Review of Books, 2009.

——. "Fosfor." In *V gorode Berdicheve*, 264–311. Ekaterinburg: U-Factoria, 2005.

——. "In the Town of Berdichev." In *The Road: Short Fiction and Essays*, translated by Robert Chandler and Elizabeth Chandler, 15–32. New York: New York Review of Books, 2010.

——. *Life and Fate*. New York: Harper & Row, 1985.

Grygiel, Stanislaw. "Extra Communionem Personarum Nulla Philosophia." *Communio* 29 (2002) 691–701.

Guber, Fedor. "Osuschestvliayuschiy zhizn' tak, kak khotelos . . . 'Iz knigi o Vasilii Grossmanie' Pamiat' y pisma." *Vaprosy Literatury* 3 (1996).

Guitton, Jean. *A Student's Guide to Intellectual Work*. Notre Dame: University of Notre Dame Press, 1964.

Gulyga, Arsenii. *Ruskaya idea i yego tvorcy* [The Russian Idea and Its Creators]. Moscow: Soratnik, 1995.

Heidegger, Martin. "Über Wesen und Begriff von Natur, Geschichte und Staat."

Henry, Michel. *L'Amour les yeux fermés*. Paris: Gallimard, 1976.

——. *Le fils du roi*. Paris: Gallimard, 1981.

——. *Seeing the Invisible: On Kadinsky*. New York: Continuum, 2009.

Herbert, Zbigniew. *Selected Poems of Zbigniew Herbert*. Oxford: Oxford University Press, 2006.

Herzen, Alexander. "Eseje filozoficzne: Rosja i stary swiat" [Philosophical Essays: Russia and the Ancient World]. In vol. 2 of *Pisma filozoficzne* [Philosophical Works]. Warsaw: PWN, 1966.

————. *Izbraniye filosofskiye proizwiedieniya* [Anthology of Philosophical Texts]. Vol. 2. Moscow: Goskomizdat, 1948.

————. *My Past and Thoughts: The Memoirs of Alexander Herzen.* Translated by Constance Garnett. Rev. ed. London: Chatto & Windus, 1968.

————. *Pisma filozoficzne* [Philosophical Works]. Warsaw: PWN, 1966.

————. *Rzeczy minione i rozmyślania.* Warsaw: Ksiazka i Wiedza, 1951.

Hippolytus of Rome. "O Antychryscie" [On the Antichrist]. In *Demonologia w nauce Ojcow Kosciola* [Demonology in the Teaching of the Fathers of the Church], 113–43. Kraków: WAM, 2002.

John Paul II. *Evangelium Vitae.* Washington, DC: United States Conference of Catholic Bishops, 1995.

Journel, M. J. Rouet de. *Une russe catholique: Madame Swetchine d'après de nombreux documents nouveaux.* Paris: Maison de la Bonne, 1929.

Junginger, Horst, editor. *The Study of Religion Under the Impact of Fascism.* Boston: Brill, 2008.

Kamieniskiy, Abram. "Paradoksy Czadayeva" [Paradoxes of Chaadayev]. Introduction to *Polnoye sobranyie sochinieniy i izbranyie pisma,* by P. Chadaayev. Moscow: Nauka, 1991.

Kandinsky, Wassily. *Point and Line to Plane.* New York: Dover, 1979.

Kantorowicz, Ernst. *The King's Two Bodies.* Princeton: Princeton University Press, 1997.

Karamzin, Nikolai. *Istoria gasudarstva Rossiyskego.* Moscow: Kniga, 1989.

————. *Letters of a Russian Traveler, 1789–1790.* Translated by Florence Jonas. New York: Oxford University Press, 1957.

Karpovich, Michael. *Imperial Russia, 1801–1917.* New York: Henry Holt, 1960.

Kertész, Imre. *Fatelessness: A Novel.* Translated by Tim Wilkinson. New York: Knopf, 2004.

Kireyevsky, Ivan. "Opyt Nauki Filosofii." In *Polnoye sobranyie sochinieniy.* Moscow, 1886.

Kladoczny, Piotr. *Prawo jako narzędzie represji w Polsce Ludowej (1944–1956).* Warsaw: IPN, 2004.

Kolakowski, Leszek. "Euro- i azjatokomunizm: jedno czy dwoje?" In *Czy diabel moze byc zbawiony i 27 innych kazan,* 375–82. Kraków: Znak, 2006.

————. *Metaphysical Horror.* Edited by Agnieska Kolakowska. Rev. ed. Chicago: University of Chicago Press, 2001.

————. "Reprodukcja kulturalna i zapominanie." In *Czy diabel moze byc zbawiony i 27 innych kazan.* Kraków: Znak, 2006.

Kondakov, Igor. *Vvedenie v istoriiu russkoi kul'tury.* Moscow: Aspekt, 1997.

Kondakov, Igor, and Lubov Shneyberg. *Ot gorkovo do Solzhenicyna.* Moscow: Vysshaya Shkola, 1997.

Koshelov, Aleksandr Ivanovich. *Zapiski* [Notes] *(1812–1883).* Berlin: B. Behr, 1884.

Koyré, Alexander. *Etudes sur l'histoire de la pensée philosophique en Russie.* Paris: Vrin, 1950.

Kozlov, Vladymir. "Status istorii v rossii v konce VXIII- pervoy chetvierti XIX v." [The Status of Russian History at the End of the Seventeenth Century to the First Quarter of the Nineteenth Century]. In *Vsemirnaya istoria i Vostok. Sbornik statiey.* Moscow: Nauka, 1989.

Krakhmalnikova, Zoya. "Mozhna li obustroit' Rossiyu biez Boga?" *Russkaya Mysl,* September 26, 1990.

Krasicki, Jan. *Bog, człowiek, zło: Studium filozofii Wlodzimierza Sołowjowa* [God, Man, and Evil: An Examination of Vladimir Soloviev's Philosophy]. Wrocław: Wydawnictwo Uniwersytetu Wrocławskiego, 2003.

———. "Bogoczlowiecznstwo i zlo" [Divine Humanity and Evil]. In W *kręgu idei Włodzimierza Solowjowa*. Kraków: Wydawnictwo Uniwersytetu Jagielloniskiego, 2002.

Kuzimin, A. "Politicheskiye i pravoviye vzgliady V. N. Tatashchieva" [The Political and Legal Ideas of V. N. Tatishchev]. *Sovetskoe gosudarstvo i pravo* 9 (1982) 101–10.

Lebiediev, A. *Chaadayev*. Moscow: Molodaya Gvardia, 1965.

Lenin, Vladimir. "Państwo a rewolucja. Nauka marksizmu o państwie a zadania proletariatu w czasie rewolucji." In vol. 25 of *Dzieła* [Works]. Warsaw, 1951.

Lepenies, Wolf. *La Seducción de la Cultura en la Historia Alemana*. Madrid: Akal, 2008.

Lira, Osvaldo. "Prologo." In *Rusia y la iglesia universal*, by Vladimir Soloviev. Madrid: Ediciones y Publicaciones Españolas SA, 1946.

Long, D. Stephen. *Divine Economy: Theology and the Market*. London: Routledge, 2000.

López Sáez, Francisco José. *La belleza, memoria de la resurrección: Teodicea y antropodicea en Pavel Florenskij*. Burgos: Monte Carmelo, 2008.

Lossky, N. O. *History of Russian Philosophy*. New York: International Universities Press, 1951.

Lossky, Vladimir. *The Mystical Theology of the Eastern Church*. London: James Clarke, 1957.

Lubac, Henri de. *Catholicism: Christ and the Common Destiny of Man*. Translated by Lancelot C. Sheppard and Elizabeth Englund. San Francisco: Ignatius, 1988.

———. *The Drama of Atheist Humanism*. Translated by Edith M. Riley, Anne Englund Nash, and Mark Sebanc. San Francisco: Ignatius, 1995.

MacIntyre, Alasdair. *After Virtue*. 2nd ed. Notre Dame: University of Notre Dame Press, 1981.

———. *Ethics and Politics*. Selected Essays 2. Cambridge: Cambridge University Press, 2006.

———. *Marxism and Christianity*. Harmondsworth, UK: Penguin, 1968.

———. "Natural Law as Subversive: The Case of Aquinas." *Journal of Medieval and Early Modern Studies* 26 (1996) 61–83.

Marion, Jean-Luc. *God Without Being: Hors-Texte*. Translated by Thomas A. Carlson. Chicago: University of Chicago Press, 1995.

———. *The Idol and Distance: Five Studies*. Translated by Thomas A. Carlson. New York: Fordham University Press, 2001.

———. *Prolegomena to Charity*. Translated by Stephen E. Lewis. New York: Fordham University Press, 2002.

Mayorov, Gennady. *Filosofia kak isaknie Absoliuta*. Moscow: URSS, 2004.

Meyendorff, John. *Byzantium and the Rise of Russia: A Study of Byzantino-Russian Relations in the Fourteenth Century*. Crestwood, NY: St. Vladimir's Seminary Press, 1997.

———. *The Orthodox Church: Its Past and Its Role in the World Today*. Crestwood, NY: St. Vladimir's Seminary Press, 1996.

Milbank, John. *Theology and Social Theory: Beyond Secular Reason*. 2nd ed. Oxford: Blackwell, 2006.

Miliband, Ralph. *The State in Capitalist Society: An Analysis of the Western System of Power*. New York: Basic, 1969.

Mill, John Stuart. "Utilitarianism." In *On Liberty and Other Essays*, edited with an introduction by John Gray, 131–201. Oxford: Oxford University Press, 1991.

Miłosz, Czesław. *The Captive Mind*. Translated by Jane Zielonko. New York: Knopf, 1953.

Mochulsky, Konstanty. *Wladimir Solowiow: Zhyzn' i ucheniye* [Vladimir Soloviev: Life and Teaching]. Paris: YMCA, 1951.

Mrówczyński-Van Allen, Artur. "Literature and the Totalitarian State—the Icon and the Idol—from Soloviev to Grossman." Paper presented at the International Vasily Grossman Convention, Life and Fate Study Center, Turin, Italy, February 19–21, 2009.

———. "Ruskiye myslitieli y Evuropa segodnia" [Russian Thinkers and Europe Today]. Paper presented at the Twentieth Annual Theological Conference, St. Tikhon's Orthodox University, Moscow, Russia, October 9–14, 2009.

Mrówczyński-Van Allen, Artur, and Sebastian Montiel. "Aspekty russkoy tradytsiy filosofsko-teologitchevskovo sinteza v postsekularnom kontekste: C. Bulgakov, G. Florovsky, A. Badiou i *karlik teologii*" [Aspects of the Philosophical-Theological Synthesis of the Russian Tradition in a Post-Secular Context: Sergius Bulgakov, Georges Florovsky, Alain Badiou, and the *Dwarf of Theology*]. Paper presented at the Twenty-Second Annual Theological Conference, St. Tikhon's Orthodox University, Moscow, Russia, November 16–22, 2011.

Nahirny, Vladimir C. "The Russian Intelligentsia: From Men of Ideas to Men of Convictions." *Society for Comparative Studies in Society and History* 4 (1962) 403–35.

Nietzsche, Friedrich. *The Anti-Christ*. New York: Soho, 2012.

Nisbet, Robert. *The Quest for Community: A Study in the Ethics of Order and Freedom*. Wilmington, DE: ISI, 2010.

Odoevsky, V. F. "A City Without Name." In *Russian Nights*. Translated by Olga Koshansky-Olienikov and Ralph E. Matlaw. New York: Dutton, 1965.

———. *Russkie nochi*. Moscow: Put', 1913.

Olbrych, Wieslawa. *Wasilij Grossman: Dramat humanisty w swiecie cywilizacji totalitarnej*. Toruń: Adam Marszalek, 2004.

Pelevin, Viktor. *Generation "P"*. Moscow: "Vagrius", 1999.

Pickstock, Catherine. *After Writing: On the Liturgical Consummation of Philosophy*. Oxford: Wiley-Blackwell, 1998.

Pierling, Paul. *L'Empereur Alexandre I est-il mort catholique?* Paris: Plon-Nourrit, 1901.

Pipes, Richard. *The Russian Revolution*. New York: Vintage, 1991.

Pseudo-Dionysius. *The Complete Works*. Translated by Colm Luibheid and Paul Rorem. New York: Paulist, 1987.

Pushkin, Alexander. *The Poems, Prose and Plays of Alexander Pushkin*. Selected and edited by Avrahm Yarmolinsky. New York: Random House, 1936.

———. *Polnoye sobranyie sochineniy* [Collected Works]. Moscow: Izdatielstvo Akademii Nauk SSSR, 1949.

Quénet, Charles. *Tchaadaev et les Lettres Philosophiques*. Paris: Champion, 1931.

Quesada, Julio. *Heidegger de camino al Holocausto*. Madrid: Biblioteca Nueva, 2008.

Raeff, Marc. *Origins of the Russian Intelligentsia: The Eighteenth-Century Nobility*. New York: Harcourt, Brace, 1966.

Rapoport, Aleksandr. "Iz protivostoyania s sistemoy otciets vyshol pobeditelem." *Lechaim* 5768–5 (2008) 24–32.

Ratzinger, Joseph Cardinal. *Introduction to Christianity.* Translated by J. R. Foster. San Francisco: Ignatius, 2004.

"Retreatants Hear of Guises of the Antichrist." *ZENIT,* 28 February 2007. Online: http://www.zenit.org/en/articles/retreatants-hear-of-guises-of-the-antichrist.

Riasanovsky, Nicholas. *Russia and the West in the Teaching of the Slavophiles: A Study of Romantic Ideology.* Cambridge: Harvard University Press, 1952.

Rolland, Romain. *Péguy.* 2 vols. Paris: A. Michel, 1944.

Saint-Simon, Henri de. *Le Nouveau Christianisme.* Paris: Éditions du Seuil, 1969.

Sakulin, Pavel. *Iz istorii russkogo idealizma.* Moscow, 1913.

Schönborn, Christopher. *God's Human Face: The Christ-Icon.* San Francisco: Ignatius, 1994.

Shakhovskoy, Dymitriy. "Niizdanyi proyekt proklamacyi P. J. Chaadayeva 1848 g." [Unedited Project of a Proclamation of P. Chaadayev, 1848]. In *Litieraturnoye Nasledstvo,* 22:679–82. Moscow, 1935.

Shentalinski, Vitali. *Crimen sin castigo: Últimos Descubrimientos en los Archivos Literarios del KGB.* Barcelona: Galaxia Gutenberg, 2007.

———. *Denuncia contra Sócrates: Nuevos Descubrimientos en los Archivos Literarios del KGB.* Barcelona: Galaxia Gutenberg, 2006.

———. *Esclavos de la libertad.* Barcelona: Galaxia Gutenberg, 2006.

Shestov, Lev. "Egzystencjalizm jako krytyka fenomenologii." In *Filozofia egzystencjalna.* Warsaw, 1963.

Soloviev, Vladimir. *Dykhovnyia osnovy zhiznii* [*The Spiritual Foundations of Life*]. 301–421.

———. "Historia i budushchnost' teokratiy" [History and the Future of Theocracy]. In vol. 4 of *Sobranyie sochinieniya* [Complete Works]. Brussels: Zhizn's Bogom, 1966.

———. "Ideya cheloviechestva u Avgusta Komta" [The Idea of Humanity in Auguste Comte]. In *Sobranyie sochinieniya,* 2:562–82. Moscow: Mysl', 1990.

———. "Ideya sverkhcheloveka" [The Idea of the Superman]. In *Sobranyie sochinieniya,* 626–34. Moscow: Mysl', 1990.

———. *The Justification of the Good: An Essay on Moral Philosophy.* Translated by Nathalie A. Duddington. Edited by Boris Jakim. 2nd ed. Grand Rapids: Eerdmans, 2005.

———. "Kritika otvliechennyh nachal." In vol. 2 of *Sobranyie sochinieniya.* Moscow: Mysl', 1990.

———. *Krizis zapadnoy filosofii. Protiv positivistov* [*The Crisis of Western Philosophy: Against the Positivists*] 3–138.

———. *Lectures on Divine Humanity.* Revised and edited by Boris Jakim. Hudson, NY: Lindisfarne, 1995.

———. *The Meaning of Love.* Edited with a revised translation by Thomas R. Beyer Jr. West Stockbridge, MA: Lindisfarne, 1985.

———. "Mitologicheskiy proces v' drevniem' yazychestvie." In vol. 1 of *Sobranyie sochinieniya.* Brussels: Zhizn's Bogom, 1966.

———. *Politics, Law, and Morality: Essays.* Translated and edited by Vladimir Wozniuk. New Haven: Yale University Press, 2000.

———. *Russia and the Universal Church.* Translated by Herbert Rees. London: G. Bles, 1948.

———. "Smysl lubvi." In vol. 7 of *Sobranyie sochinieniya.* Brussels: Zhizn's Bogom, 1966.

————. "Tri razgavora, Kratkaya poviest' ob anticristie." In *Sobranyie sochinieniya*, 2:635–763. Moscow: Mysl', 1990.

————. "Vielkiy spor i christianska política" [The Great Controversy and Christian Politics]. In vol. 4 of *Sobranyie sochinieniya*. Brussels: Zhizn's Bogom, 1966.

————. "Vladimir Soloviev's Letter to L. Tolstoy on the Resurrection of Christ." *Sobornost'* 1 (1935) 8–12.

————. *War, Progress, and the End of History: Three Conversations, Including a Short Story of the Anti-Christ.* Hudson, NY: Lindisfarne, 1990.

————. "Zapadniki y zapdnichestvo." In *Sobranyie sochinieniya*. Brussels: Zhizn's Bogom, 1970.

Solovyov, Sergey M. *Vladimir Solovyov: His Life and Creative Evolution*. Faifax, VA: Eastern Christian, 2000.

————. *Życie i ewolucja twórcza Włodzimierza Solowiowa* [The Life and Creative Evolution of Vladimir Soloviev]. Poznań: W drodze, 1986.

Solzhenitsyn, Aleksandr. "Kak nam obustroit' Rossiyu?" *Konsomolskaya Pravda*, September 18, 1990.

Spaemann, Robert. *Der Ursprung der Soziologie aus dem Geist der Restauration*. Munich: Kosel, 1959.

Stobiecki, Rafal. *Bolszewizm a historia: Proba rekonstrukcji bolszewickiej filozofii dziejow*. Lodz: Wydawnictwo Uniwersytetu Ludzkiego, 1998.

Suslov, Ivan. "Pochiemu moltchitie, Mastier?" *Novoye Russkoye Slovo*, June 23, 1987.

Tischner, Józef. *Etyka solidarności oraz Homo sovieticus* [The Ethic of Solidarity and Homo Sovieticus]. Kraków: Znak, 1992.

————. "For the Existence of Man: An Ontological Argument." In *Spór O Istnienie Człowieka*. Kraków: Znak, 1998.

Todorov, Tzvetan. "Les combats de Vassili Grossman." Introduction to *Œuvres*, by Vasily Grossman. Paris: Robert Laffont, 2006.

Tolstoy, Leo. *Tolstoy's Letters*. Vol. 1, *1828–1879*. Selected, edited, and translated by R. F. Christian. New York: Scribner's, 1978.

Uspienski, Boris. *Religia i semiotyka*. Gdansk: Slowo/Obraz Terytoria, 2001.

Valliere, Paul. *Modern Russian Theology: Bukharev, Soloviev, Bulgakov*. Grand Rapids: Eerdmans, 2000.

Vasilenko, Leonid. *Vvedenie v russkuyu religioznuyu filosofiyu*. Moscow: Izdatielstvo PSTGU, 2010.

Vernadsky, George. *Russian Historiography: A History*. Edited by Sergeï Pushkarev. Belmont, MA: Nordland, 1978.

Voegelin, Eric. "Gnostic Politics." In *Published Essays, 1940–1952*, 223–40. Edited by Ellis Sandoz. Collected Works of Eric Voegelin 10. Columbia: University of Missouri Press, 2000.

————. *The New Science of Politics: An Introduction*. Chicago: University of Chicago Press, 1952.

————. *The Political Religions*. Translated by Virginia Ann Schildhauer. In *Modernity Without Restraint*, edited by Manfred Henningsen, 19–72. Collected Works of Eric Voegelin 5. Columbia: University of Missouri Press, 1999.

Vysheslavtsev, Boris. "Viechnoye w russkoy filosofii." In *Etika prieobrazhonnovo Erosa*, 154–228. Moscow: Rspublika, 1994.

Wachtel, Michael, editor. *The Cambridge Introduction to Russian Poetry*. Cambridge: Cambridge University Press, 2004.

Walicki, Andrzej. *Rosja, katolicyzm i sprawa polska* [Russia, Catholicism, and the Polish Question]. Warsaw: Pruszynski i S-ka, 2003.

———. *The Slavophile Controversy: History of a Conservative Utopia in Nineteenth-Century Russian Thought.* Translated by Hilda Andrews-Rusiecka. Notre Dame: University of Notre Dame Press, 1989.

Wiener, Leo, editor. *Anthology of Russian Literature from the Earliest Period to the Present Time.* 2 vols. New York: Putnam's, 1902–1903.

Wojytla, Karol. *Sign of Contradiction.* Strathfield, New South Wales: St. Paul, 1977.

Zander, Lev. *Bog i mir: Mirosozerrcanie otca Sergia Bulgakova.* Vol. 1. Paris: YMCA, 1948.

Zaremba, Marcin. "Nieboszczyk w służbie partii." *Mówia Wieki* 11 (1999) 16–20.

Zdybel, Jolanta. "Intelektualna droga Isaiaha Berlina." In *Miedzy wolnoscia a powinnoscia: Filosofía polityczna Isaiaha Berlina i Alasdaira MacIntyr'a.* Lubin: UMCS, 2005.

Zenkovsky, V. V. *A History of Russian Philosophy.* Translated by George L. Kline. 2 vols. New York: Columbia University Press, 1953.

———. "N. V. Gogol." In *Ruskiye myslitieli i Evropa.* Paris: YMCA, 1955.

———. *Russkie mysliteli i Evropa.* Paris: YMCA, 1955.

Zinoviev, Alexander. *Homo Sovieticus.* Translated by Charles Janson. London: V. Gollancz, 1985.

———. *The Radiant Future.* Translated by Gordon Clough. New York: Random House, 1980.

Zinoviev, G., and N. Lenin. *Lenin Vladimir Ilich: Ocherki zhizni i deiatielnosti.* Petrograd, 1918.

Zizioulas, John. *Communion and Otherness: Further Studies in Personhood and the Church.* Edited by Paul McPartlan. New York: T. & T. Clark, 2006.

Zweig, Stefan. *The World of Yesterday: An Autobiography of Stefan Zweig.* New York: Viking, 1943.

www.ingramcontent.com/pod-product-compliance
Lightning Source LLC
Chambersburg PA
CBHW020333100426
42812CB00029B/3115/J